RECLAIM *Your* SOUL

DESTINY IMAGE BOOKS BY DR. CINDY TRIMM

The 40 Day Soul Fast

40 Days to Discovering the Real You

40 Day Soul Fast Curriculum

RECLAIM
Your SOUL

Your Journey to Personal Empowerment

DR. CINDY TRIMM

Manuscript prepared by Rick and Melissa Killian, Killian Creative, Boulder, Colorado. www.killiancreative.com.

DESTINY IMAGE® PUBLISHERS, INC.

P.O. Box 310, Shippensburg, PA 17257-0310

"Promoting Inspired Lives."

This book and all other Destiny Image, Revival Press, MercyPlace, Fresh Bread, Destiny Image Fiction, and Treasure House books are available at Christian bookstores and distributors worldwide.

For a U.S. bookstore nearest you, call 1-800-722-6774.

For more information on foreign distributors, call 717-532-3040.

Reach us on the Internet: www.destinyimage.com.

ISBN 13 TP: 978-0-7684-0348-0

ISBN 13 Ebook: 978-0-7684-8478-6

For Worldwide Distribution, Printed in the U.S.A.

3 4 5 6 7 8 / 23 22 21 20

What would you give to get back your soul?
(Matthew 16:26 CEV).

For freedom Christ has set us free;
stand firm therefore, and do not submit again
to a yoke of slavery (Galatians 5:1 ESV).

Be careless in your dress if you must,
but keep a tidy soul. —Mark Twain

DEDICATION AND ACKNOWLEDGMENTS

First and foremost, I dedicate this book to my Lord and Savior Jesus Christ. Thank you for gifting me with the skill of effective communication.

To all who are in search of a practical guide for living an unencumbered life with meaning and purpose.

To my mother who gave me my first map in life by living exemplarily before me.

To my brothers and sisters Stanley, Charlene, Winston, Marilyn, Deborah, and Freda, who have been the best traveling companions any one could have asked for.

To the next generation of movers and shakers and history makers: Marvin Trimm, Leticia Seymour, Savon Stowe, Winnette Trimm, Laquita Trimm, Ashaunte Trimm, Aaron Trimm, Rachel Ball, Reaia Ball, Ashe Trimm, Asia Trimm, Riel Trimm. To Mitzy, Andrea, Nadine, Robert, Paul, Cyril, and Derrick, you have contributed so much to my life by playing a role in helping to produce the next generation of "Trimms," my beautiful nieces and nephews.

To Dr. Jacque DelRosario, Vincent DelRosario, Dr. Fran Pinder, Dr. Dorie McKnight, Gina Roberts, Jim and Rochelle Moech, Lisa Palmer, Malcom and Terisita Harris, Pamela Shillingford, Marion Tanock, D. Myron Brangman, Beverley Jones, Lynette Webb, Merle Williams, Sandra Ming, Gloria-Jean Dickerson, Deneise Lightbourne, Adriann Tucker-Raynor, Jonelle Christopher, Lorna MaGowen, Albert Lightbourn, Angria Bassette,

Theresa Tucker, Donna-Mae Hinds, Deborah Stead, Robin Tota, Rhonda Lambert, Miriam Simmons, Muriel Santucci, Katherine, Melissa Butterfield, and the entire KU Bermuda staff; your generous contributions have made my dream of publishing this book a reality.

To Wendy Williams, A. Monica Jackson, Sharon Harris, Holley Richardson, Jewel Edwards, Melva Hodge, Debbie Leakey, Dolores Hughes, Claudette McAlpin, Claudette Hinds, Shamerra Brown, Elke Smith-Pettiford, Janice Ruff, Tonya Parker, Treniece Griffin, Marcus Green, Yamia Green, Jimmie Green, Robin Green, "Uncle" Larry, Darlene Pachot, Anette Ortega, Dr. Jonie Dodgens, Lisa Saddleburgh, Lisa Washington, Abraham Thomas, Dr. Rita Claxton, Dr. Lori Johnston, Beverley Moore, Marie Butler, Jeannette Bayardell, Shamalia Willis, Dennis Worden, Kelly Umstead, Andrea and Apostle Carter; you have been the best executive, administrative, and volunteer staff (past and present) in the world. Thank you for standing with me and exemplifying true commitment.

To my publishing team at Destiny Image, most especially Ronda Ranalli, Terri Meckes, and Larry Sparks, I am ever grateful for your enduring patience, diligence, support, and partnership.

To Rick & Melissa Killian, you waded through hundreds of pages of what I called a manuscript and helped me to turn it into a book. Thank you for your literary brilliance.

To all those who prayed for me and contributed to our efforts and initiatives to make this world a better place; those too numerous to name, because your names would constitute writing a book just to say, "Thanks"... I dedicate this book to you.

You are all the wind beneath my wings.

CONTENTS

INTRODUCTION

Every moment and every event of every man's
life on earth plants something in his soul.
—Thomas Merton

We are all a product of the stories we tell ourselves. We live
in an invisible framework constructed by our past experiences, upheld by the unconscious mechanisms we put into place
to protect our conscious minds. The reality we experience is created by the thoughts we think. "The world as we have created it
is a process of our thinking," observed Albert Einstein. "It cannot be changed without changing our thinking." It is a universal
principle, indeed— *"As* [a man] *thinketh in his heart so is he."*[1]

This series of books, beginning with *The 40 Day Soul Fast:
Your Journey to Authentic Living,* has been written with the
soul-purpose of helping you change the process of your thinking by finding *soul*-utions. Why? Because, as we are told in Proverbs, the machination of the soul *"determines the course or your
life."*[2] Further down we read, *"don't get side-tracked."*[3] You, your
reality, your world—at least how you interpret your experience
of being alive on the earth—is a product of your mental state.
Many are operating from a state of repression or suppression—
subconsciously or consciously choosing to forget, ignore, or
avoid painful or negative experiences. By doing so, the same
patterns, scripts, events, traumas, difficulties, and obstacles to
growth continually repeat themselves.

If you are not growing, maturing, and building your capacity to be and do more with every passing day, you are stagnating. That river of living water that Jesus said would flow out from within each of us[4] becomes blocked; psychological barricades, protective barriers, and defense mechanisms are erected on the internal landscape of our minds. Like stagnant waters that become foul and brackish—providing the perfect environment for dangerous parasites and pests to breed—an unhealthy soul threatens the beauty of the natural order and undermines the health of both our spiritual and social ecosystem. This may seem over-dramatic, but don't you know the health of society is determined by the health of its members?

The soul of a society is a reflection of the souls of its people. If the world you see around you is broken, it is because the people within it are broken. Likewise, broken relationships are a result of broken people.

It's not hard to believe, therefore, that what we might call "cesspools of the mind" threaten the health of your body as well as your soul, and that this "dis-ease" ultimately threatens your relationships. As with any water source, it needs to be kept clean and flowing freely—the wellspring of living water available to you must remain free of junk and clutter. That takes work. You've got to do the heavy lifting of clearing away debris, breaking up dams, and maintaining well-defined channels. It is much like tending a garden. To enjoy the beauty of it, you must get your hands dirty. You must cultivate it, prune and weed it, water and nourish the soil. If you let it go unattended, you risk it being overgrown by weeds and thistles—worse, under the ground hidden from sight, those roots are choking out and binding up the entire root system. The beautiful garden you intended becomes root-bound, withers, and eventually dies. If, however, you did a little weeding each day, nothing would keep your garden from flourishing.

That is why I've written this book—to help you successfully

tend the garden of your soul. You need to know how to identify the tares from the wheat in your life, how to create an environment where your best self can flourish, and where and when to plant for a better future.

The Journey

The book you are presently reading is the second install-ment of The Soul Series, which is designed to take you on a transformative journey from soul to body to world. In book one, *The 40 Day Soul Fast: Your Journey to Authentic Living,* I talked about the importance of embracing your true identity—the authentic, divinely created unique self. We began by exploring your incredible potential, extraordinary worth, and the pro-found expression of the divine nature that you are called to reveal in your daily life. We discussed the effects of negative words, mental scripts, and the clutter that accumulates in your soul muddying the luster of your soul's inherent beauty. By rid-ding your soul of those "soul toxins"—the daily minutia and negativity that produce corrosive thought patterns and limiting beliefs—you are able to break free from the scar tissue of the mind. You can change the mental habits that keep you from liv-ing authentically. To help you in the process of renewing your mind and embracing your true self, we explored the forty char-acteristics of an authentic person.

As so many have attested, *The 40 Day Soul Fast* created a space for meaningful self-reflection and tremendous inner healing—a map and a compass for living more authentically—and yet, while the groundwork was laid for cultivating the life of the soul, this was only the beginning.

After having read *The 40 Day Soul Fast,* and hopefully taken the free AQ (Authenticity Quotient) Assessment at www.soul fast.com, you should have a clearer understanding of who you were created to be—a blueprint of what your most authentic self would look like. If you have not taken the free AQ Assessment, I strongly recommend that you take a few minutes to do so now.

As with any other fasting or detox regimen, if you return to the same old habits, behaviors, and coping mechanisms that caused the disequilibrium or *dis*-ease in the first place, than in the end you will have defeated the purpose. You must learn to identify and change the behavioral patterns that continually threaten to oppress and debilitate your soul. What are the habits and practices you engage in that cause you to erect those facades and defense mechanisms—the false self that casts a shadow repressing your divine potential and pulling you away from the freedom of authentic living?

In book three of this series, you will learn about the physiological effects of your thought life; how emotional "disorder" manifests as disorders in your body—how much of the *dis*-ease we experience begins in the corridors of the mind. But to have that conversation, we must first have this one. How, then, do you reclaim your soul? How do you sever unhealthy soul ties—those destiny altering and purpose undermining emotional attachments? How do you unblock those rivers of living water so you can flush away the stagnant pools that have pocketed in the hidden recesses of your psyche? How do you recapture and reveal the brilliance of your own soul?

EMPOWERMENT THROUGH RESILIENCY

You must build into your life a new skill set, a new discipline for acting and reacting to people and circumstances, so that you don't again fall prey to the hidden repressions of the soul. You must learn to deliberately reclaim your soul every moment of every day. This is what empowerment is all about. This is the path to true and lasting empowerment and why I have written this book—as a field guide, so to speak, of how to move from a mind renewed through the practice of soul fasting, into a life empowered by new habits and behavioral patterns. This is the foundation of building your capacity to not only achieve your goals and live the life of your dreams, but also to grow into becoming a person of influence—and it is the "empowerment process" I have taught about and coached thousands through around the world (visit www.explorecore4.com to learn more).

Why is this empowerment process so important? Because until you are able to shift your mindset about who you are and what you are capable of, and translate that into the daily habits, behaviors, and practices that will point you toward success, you will never be in a position to maximize your potential as a leader and change catalyst. At the end of the day, that is what empowerment is all about—giving you the tools, strategies, and encouragement you need to be a positive force for the good of all. And that requires resiliency.

Empowerment is the fruit of resiliency. That is why I want to take you from living more authentically to living more resiliently. In *The 40 Day Soul Fast* we talked about the key characteristics of an *authentic* person, in this book we will be talking about the key disciplines—or best practices—of a *resilient* person. What are the types of behaviors and habits practiced by resilient people? What are the skills you need to develop on a daily basis to keep you free from emotional entanglements and toxic thought patterns? These are eclipsed aspects of our selves—psychological strongholds that result in infantile tendencies, neurotic thoughts, and repressed feelings that threaten to erupt at any time.

I know what it's like to battle for the peace and life of my soul on a daily basis. We all do. We are all responsible for the ongoing reclamation process when it comes to the health and wholeness of our souls. It is with patience we are instructed by Jesus to possess our souls.[5] But how do you actually "take possession" of your soul?

You begin by understanding what is threatening to lay claim to it. In this eight-week study, you will learn the types of soul exchanges that can derail your best intentions to protect it. You will learn how to navigate and circumvent the kinds of inter-actions, agreements, associations, and communication patterns that undermine your attempts to preserve the health of your soul. I will show you how to recognize the various channels that the forces opposing your soul use to entrap and oppress it.

But more importantly, I will show you how to tell a new story—how to shift reality by reconstructing the framework you have created for your mind to operate within, the artificial shelter you've erected to protect your soul. Yes, you are uncon-sciously doing your best to safeguard your most prized posses-sion, but like an overprotective father who ends up jailing his daughter in a high tower, you must learn to trust the voice of your soul, learn to be led by its wisdom, and lean on its profound ability to intuit the best direction to take in every situation. It is in the realm of your soul that the Spirit of God gives wisdom for living—timeless strategies for living the best life possible. God will empower you to shift from making instinct-based decisions to inspiration-based decisions. "Inspiration is the voice of your soul giving you direction in your life; it is the voice of your soul in the world," teaches Richard Barrett, founder of the Barrett Values Center. "When you learn to hear the voice of your soul, you can begin to lead a values-driven life [rather than an ego-driven life]—when you understand the values held in your soul, you can lead a life of meaning and purpose by avoiding the behaviors rooted in fear-based beliefs." He admonishes us all to "begin living the life of the soul."

As you begin this next soul journey, I want you to remember that every behavior is learned; and likewise, every new practice, discipline, and habit can be mastered. You are where you are today because of the habits you are currently practicing, so all you need to do is learn what to do differently. It's not complicated. You'll begin exercising a new discipline one day at a time. Step by step. One week will turn into two weeks, and then a month, and then two months. As I so often say, thirty days creates a discipline, sixty days a habit, and ninety days a lifestyle. In forty days from now, you will be well on your way to mastering the practices that will equip you to become the kind of resilient person that is empowered for life.

That is my prayer for you.

> A man sooner or later discovers that he is the master-gardener of his soul, the director of his life. —James Allen

PREFACE

Just as a mirror, which reflects all things, is set in its own container, so too the rational soul is placed in the fragile container of the body. In this way, the body is governed in its earthly life by the soul, and the soul contemplates heavenly things through faith. —Hildegard of Binden

Human beings are not just bodies, but *souls* wearing bodies. To be more accurate, we are souls who interact with the physical world through our physical bodies. We are also souls who interact with the spiritual world through our spirits. Though science has yet to discover a way to determine where our physical bodies end and where our souls begin, we are still more soul than body. One day our bodies will pass away and return to dust, but our souls will go on into eternity.

Our souls operate on a spiritual plane—what quantum physicists have identified as the fourth dimension—the unseen quantum world that lies beyond time and space and shapes all that we see in the physical world. Our souls bridge the eternal with the temporal, pick up on the frequencies of heaven, and translate spiritual truths into the language that our minds can comprehend. Your soul is the source of your healing, purpose, and success when it has been seeded by the Spirit of Christ and watered by the Word of God. When your soul comes alive in Christ, a genesis takes place. A new world of possibilities emerges—a kind of alternate reality, which the Bible calls the Kingdom of Heaven. This Kingdom is received in seed form when it is birthed in you upon salvation. You become a multi-dimensional being—a child of the Creator of the World—a child of Light.

Your soul having been seeded with light—with divine love—carries the DNA of Love Himself (see 1 John 4:16). The Father of Light—*"all light"* (James 1:17 AMP)—deliberately fashioned and formed your soul as a unique reflection of His light—your extraordinary unique self—to be revealed at this very time in history.

> *Your soul is the source of what makes you alive.*

Your soul is the source of what makes you alive. It is what transmits light to your life. This is why Apostle Paul gave the instruction: *"Awake you who sleep, arise from the dead, and Christ will give you light"* (Eph. 5:14). Paul doesn't mean that when you jump out of bed Christ will shine down a beam of light on your pajama-clad body; but rather, it is you who must discipline your soul to harness the light that Christ gives. Paul offers step-by-step instructions about how to do just that:

> *...Live purposefully and worthily and accurately, not as the unwise and witless, but as wise (sensible, intelligent people), making the very most of the time [buying up each opportunity], because the days are evil. Therefore do not be vague and thoughtless and foolish, but understanding and firmly grasping what the will of the Lord is. And do not get drunk with wine, for that is debauchery; but ever be filled and stimulated with the [Holy] Spirit. Speak out to one another in psalms and hymns and spiritual songs, offering praise with voices [and instruments] and making melody with all your heart to the Lord, at all times and for everything giving thanks in the name of our Lord Jesus Christ to God the Father* (Ephesians 5:15-20 AMP).

STEWARDING YOUR SOUL

Living on purpose, making the most of the time, being led by the Spirit, offering praise, and giving thanks are some of the ways to enlighten—as well as *lighten*—your soul. Your soul,

then, is a transmitter of light that is either positioned to capture and harness the light, or to repel it. You are in the conduc-
tor's seat. You can choose to position your soul by aligning it
with behavioral best practices as outlined by Paul, or to remain
spiritually asleep—sleepwalking through life among the clutter
of the living dead. There will always be negative forces pulling
you away from the light, attempting to suppress or diminish
the light you carry, for as Paul wrote, *"the days are evil."* But
you have the power within you to overcome any darkness with
the light emanating from your soul. Celtic priest and philosopher John O'Donohue wrote, "Negativity is an addiction to
the bleak shadow that lingers around every human form. You
can transfigure negativity by turning it toward the light of your
soul."

You may feel like only a small flicker in a dark world, but
you are not alone. Imagine a football stadium filled with people
holding up their lighters—all those tiny flickers, lighting up the
whole field! You may feel like a lonely lighthouse on an island
amidst a dark, raging sea, but you are among many positioned
to light up the shoreline. Your soul gives you more than the
light of self-knowledge—it gives you the ability to be known by
others as well. You are able to influence and to be influenced,
"because to influence a person is to give him one's own soul,"
wrote Oscar Wilde.

But Wilde also warns of the danger. Although we long to
come together and connect on a deep level—to know and be
known—we must be careful to maintain the integrity of our
own souls. Wilde goes on to write that when an exchange takes
place at the level of the soul, "[One] does not think his natural
thoughts, or burn with his natural passions. His virtues are not
real to him. His sins…are borrowed. He becomes an echo of
someone else's music, an actor of a part that has not been written
for him." We will discuss this concept of *exchange* in great detail
throughout this book, as these are the soul-level connections

that need to be evaluated, and if unhealthy, broken in order for us to reclaim our souls and live resilient lives.

Wilde concludes by making the following observation:

> The aim of life is self-development. To realize one's nature perfectly—that is what each of us is here for. People are afraid of themselves, nowadays. They have forgotten the highest of all duties, the duty that one owes to oneself. Of course they are charitable. They feed the hungry, and clothe the beggar. But their own souls starve, and are naked. Courage has gone out of our race.
> —The Picture of Dorian Gray

This reminds me of a verse from Ecclesiastes which states, *"We work to feed our appetites; meanwhile our souls go hungry"* (Eccles. 6:7 MSG). How do we keep our own souls from starving? How do we not neglect the highest of all duties—to properly care for, nourish, and protect our own souls? Could this be at the root of humanity's woes? Could the hunger, conflict, and darkness we see in the world be a reflection of the condition of our inner lives? Have we failed to take possession of the kingdoms of this world for our Lord Jesus Christ because we have failed to take full possession of our own souls? This is what we will explore in the fourth and final book of this series. But for now, we will look at how you can begin to possess your soul by learning to practice the disciplines and behaviors that will establish the environment your soul needs to thrive.

What is True Freedom?

To review, your soul is the seat of your reflective consciousness housing your mind, will, and emotions, also your intellect, decision-making ability, and your heart. Proverbs 4:23 exhorts you to, *"Keep your heart with all diligence, for out of it spring the issues of life."* The word *issue* in this verse is used to denote a

PREFACE

"place of departure."[1] I picture it like the source or headwaters of a spring that flows into a stream and then into a mighty river. From it come waters that, though they start small, have the capacity to grow to sustain and nurture life in plateaus and valleys for miles on end. Our souls are the *"the source of true life"* (Prov. 4:23 CEV).

The soul is the seat of ideas and inventions, any one of which can light the world, transform a generation, or free a continent. While it is the center of our being, it is also what keeps us centered, balanced between physical and spiritual needs and desires—between cold intellectual calculations, strength of will, and compassionate justice. It is the cradle of prosperity and health, the womb of inspiration and aspiration, and the lathe of policy and programs. It is the conduit through which all good things come into the world.

But if our souls are not free to be their best, none of this comes about. Some exercise their physical freedom only to find they do things that enslave their souls to substances, behaviors, or relationships that eat away at their very core and are incredibly difficult to escape. They exercise a "freedom" that inhibits their own success—developing habits that hold them back and keep them from their own promotion, prosperity, and fulfillment in life because they quench the true life that pours out from their hearts.

They think discipline is the opposite of freedom—that ethics and morals are meant to inhibit their pleasure and enjoyment rather than enhance them. They resist letting others tell them what to do only to be placed in bondage to laziness, sensuality, or addiction. They seek comfort at the expense of their own achievement and growth. They seek reward in trying to obtain a certain lifestyle while diminishing every life they touch. They end up in a prison that is of their own making, whether it is figurative or literal. They live a life that sounds like an old country song:

You load sixteen tons, what do you get?
Another day older and deeper in debt
Saint Peter don't you call me 'cause I can't go
I owe my soul to the company store.
—Merle Travis ("Sixteen Tons")

The harder you work, the further you get behind. Little compromises you make every day are like trading little bits of your self away, selling your soul for nickels and dimes until you feel like you don't own your own life anymore. All your hopes and dreams have been given to someone or something else— you've sold your soul for a flimsy "success" that is of significantly less value than advertised.

What's got you locked up in its grip? What is keeping you from being the person deep down you know you are supposed to be? Are you free—really free? Or are you trapped in something you feel you can never escape? What is it you have traded your soul for? And is there a way to get it back? Just what would you give to get back your soul?

The human soul is God's treasury, out of which He coins unspeakable riches. —Henry Ward Beecher

Christ asks for a home in your soul, where he can be at rest with you, where he can talk easily to you, where you and he, alone together, can laugh and be silent and be delighted with one another. —Caryll Houselander

Part One

THE POWER THAT WORKS IN YOU

We must walk into the arena, whatever it may be—a new relationship, an important meeting, our creative process, or a difficult family conversation—with courage and the willingness to engage. Rather than sitting on the sidelines...we must dare to show up and let ourselves be seen.
—Brene Brown

Now to Him who is able to do exceedingly abundantly above all that we ask or think, according to the power that works in us (Ephesians 3:20).

Chapter One

GOD'S PLAN A

Then God saw everything that He had made, and indeed it was very good (Genesis 1:31).

I n the beginning, everything God made was good. This included humanity. Humankind existed in a realm that was not only abundant, but also balanced. The environment was designed to blossom and prosper—there were no storms, no deserts, no earthquakes, or natural disasters. The world was a lush, subtropical paradise, even at the north and south poles. It's possible as well that oceans were much smaller and there was much more land to live on.[1] What extravagance! A vast, fertile, bountiful planet; a cornucopia of fruits and vegetables growing wild, with livestock blanketing the hills, birds filling the air, trees laden with a plethora of fruit, and fish packed into the waterways, lakes, and seas. All of this, dropped into the center of a universe so large that the light from its edges has yet to reach us after 13.7 billion years—made as the home for two people, Adam and Eve, all so they could share it with their family. The sky was their roof, the grass, stapled down with roses and daffodils became their carpet. Organic was not a brand, nutritional supplements were not necessary, and Prozac was not their source of peace.

After creating Adam, the first thing God did was to give him an assignment—to care for the Garden and name all of the animals. What an incredible mind Adam must have had to do that! He imagined, theorized, postulated, innovated, engineered, and created—all without a formal education. He was born with divine genius. God also gave human beings emotions, just as He had Himself, which meant they could empathize, desire, long for, build loyalties, trust, and have soulish ties of affection and affinities. They could love, be loved, know, be known, worship, discern, and prefer. They could connect on a level no other of God's creation could. It was a gift unique in all of creation that God gave to humanity—all so each human being could have a relationship with Him, with each other, and with their environment. It is this ability that allows each of us to know and be known by God, as well as to know and be known by each other. It was only after Adam was settled into his responsibilities and created a comfortable living that God decided to give him a wife.

> *Every human is unique and individual, a divine masterpiece, a special piece of God's manifold imagination—a revelation of God's majesty, sovereignty, glory, ingenuity, and mystery.*

The abilities of the human beings God created were second only to God Himself. Although the angels He created as His messengers, warriors, and servants were awesome, beautiful, and powerful, human beings had something that angels did not: free will—the right to choose for themselves whatever they did or didn't do. God gave humans the ability to think for themselves—to have ideas, dreams, and imaginings no other being besides God had ever had before. Divine creativity is imprinted into humanity's DNA to such an extent that from the first formation of a human, the life process has moved forward in perpetual motion ever since. This process has gone through millennia without ever creating a duplicate. Each and every new human is unique and individual, a divine masterpiece in and of him or herself, a special piece of the overall puzzle of God's manifold imagination—a revelation of God's majesty, sovereignty, glory, ingenuity, and mystery.

But this is what I find most fascinating: the universes—physical, spiritual, and whatever else God has yet to tell us about—observe those of us who have pledged ourselves to God to see what *He* will come up with next. No, you didn't read that wrong. The angels and powers and principalities of the multiverse don't watch God to see what He will do next, they watch us! (See Psalm 8:3-6.) They look to the people of God on the earth to see the multifaceted wisdom of God revealed! How do I know? Because God told us through Apostle Paul:

> *So here I* [Paul] *am, preaching and writing about things that are way over my head, the inexhaustible riches and generosity of Christ. My task is to bring out in the open and make plain what God, who created all this in the first place, has been doing in secret and behind the scenes all along. Through followers of Jesus like yourselves gathered in churches, this extraordinary plan of God is becoming known and talked about even among the angels!* (Ephesians 3:8-10 MSG)

This mystery is revealed through individuals connected with God who connect with one another in the Church—what the Bible also calls "the Body of Christ." In other words, the mysteries of God are only revealed in genuine connection—our connecting with God and our coming together as Christ's Body on the earth to do His will. This is how the Kingdom of God is manifest or made real. This is the power of intimacy.

THE POWER OF INTIMACY

When a man and a woman physically connect through intercourse, there is the possibility of new life being born—an incredible miracle, but at the same time the most shallow of intimate connections available to us as human beings. Conversely, when two souls connect, for example, music, art, and movements are conceived and then born. When minds connect—or ideas connect in a mind—inventions and innovations are born. When spirits connect, the possibilities are endless; imagine what happens when the spirit of a person connects with the Spirit of God. The impossible, becomes possible. Such a person enters the zone of unlimited potentialities and possibilities (see 1 Cor. 2:9-12). Like the difference between nuclear fission (division) and nuclear fusion (joining together), connection is always several times more powerful than dividing apart.

The Bible goes on to tell us that each of us was an incredible miracle of God from the moment we were conceived in our mother's womb. As the psalmist wrote,

> *For You formed my inward parts; You wove me in my mother's womb. I will give thanks to You, for I am fearfully and wonderfully made; wonderful are Your works, And my soul knows it very well* (Psalm 139:13-14 NASB).

The word "wove" in this Scripture is akin to the word *crocheted*. In other words, as you were being conceived in your mother's womb, God directed the "crocheting" or "knitting" together of your mother and father's DNA double helixes to release into the universe something that had never existed before. The *YOU* God created has unique and special gifts to fulfill a unique and special purpose. You have destiny stitched into the very building blocks of your cells. Fearfully and wonderfully made indeed!

> " *The keys to unlocking all you are supposed to be is in the relationships you make in life.* "

Once God formed you in the womb, He breathed life into you and with that made you a receptacle of a unique part of the mysteries, wisdom, creativity, and ingenuity He wanted to reveal into the multiverse. He locked these things away within you in pieces, pieces that could only be put together or completed through connection with others. The keys to unlocking all you are supposed to be is in the relationships you make in life—first your relationship with God, and then your relationship with others who are in tune with Him, from intimate marriage partners to acquaintances. Some have major, permanent roles in our lives; others we will learn from along the way, picking up truths we didn't know before or the thoughts needed to complete the ideas God has been developing in us. These could lead to inventions, works of art, new healing technologies, or breakthroughs in any number of fields including business, medicine, social justice, personal development, or politics. Great and wonderful things are to be released through our connections with each other!

We are wheels within wheels in design—systems meant to work within other systems, everything functioning together in healthy and mutually beneficial relationships. The very core of our existence illustrates this to a Tee.

The human body is made up of billions of cells in relationship to one another, and each cell is made up of molecules, each a collection of atoms connected together. Healthy connections of atoms at the basest level are important for the overall health of the body. Unhealthy connections lead to dysfunctions like cardiovascular disease and cancer. Atoms "need each other" to form molecules. This "neediness" is built into their very structure. As you probably remember from high school chemistry, atoms are made up of protons, neutrons, and electrons working together in a nucleus and orbiting around that center. Each orbit—or "shell"—around the nucleus has a "number of completion": the innermost shell requires two electrons; the next shell requires eight electrons, and so on. Atoms rarely come with completed shells, so they look to find completion by combining with other atoms to form molecules. One of the most basic molecular structures is created when two hydrogen atoms connect with an oxygen atom to form H_2O, more commonly known as water, a key ingredient for sustaining life. Another is when two oxygen atoms find each other to form O_2, or an oxygen molecule, something none of us can live without. Life on earth, or anywhere else in the universe, would be impossible without connections like these.

THE CELLULAR PARALLEL

However, this process is short-circuited and becomes unhealthy when, instead of connecting with the atoms they need, atoms connect or interact with what are called "free radicals." Free radicals are dysfunctional atoms that don't have the right number of electrons in their shells for the atom they are supposed to be—they are atoms with something missing; they have been corrupted in some way, shape, or form—and when they interact with other atoms, instead of staying connected to form molecules, they "steal" completeness from the other atoms, turning them into corrupted free radicals as well. Some of this happens normally in the process of atoms interacting with each other and can be handled by the body, but it can be an overwhelming problem when those free radicals reach a tipping point—as happens when the body is exposed to pollution, radiation, cigarette smoke, or herbicides, for example.

The word "radical" should let you know that they are essentially aberrant and abnormal. Free radicals deviate from the norm—they don't connect with others without doing damage to both parties, and thus tend toward isolation and the incubation of unhealthy characteristics. If this happens enough, it will cause disruption in the cell. When cellular corruption happens in the lining of a blood vessel, it causes arteriosclerosis, or hardening of the arteries, which can lead to strokes or heart attacks. When other cells are corrupted by free radicals, they can turn cancerous and metastasize, spreading throughout the body so fast that, depending on the type of cancer, a person could die in a matter of months.

To combat free radicals in our bodies, health experts tell us we need a steady dose of antioxidants, which are found primarily in fruits and vegetables. Antioxidants have the ability to "heal" free radicals by giving them electrons without becoming unstable free radicals themselves. Thus they have the ability to keep the body function healthy on every level by healing the most basic of relationships within the body. While we can take supplements to give our bodies mass doses of antioxidants— and this can be good, like when you take extra vitamin C (a potent antioxidant) to fight off an oncoming cold—researchers find it is not as effective to take occasional large doses as it is to consume five to eight servings of fruits and vegetables throughout the day every day, giving you a steady intake of antioxidants. It is now widely believed that doing so will fight cancer and cardiovascular disease—two of the biggest killers in our world— giving people longer, healthier lives.

FREE RADICALS OF THE SOUL

Why is all this important to our discussion of the soul? I believe what happens in our bodies on the cellular level is a direct parallel to what happens in the spirit on the *soulular* level. Again, these are systems of relationships within systems of relationships, wheels within wheels as Ezekiel saw in his visions from God.[2] Each of us is created with certain needs and desires, talents and gifts, dreams and purposes that cannot be fulfilled in a vacuum. We do not grow into healthy adults without parents and families, and communities do not function well without the basic building blocks of functional families. Prospering communities are then the bedrock of prospering towns, cities, states or provinces, and nations. We find "completion" for certain areas of our lives through connections with others.

Some connections are more intimate—with God, marriage, family, and deep friendships; and others are more superficial—classmates, colleagues, teachers, students, pastors, mentors, and so on. There are personality aspects within us that need interaction with others to be healthy—rough spots to wear down or deficiencies to be made up. There are ideas that we need for success in life that need other ideas for completion. There is knowledge and wisdom that needs other knowledge and wisdom. There is insight that needs other insight and revelation that needs other revelation for wholeness. The Bible tells us, *"For we know in part and we prophesy in part. But when that which is perfect has come, then that which is in part will be done away"* (1 Cor. 13:9-10). Completion brings resolution, and salvation and transformation. Completion is necessary for healthy, prosperous living.

The problem is, in life—even more than inside of our bodies—there are *free radical* types of individuals, who we connect with (or who connect with us) and create dysfunctional relationships characterized by toxic exchanges of ideas, self-destructive habits, exploitive allegiances, blinding selfishness, abusive guardianship, belittling opinions, codependent companionship, potential-squandering amusements, suffocating ignorance, violence-inflaming ideologies, crippling emotions, traumatically stressful experiences, and again, the list goes on. By connecting and tying ourselves to the wrong things—especially dysfunctional people—our lives and purposes are put in jeopardy. The great part you have in revealing God's manifold wisdom to the universe could be frittered away like pearls tossed into the mud before swine.

Such things may affect us to the point that we are like the person Paul described in Romans 7 and we begin to think, *"I know that nothing good lives in me"* (Rom. 7:18 NLT). We accept that we are worthless, we are undeserving of anything good, and we even begin to accept that the world would be a better place without us. This is far from the truth. I am here to tell you that such thoughts are toxic free radicals in your soul—they are out-and-out lies. If you accept them, they will steal from you and leave you even more incomplete than you were before. They are cancers of the mind, hardeners of your heart, assassins of your destiny. God never intended them to be in your life, but when we allow

> *By connecting and tying ourselves to the wrong things—especially dysfunctional people—our lives and purposes are put in jeopardy.*

them in through our choices or mistakes, they want to grab your potential by the throat and choke the life out of it.

Thus we are in an interesting dilemma that happens day by day, hour by hour, and moment by moment. As we walk through life, we constantly have choices before us. Every decision counts, even though some decisions count more than others. From "Do I have a Danish with my coffee this morning?" to "Is this the person I am supposed to marry?" or "Should I look for another job?" we make decisions, form habits, follow paths, and create our life one choice at a time.

IT IS UP TO YOU

The bad news is that if you don't like the life you are currently living, you are responsible for that. The good news is that if you don't like the life you are currently living, you are responsible for that too. No, I didn't leave something out there, nor did I make a mistake—what I want you to understand is that if you are responsible for something, it's not about guilt, it's about the fact that you have the ability to change things. Once you accept responsibility for where you are today, you have the power to change everything. Everything in life is connected to a decision. If one decision got you here, you are only one decision from being somewhere else. No matter how bad your past or how stuck you feel, there is a path to lasting change. There is a way to get back to what God has for you.

You see there is no plan B with God. He is always trying to get you back to His best—His original plan A for your life.

> When God created man, He created man as a free moral agent—a decision-making being. Refuse to see yourself as a victim of circumstance.

Choose His plan over yours for healthy living and healthy relationships. Don't settle for less than the best for your life. Make the decision not to allow your past to define your present and future. Refuse to allow temporary crises to become a permanent condition. Your destiny is inextricably connected to your decisions. If you do not like what is going on in your life, make a decision to change it. Everything in the universe rises and falls on your power of choice. When God created man, he created man as a free moral agent—a decision-making being. Refuse to see yourself as a victim of circumstance. You have the power to:

- choose to do something or not to do something,
- choose to be something or not to be something,
- choose to believe or not to believe,
- choose to live or not to live,
- choose what you focus on,
- choose who you marry,
- choose what you accomplish,
- choose where you live,
- choose who you live with,
- choose the quality of your life,
- choose what you address and what you ignore,
- choose life or death,
- choose blessing or cursing,
- choose what you believe in,

- choose who you believe in,
- choose what or who you worship,
- choose how you respond to people or circumstances,
- choose to live inside out or outside in,
- choose good or evil,
- choose health or sickness,
- choose to conform or to be proactive,
- choose your future, and
- choose your destiny.

Remember, where you are today is based on the sum total of decisions you made yesterday. I heard someone describe it this way: the day you were born you were given two proverbial envelopes. On the front of one was written "pleasure, faith, and prosperity"; on the other envelope was written "pain, fear, and disease." When opened, each contained the same blank pages labeled "destiny." You get to choose which pages you will write on.

God has given you the power of decision making, to change circumstances, to reverse negative human conditions. *Wistful and wishful thinking never changes anything. You must be the change you want to see. Change is not just a process or a principle, but a person—Jesus Christ is our agent of change who gives you the power to be different tomorrow than you are today.*

CREATE YOUR DESTINY WITH A DECISION

As an individual *you must be intentional* about the kinds of changes you want to make in your life, your home, your community, your ministry, your business, your government, your school, your health care system, and your nation. You must be intentional when it comes to your relationships. Intentionality is powerful because it refuses to be limited by what is. When you are intentional, it refocuses you in such a way that you are more inclined to see the possibilities that lie ahead rather than the obstacles that lay behind—you are able to identify and capitalize on the resources to bring to pass what could be. It forces you to have hope in the future as you leave things, behaviors, habits, and dysfunctional relationships behind.

This is the very essence of resiliency, the very lifestyle I want to help you develop. Resilient people do not get left behind as they are leaving behind the negativities of their past. We get stuck in our grieving process when we have to walk away from maladaptive sets of behaviors and undermining habits. At the same time, you must resist the temptation to feel victimized, because it will stagnate your growth and development through its seductive wooing.

My goal is not to help you go from victory to valley, victory to valley—like a yo-yo oscillating between highs and lows and ups and downs. Resiliency never allows a valley to become a habit—although it is often the path of least resistance. Yes, we must acknowledge the challenges we are facing. It is foolish to ignore them or try to pretend our problems away. However, the key is not overcoming something only to fall right back into the same old habit or dysfunctional relationship shortly thereafter. To truly reclaim your soul, you must be committed to breaking the cycle and inaugurating a whole new way of life. *The decision to break these destructive cycles will shape your life and define your destiny.*

The book of Ruth is dedicated to the journey of a young widow. Ruth intentionally chose to move beyond her situation and not allow her past or present to define her future. Ruth chose not to allow her temporary crises to become a permanent condition. She made a decision, and in so doing, she changed her destiny.

Our destiny is connected to our decisions. If you do not like what is going on, make a decision to change and to shift. The earth is a domain characterized by decisions. Refuse to see yourself as a victim of circumstance. Make a choice to be something better—a victor *over* circumstances.

The greatest gift you can give yourself is the gift change. Don't be afraid. Face forward; move on. *Lot's wife was different from Ruth.* Because she lacked the resiliency necessary to forge ahead, she couldn't resist looking back, thus she never moved forward again—she was turned into a pillar of salt. What this means is that she never got past her past or moved beyond her present state (see Gen. 19:26). But you can move beyond your present state. You don't have to be a victim of current conditions, surroundings, situations, or positions. Poise yourself for success by elevating your mind. You will never go where you thoughts can't take you. Likewise, wherever your head turns, your body follows suit. *Protect your thought life:*

> *Let your eyes look straight ahead, and your eyelids look right before you. Ponder the path of your feet, and let all your ways be established. Do not turn to the right or the left; remove your foot from evil* (Proverbs 4:25-27).

MANKIND'S COMPROMISE

As human beings, we have fallen from a place of dominion: that place where we manifested our true divine nature in God. When Adam fell, he did not fall from heaven. He fell from his place of dominion over the earth. This is why the message of the Kingdom is important. It is not about getting you to heaven, but about bringing heaven to earth. Even Jesus' prayer emphasizes this (see Matt. 6:10). The Kingdom of Heaven is a literal spiritual realm that believers have the privilege to live in, characterized by righteousness, peace, and joy in the Holy Spirit (see Rom. 14:17). When Adam fell he lost the capacity to think like a representative of God. This meant he lost:

1. Psychological congruency: his values, ethics and morals; motives, intentions, and drives; perception became misaligned with the reality of heaven.

2. Personal individuality: he became enmeshed in a dysfunctional state.

3. Uniqueness of his true identity: he was stripped of the knowledge of his true identity and authentic self, losing touch with what it means to be like God.

4. Intellectual and divine genius: consumption and dependency replaced production and problem solving.

5. Spiritual bandwidth: facts and rationalization replaced faith and revelation. Jabez prayed, *"enlarge my territory"* (1 Chron. 4:10)—in other words, expand my spiritual bandwidth and take the limits off my thinking.

6. Relational/interpersonal health: the first thing that was compromised after the fall was how Adam related to God, to his spouse, and to his environment.

When Adam fell, he was sentenced to a realm that was unnatural to his nature. He fell from a realm of being one with God to being alienated from God, from living in the Spirit to living controlled by five physical senses, from a realm of:

- Dominion to Deception
- Thriving to Struggling
- Faith to Facts
- Revelation to Education
- Inspiration to Information
- Creativity to Consumerism
- God-consciousness to Self-consciousness
- Empowerment to Bondage

- Cooperation to Competition
- Knowing to Doubt
- Truth to Lies
- Life to Death

After the fall, the trees, earth, moon, and animals continued to follow the assignments given to them in Genesis chapter 1—only humanity changed; only humans lost touch with their natural, God-given assignments. When Adam fell:

- The landlord became the renter
- The entrepreneur became the employee
- The leader became the follower
- The victor became the victim
- The benefactor became the beggar
- The lender became the borrower
- The co-creator became the consumer
- The problem-solver became the problem
- The head became the tail
- The first became the last
- The overcomer was subdued
- The hunter became the hunted

GETTING BACK ON COURSE

God's solution for us is not only spiritual salvation, but also our real-time relationship with the Holy Spirit. I once heard Pete Greig teach that the Spirit of God is like one of those GPS navigational systems—we could call it "God's Positioning System." The Holy Spirit, like our modern-day GPS when you take a wrong turn, doesn't throw up its hands and say, "Well, now you've done it! You're lost! There is no way I can help you now!" No, instead it simply says, "Recalculating...recalculating...." God considers where you are now—no matter how far off course you get—and determines a way to get you to where you were originally supposed to be. That doesn't mean there won't be some backtracking or traveling through parts of town you would prefer to avoid, but if you follow that still small voice of God within you, He will get you back on course to your intended destination. It won't happen overnight, but it will happen if you walk with Him step by step. There might be some retraining involved—or some self-disciplining required—but as the Bible promises:

> *For the moment all discipline seems painful rather than pleasant, but later it yields the peaceful fruit of righteousness to those who have been trained by it* (Hebrews 12:11 ESV).

God has big plans for you, and it is time to put the past behind you and like the prodigal son, get on with your personal journey back toward that place within your heavenly Father's Kingdom—that place where purpose is fulfilled and you are able to become and do all that you were created for. It is time to let the Spirit of God "recalibrate" your course. But before you start any journey, it is good to know the terrain over which you will be traveling. Just as when you start any training regime, it helps to know the purpose of each exercise and how each one relates to the changes you want to make. For that, we need to dig a little deeper into the person God created you to be in order to reach toward the one He hoped you would become!

> The soul is placed in the body like a rough diamond; and must be polished, or the luster of it will never appear.
> —Daniel Defoe

Soul. The word rebounded to me, and I wondered, as I often had, what it was exactly. People talked about it all the time, but did anybody actually know? Sometimes I'd pictured it like a pilot light burning inside a person—a drop of fire from the invisible inferno people called God. Or a squashy substance, like a piece of clay or dental mold, which collected the sum of a person's experiences—a million indentations of happiness, desperation, fear, all the small piercings of beauty we've ever known. —Sue Monk Kidd

Chapter Two

YOU BY DIVINE DESIGN

Then God said, "Let us make human beings in our image, to be like us. They will reign over the fish in the sea, the birds in the sky, the livestock, all the wild animals on the earth, and the small animals that scurry along the ground" (Genesis 1:26 NLT).

God created human beings to reflect His image and likeness, to have dominion in the earth realm—to *reign* over our world as He reigns over the heavens and the universes. As God is three—Father, Son, and Holy Spirit, so we are three in one—spirit, soul, and body. We see outlined in First Thessalonians 5:23 ESV:

Now may the God of peace Himself sanctify you completely, and may your whole spirit and soul and body be kept blameless....

There are a number of ways to look at this. I like to think of it as the soul being sandwiched between two realms: a physical body on one side that interacts with the physical reality of the natural universe and a spiritual "body" on the other side that interacts with the supernatural, or spiritual, universe (see Diagram A). In referring to "supernatural," we're talking about something that supersedes the natural—that's actually more real, if you will, because everything seen in the natural world comes from the unseen world of the spirit. Only the things of the spirit are eternal: *"For the things which are seen are temporary, but the things which are not seen are eternal"* (2 Cor. 4:18).

Another way I like to view our make-up is as a series of concentric circles, with the spirit as our innermost part and our body as the outer layer (see Diagram B). Though this gives the illusion that the inner world of the spirit is perceived to be smaller than the outer world of the body, this is simply not true. It might be better to think of the soul like a scientist thinks of a wormhole in space that exists between two universes; one being the physical realm, the other the spiritual. In physics, the wormhole is the communication conduit between the two realms, while also having a personality and traits or characteristics of its own.

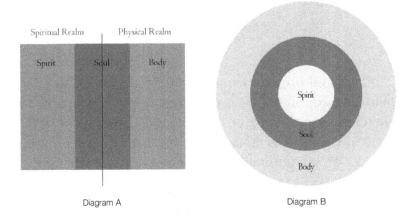

Diagram A   Diagram B

The soul is made up of another three elements: mind, will, and emotions. These are somewhat broken out in the first of the great commandments:

*You shall love the Lord your God with all your **heart**, with all your **soul**, and with all your **mind**, and with all your strength* (Mark 12:30).

In this Scripture, I believe *"heart"* represents emotions emanating from the subconscious mind (heart also frequently refers to the human spirit, however, since the human spirit is the part of us through which we connect to the spiritual realm and thus to God, our human spirits will naturally love God, which is not the same case with our emotions). I believe *"soul"* and *"mind"* in this Scripture each represent themselves. The word for *soul* here is the Greek word, ψυχή *(psuche)* from which we get the word psyche, referring to our human consciousness or personality. *Psychology*, which has *psyche* at its root, is the study of personality and behavior—you could call it the study of the soul. The mind comprises the inner world of our intellect, rational analysis, and our thought life. While *"strength"* does speak of physical strength, our greatest strength is not in our muscles, but in our choices, thus I think

> *Our greatest strength is not in our muscles, but in our choices.*

it also refers to our wills and what you would call "will power." Because the power to choose decides and controls everything in our lives, it can be viewed as our greatest asset as well as potential liability. It is with our souls that we decide to move toward God or away from Him—to love the Lord and other people, or not to—and thus from the soul flows all that leads to life.

The Difference between Soul and Spirit

It is difficult to divide the inner world of the soul from the innermost world of the spirit—it is so difficult, in fact, that the *"word of God"* is the only thing that can pierce *"to the division of soul and of spirit...discerner of the thoughts and intents of the heart"* (Heb. 4:12). The reason for this is that to the exterior world, the voice of the spirit sounds just like the voice of our own minds or consciences. We appear to have an "outer" world of the body and an "inner" one of the soul because the spirit and soul are so easily confused as one.

However, the Word of God teaches differently, and through time and study in the Scriptures, we learn to discern the difference between the voice of our own thoughts and the voice of our consciences—"that still small voice" that teaches us the depth of truth we find in the Bible. As Jesus told us: *"When He, the Spirit of truth, comes, He will guide you into all the truth"* (John 16:13) and *"the anointing which you have received from Him abides in you, and you do not need that anyone teach you"* (1 John 2:27). You see, that *"anointing"* is the Spirit of God—the Holy Spirit—living within our human spirits. When He speaks to our hearts, His voice is not easily distinguished from our own thoughts or emotions, so it takes some practice to tell one from the other. The more time we spend reading the Bible, the more practice we will have in learning to understand the voice of the Holy Spirit compared to what we are thinking and wondering in our own minds.

You see, before we are born again (see John 3:3), our human spirits are disconnected from God and the spiritual realm. Some say our spirits are dead at that point, but I would say they are more embryonic. Even those who are not born again have a sense of spiritual things, however, they've not yet developed the ability to discern in their spirits between voices that are good or those that are evil. They develop a sense of spirituality that is corrupted because its source is not the one true God.

When we become born again—or "born of the Spirit" as Jesus put it in John 3:6-7—it is as if our spirits go from being embryos to newborn babes. Suddenly, our spiritual senses start to function outside of the womb where before they were dormant, and we start to take in the spiritual world in the same way we did the physical world when we were first born from our mothers' wombs.

AWAKEN YOUR SPIRITUAL SENSES

As I have discussed in some of my other books, we learned a bit about this process when doctors first learned to do cataract surgery on people who had been born blind. By removing the cataracts—like taking the lens cap off of a camera—what was blackness before suddenly revealed the shapes and shadows of a three-dimensional world. Because these people had grown up without doing what sighted people do as infants—learn to interpret the things that come through our eyes to our brains as people, places, animals, or objects—these newly sighted people only saw what they understood to be bright and dark splotches in a myriad of colors in a world that appeared as flat as a piece of paper. It was confusing and disorienting.

As infants, in those first few months of development, we are learning to roll over, sit up, crawl, walk, and eventually speak, absorbing information that we have no idea what to do with. We first learn the faces of our caregivers as they cradle us and rock us to sleep. During this time, it doesn't matter much that everything is confusing, we don't have anything to do but ponder our world and the various sensations it offers.

This process is dramatically different for adults learning to see for the first time. Having grown up in a world without sight, they learned to get along without it. They learned to hear, to speak, to get around, and to do everything other people did as best they could without being able to see. Newly introduced to sight, the sensation was utterly confusing. The idea that there were faces connected to the voices they heard was a marvelous discovery. Color was a completely new concept to be understood. The idea of navigating around stationary objects or through doorways by sight instead of touch was so disorienting that many reverted to closing their eyes to move about. One man practiced learning depth perception by taking a shoe, tossing it out on the floor from where he sat on his bed, and then estimating how many steps he needed to take to get the shoe before getting up to retrieve it. Often, it was still out of reach after he had finished pacing off the estimated distance. One young woman was so disoriented by sight that she firmly closed her eyes and refused to open them again, much to the chagrin of her parents who had hoped for so much from the operation.

I think we do the same thing with our newly awakened spiritual senses. As a "born again" newborn, it takes some time before the input from our spiritual senses can be readily and correctly interpreted in our minds. As a baby learns by being in the world and sensing it, so our spiritual senses are trained and honed through being "in the spirit"—

> As a baby learns by being in the world and sensing it, so our spiritual senses are trained and honed through being "in the spirit."

this means in prayer, in the Word, in praise and worship, and in listening to good Bible teaching.

This is not a comfortable process for those of us who were born into the physical world and have been trained solely by it all of our lives (which is all of us). Like the young girl who chose to close her eyes to get around the house rather than face the discomfort and confusion of learning to see, many who become born-again followers of Jesus choose to live only by their natural senses rather than learning to navigate by their spiritual senses. We think for some reason that making mistakes in interpreting our spiritual sensing is somehow evil, though we would never condemn a toddler for falling down as he or she is learning to walk. We fully expect a toddler to "toddle." Likewise, we will certainly make mistakes in learning to *"walk by the Spirit"* (Gal. 5:16), but as any parent knows, there is no way to learn but by doing.

WALKING WITH THE SPIRIT

Many of Paul's writings in the New Testament, particularly his letters to the Galatians and Romans, wrestle with the duality of living by our natural senses—following some kind of strict moral philosophy based upon laws and rules—or following the living spiritual guidance of God by being led of His Spirit. Not only did Paul talk about walking by the Spirit in Galatians 5:16, but also about being led by the Spirit (see Gal. 5:18 and Rom. 8:14) and living by the Spirit (see Gal. 5:25). In another translation we are told to *"keep in step with the Spirit"* (Gal. 5:25 NIV).

Of course, this is much more easily said or written about than done. Very few Christians, in my experience, have mastered the art of living according to the dictates of the Holy Spirit rather than their own sense of right and wrong or some systematic approach to "being a Christian." Everyone I know struggles with how best to "live by the Spirit," including myself. At the same time, I can confidently tell you that in many instances I am led by the Spirit—and the ability to discern those promptings is a wonderful, powerful thing. It is the key to success, to living out your destiny, and to knowing and experiencing God. Just because you fall down along the way, doesn't mean you are on the wrong road. I would rather fall down a million times on God's road and get up again to keep following—sometimes toddling—after Him, than run expertly along on the wrong road, cruising smoothly into a life void of purpose and God's presence.

The ability to grab hold of heaven's perspective of who we are—the fullness of our authentic selves comprised of our personalities, desires, emotions, intellect, and will—all come from our soul. Though our bodies are part of who we are and we are influenced by their appetites, needs, sensations, perspective, and appearance, our bodies will one day pass away. If we are born again, our spirits will grow and mature throughout our lifetimes on earth and into eternity with God, and I wouldn't be surprised—if you could see your spirit—that it will appear in the eternal, spiritual realm much like your earthly body does in the temporal, physical realm. It might be, of course, that our spiritual age is very different from our physical one—far too many

Christians never spend enough time nurturing their spirits for them to grow up healthy and strong. The way we do that is to focus our souls on the spiritual side of us as much as we focused our minds on the physical side of us as we grew up from infancy.

> When we come to Christ for renewal, we come with some serious "soulish" problems.

The dilemma is that with our upbringing in a physical, fallen world full of corruption and trauma, we have, to put it mildly, picked up some bad habits along the way. When we come to Christ for renewal, we come with some serious "soulish" problems—ties to limiting things in the soul that keep us from the potential of who we actually are by divine design. These "soul ties" can be from any number of things: physical or emotional addictions, situations of oppression or exploitation, trauma from abuse or violent experiences, codependent or dysfunctional relationships, counter productive habits, ignorance, selfishness, cowardice or any other behavior or attitude the Bible refers to as *"works of the flesh"* rather than the *"fruit of the Spirit"* (Gal. 5:19,22). These ties hinder us by filtering or blocking the fullness of the Spirit from being manifested in our lives.

Interestingly, negative influences and thought patterns have been proven to have a stronger and longer lasting impact on the mind than do positive thoughts and experiences. In fact, frustration, conflict, and adversity are three times more powerful in affecting a person's attitude than are positive feedback and good fortune. People are more likely to remember a negative experience than they are a positive one. With a fallen world came a mental bias for negativity.

REWIRING YOUR MIND

Our brains have become conditioned to interpret the world, our circumstances, and other people negatively—to pay more attention to negative experiences than positive ones. They are wired to emphasize the negative as a self-protective survival response—always scanning for threats as was necessary during less peaceful times in human history. "Fortunately," writes entrepreneur Walter Chen, "we aren't doomed by our natural disposition toward negativity—we have the ability to break out of that negative feedback loop and rewire our brains to think positively." Daily, God wants you to renew the spirit of your mind (see Eph. 4:20-32).

This is the science of neuroplasticity—or the brain's ability to change structurally. "Neurons, or nerve cells, in your brain make connections, communicating through synapses. When you learn something, you change those neural connections. Every time you reactivate a circuit, synaptic efficiency increases, and connections become more durable and easier to reactivate."[1]

Chen explains that, "When we practice looking for and being more aware of positive aspects of life, we fight off the brain's natural tendency to scan for and spot the negatives. We can harness the brain's plasticity by training our brain to make positive patterns more automatic." Author of *The Happiness Advantage*, Shawn Achor, concurs. "We can retrain the brain to [look] for the good things in life—to help us see more possibility, to feel more energy, and to succeed at higher levels."

Success, therefore, is a frame of mind—an outcome of repeated thought patterns that result in how your brain makes connections. Rewiring your brain is what scientists and psychotherapists have come to call neurosculpting. It is what Paul revealed to the Romans when he wrote, *"Do not be conformed to this world, but be transformed by the renewing of your mind"* (Rom. 12:2). Paul understood that the only way to counteract our proclivity to negativity—to move beyond fear-based beliefs and decision making—was to rewire the mind. By doing so, one might *"prove what is that good and acceptable and perfect will of God."* I like how the New Life Version translates this verse:

Do not act like the sinful people of the world. Let God change your life. First of all, let Him give you a new mind. Then you will know what God wants you to do. And the things you do will be good and pleasing and perfect (Romans 12:2).

So let's look again at the fruit of the Spirit in light of its potential effects on your soul. Like any fruit that provides powerful antioxidants that build your body's immune system, so the fruit of the Spirit is a powerhouse of *dis*-ease fighting nutrients undergirding the health of your soul. When you look at the effects negative emotions have on not only your psyche, but also your physiology, it's no wonder that God would instruct you to fill up on ample servings of *"love, joy, peace, patience, kindness, goodness, faithfulness, gentleness, and self-control"* (Gal. 5:22). As we've just learned, positive attitudes and behaviors are the tools you use to rewire your brain. "The impact of practicing and retaining a more positive thinking pattern," concludes Chen, "especially on our well-being and happiness, [is] powerful."

Emotional disciplines are important because they dictate how we feel about who we are. They are the bridge between the mind and the body. "Emotions that have been suppressed do not just disappear into the ethers," writes author Janet Reed. "They collect in the body."

When emotions of fear, anger, lack, or pain are held in the body they impede the ability for the affected organs to do their job efficiently. Science now knows that receptor sites on cells for particular peptides are disrupted or close down altogether. Since the body is a network of interconnected physical expression, any organ system that has been compromised will weaken the entire system, and reduce mental clarity.[2]

Clarity of mind is essential to overcoming the emotional habits that lead to dangerous soul ties and critical to the pro-

YOU BY DIVINE DESIGN

cess of reclaiming your soul. Knowledge is indeed power. Your ability to recognize and then influence the functioning of your brain through the conscious use of directed thoughts and experiences is the power of neuroplasticity. The latest research indicates that the adult brain not only has the ability to repair regions damaged by emotional trauma, but to also grow new neurons. "In the not-too-distant future," writes Reed, "we will begin hearing more about the effects of the mind on the mind, and the power of the mind to direct and master its own fate."

The science of the mind and the physiology of the brain have come to the forefront in recent years as we explore why we do what we do. Yet through spiritual discernment, Apostle Paul understood the dynamics of neuroplasticity—the power of belief, attitudes, and mindsets—as an essential key to empowering individuals to press toward their highest calling. And as Apostle Peter wrote, to *"obtaining the outcome of your faith, the salvation of your souls"* (1 Pet. 1:9 ESV).

Hundreds of books have been written about the issues keeping us from fulfilling our potential or experiencing greater success—and many are indeed helpful; yet, until we understand the true causes of what is holding us back, we are putting a bandage over problems whose roots lie deep within us—even within the neural structures of our brains.

Understanding the power of our minds to redirect the course of our lives—combining knowledge of scientific truths with knowledge of the Word of Truth, founded on our belief in the redemption provided by the blood of Jesus—can deliver us from any emotional strongholds and set us free to be who we really are. We must not be complacent. We cannot fulfill our purpose and maximize our potential as the salt and light of the earth if we continue in our old thought patterns and ways of interacting with the world and people around us. We must continue to pursue understanding as we unveil the nature of our human dilemma. For until we can embrace and fully own our deeply rooted perceptions and beliefs, we will remain captive to our own misconceptions.

> Education...is the leading of human souls to what is best, and making what is best out of them; and these two objects are always attainable together, and by the same means; the training which makes men happiest in themselves, also makes them most serviceable to others.
> —John Ruskin

Chapter Three

LONGING
FOR BELONGING

Man is a knot into which relationships are tied.
—Antoine de Saint-Exupéry

Once the realization is accepted that even between
the closest human beings infinite distances continue, a wonderful living side by side can grow, if
they succeed in loving the distance between them
which makes it possible for each to see the other
whole against the sky. —Rainer Maria Rilke

Righting our relationships is a primary goal of this book. If
we have unhealthy soul ties in our relationships, we remain
restrained from living a resilient life. Relationships are a key
factor that either propel us forward toward resiliency or hold
us back from fulfilling our destiny. There is no such thing as
a healthy relationship that produces stagnation. On the other
hand, we can cultivate ties with people who propel us into
new seasons, help us embrace greater levels of success, offer
strengths for our weaknesses, and partner with us in our vision
to change the world. Whether we change the world, change our
lives, or simply continue living life as we always have, the soul
ties formed through relationships are essential contributors to
which type of reality we experience.

In this chapter, we are going to explore the connection between relational attachments and the state of our souls.

We come into the world with a deficit—a kind of hole in our souls that can only be filled as we relate to God and to each other in a healthy way. There is something that we all need from the very beginning, and all of us spend a lifetime trying to compensate for it through our relationships. It is a need that can only be met a little at a time, a day at a time, for we can't go very long without feeling the need to connect to someone else. This is why social media has become so successful—people want to feel connected. It is a need that, unless met in the right ways, can drive us to take desperate action and make destructive choices. What is this divine deficit? It is the need for acceptance, belonging, and genuine connection with others. It is the longing for belonging without which we are incomplete.

> *Relationships are a key factor that either propel us forward toward resiliency or hold us back from fulfilling our destiny.*

When we are infants, we cry out for it. As we enter the toddler years, we run toward it as fast as our little legs can carry us. Throughout our childhood and into our teen years we search it out wherever we go making friends, finding mentors, and emulating role models. As we reach adulthood, we look for soul mates to partner with—most intimately in marriage, but also in business, society, and in pursuit of building a better world. We attach to political parties, community organizations, add our names to social causes, even become fans of certain sports teams or celebrities in order to find a place to fit in with like-minded people. We long to belong, and this driving force can lead us to great things. In fact, we can't find true success without it; but it can also lead us to despair, heartache, and defeat and we sometimes go, as the song says, "looking for love in all the wrong places."

In 2003, The Commission on Children at Risk issued a report they titled *Hardwired to Connect*. Through their research, they put forward the following theory outlining the two basic needs of every human soul:

> First, a great deal of evidence shows that we are hard-wired for close attachments to other people, beginning with our mothers, fathers, and extended family, and then moving out to the broader community.
>
> Second, a less definitive but still significant body of evidence suggests that we are hardwired for meaning, born with a built-in capacity and drive to search for purpose and reflect on life's ultimate ends.[1]

Another way to look at this is when God created us, He built into us a soulish cavity where He Himself would fit into our lives. Many Christian teachers have called this "a God-sized hole." We were created so we would never be complete without connecting with God, and by extension, we would then have dreams and aspirations so great that we could never accomplish them on our own.

For example, having a family, building a business, or changing a community or nation will rarely happen by someone who lives as a hermit. This need to connect in order to live for a purpose greater than simply meeting our own basic needs and desires is stitched into the very fabric of our souls. We are very much like those atoms floating around in the universe that require other atoms so that they can join together and create the building blocks of the cosmos. The molecules of everything that we see and that allow life to exist are dependent on these atoms finding each

> *This need to live for a purpose greater than simply meeting our own basic needs and desires is stitched into the very fabric of our souls.*

other and joining together. Our relationships seem to have the same significance.

UNDERSTANDING RELATIONAL SOUL TIES

So, what exactly is it about our relationships that ensnares and ties up our souls? No other dynamic in the universe has the power to so utterly bind our minds than our interpersonal relations. The world wouldn't be a problem to live in if it weren't for other people! However, it is also our connection with those people that makes our lives abundant and joyful.

The fact is, your soul is an electromagnetic life force that, as the term implies, creates a magnetic field of energy. *Electromagnetism*—or an *electromagnetic field*—is defined as "a fundamental physical force that is responsible for interactions between charged particles."[2] Electromagnetic energy is a powerful attractor—especially of other electromagnetic forces, such as other souls. This is why attachments between people can be so particularly strong. In the case of marriage, the "one flesh" paradigm that God intended is an incredibly potent and beautiful thing. Entering into a covenant agreement—"tying the knot" so to speak—is a biblical mechanism for creating divinely ordained *soulular* connections. It is supernaturally ordained and powerfully influential.

There are many examples in the Bible of these types of divinely inspired "soul ties" between people. One of the best-known examples of an honorable soul tie was between David and Jonathan: *"The soul of Jonathan was knit to the soul of David, and Jonathan loved him as his own soul"* (1 Sam. 18:1). There are also many examples of dishonorable soul ties, such as what took place between David and Bathsheba when he *"took her; and she came to him, and he lay with her"* (2 Sam. 11:4). Adultery and fornication always result in powerfully destructive attachments. In David's case, things went from bad to worse when after he slept with Bathsheba, he arranged for her husband to be killed in battle. The consequence was the loss of their infant son and ongoing conflict within his family for the rest of his days.

The story of Ruth, on the other hand, provides a beautiful illustration of how a divinely inspired connection is established. Ruth was Naomi's daughter-in-law who refused to leave her side even after the death of her husband, Naomi's son. Ruth said to Naomi,

> *Do not urge me to leave you or to return from following you. For where you go I will go, and where you lodge I will lodge. Your people shall be my people, and your God my God. Where you die I will die, and there will I be buried. May the Lord do so to me and more also if anything but death parts me from you* (Ruth 1:16-17 ESV).

God blessed the covenant Ruth made with Naomi by giving her the distinguished honor of becoming the great-grandmother of David—through whose descendants came Jesus.

From this passage in Ruth, we see that a soul tie is both a psychological and an emotional attachment that creates a kind of interdependency between one person and another person, tribe, community, culture, or other social group. These attachments bind in such a way that the strengths, weaknesses, habits, handicaps, iniquities, inadequacies, temptations, mindsets, beliefs, perceptions, persuasions, likes, dislikes, proclivities, propensities, etc. of an individual or group affect the emotions, mindset, beliefs, perceptions, destiny, and so on of another individual. Soul ties keep you connected spiritually, intellectually, emotionally, psychologically, mentally, and sometimes even socioeconomically. Soul ties empower or exploit, emancipate or dominate, enable or burden. This is why family and cultural ties are so powerful.

Soul ties empower or exploit, emancipate or dominate, enable or burden.

The ties you have with your church community are, or should be, a source of empowerment on every level, while the ties you have with the world, if you look closely, are most often disempowering and debilitating. The world is not looking to build you up, but like the enemy, is predisposed to "devouring" you! (See First Peter 5:8.)

UNHOLY SOUL TIES

This is why Paul told the believers in Corinth not to be unequally attached to people who do not know Jesus. He knew the power a soul tie has in determining the direction of a life. Yes, you have the saving grace of God at work within you, but your soul can still be yoked to the enslaving grip of the world if you don't choose to reject the ways of the world and follow Jesus *"with all your heart, with all your soul, with all your mind, and with all your strength"* (Mark 12:30). Paul warned the Corinthians:

> *Don't team up with those who are unbelievers. How can righteousness be a partner with wickedness? How can light live with darkness? What harmony can there be between Christ and the devil? How can a believer be a partner with an unbeliever? And what union can there be between God's temple and idols?* (2 Corinthians 6:14-16 NLT).

And then Paul brings it home with this amazing truth:

> *For we are the temple of the living God. As God said: "I will live in them and walk among them. **I will be their God, and they will be my people.** Therefore, come out from among unbelievers, and separate yourselves from them, says the Lord. Don't touch their filthy things, and I will welcome you"* (2 Corinthians 6:16-17 NLT).

You—your soul—can't house the living God and at the same time play host to evil. The peace of God cannot reign supreme in that environment. Where God is in His fullness, however, evil must flee.

In several other translations of Second Corinthians 6:14, you will see this instruction worded as *"do not be unequally yoked."* This gives the perfect illustration of how a soulish connection works. A *yoke* was used to tie two animals together to pull something—it was a crossbar fitted to their necks that bound them together so wherever one went the other was forced to go alongside. The implication is that whenever relationships are formed, you mutually travel in the same realms and dimensions of success or failure, prosperity or poverty, honor or degradation, peace or conflict, strength or weakness, righteousness or perversion. It's critically important to whom, or to what, you become yoked. When you are in close fellowship with unbelievers, you are yoking yourself to faithlessness, unbelief, mistrust, rebellion, separation from God, selfishness, and guilt. Why is that? Because *fellowship* means to commune with, agree to, share in, and in a sense, *become one with.* Wherever the person, organization, or culture you fellowship with moves in the earth or spirit realm is where you will go as well. Whoever is yoked with that entity ultimately "travels" with it into blessing or cursing, prosperity or lack, favor or hardship, life or death, or gain or loss.

Yokes of fellowship can manifest in a whole host of ways and on a multitude of levels which include, but are not limited to: physical, psychological, systemic, spiritual, emotional, interpersonal, intrapersonal, transpersonal, social, economic, intellectual, institutional, behavioral, neurological, familial, or professional. Unholy soul attachments create instability in relations, finances, business, and friendships. They connect you *soulishly* and spiritually; frustrating purpose, undermining potential, and constricting you like a boa that cunningly wraps itself around you and then snuffs the life out of you when you least expect it.

Unhealthy emotional ties not only drain the life out of you

personally, but are also a drain on the life of organizations, companies, and even communities. Dysfunctional relationship patterns affect the profitability of corporations and the effectiveness of institutions, including, most especially, national governments. Often, these patterns are the result of the stories we repeatedly tell ourselves and come to believe, regardless of their truth. In a cultural context, whether in an organization or a nation, these stories predispose the collective mind to make decisions based on limiting perceptions and fear-based beliefs. In fact, the power of the collective conscious can be so great that it overrides individual conscious. History is replete with examples of the destructive force of "group think."

RE-SCRIPT YOUR STORY

For now, suffice it to say that we, and the groups we associate with, are products of the scripts and stories we have come to accept about who we are. Author of *New Beliefs, New Brain,* Lisa Wimberger, observes: "We tell ourselves stories every minute of every day—stories of who we are, who we've been, and who we should be. Those stories drift out from us, spreading their seeds to take root and create a history into which we anchor." Furthermore, Wimberger writes, "When the mind tells us a story, we believe it. But what if the story you're telling yourself right now is the driving force behind your pain, stress, and fear? What would you do differently?"[3] Many stories play over and over in our subconscious minds. They are repressed so deeply that it requires an encounter with God Himself to access, reveal, and heal these ingrained scripts.

Again, knowledge—self-knowledge—is power. We can't change what we are not aware of. We have the inherent power to re-script our stories—to re-script our relationships and our lives. Our brains don't care if what we think or choose to believe is real or not; they are wired to respond to thoughts and images as if they are real. We've seen the effects of the stories we repeat and the emotions they produce in our physiology—how much more will we see these effects in our relationships? If they show up in our physical bodies as disorders and disease, certainly they will manifest as disorders in the Body of Christ.

Wimberger asks her readers to consider the following questions: "How many silent sub-stories do you tell yourself, just under the surface, which literally alter the images you see and the reality you perceive? ...If the brain makes up stories and we claim those stories to be truth, then why not consciously create new stories—equally plausible—to rewrite our truths? It is our choice."

God has given you the power to choose—and the power to change. He has given you power to rewire your mind with the Truth of His Word. What does God say about who you are? What does the Word say about your potential, your purpose, your identity, your circumstances? There is a higher order, a higher truth, a higher reality than what your senses are prone to tell your brain, or what your brain is prone to tell your senses. Not only are you working against the natural tendencies of your flesh in a corrupt and fallen world, but you also have an adversary *"seeking whom he may devour"* (1 Pet. 5:8).

For every good gift that God has created, the enemy has a perversion meant for evil. The brain's ability to make new connections and create fresh neural pathways is a gift, but it can also work against you. Likewise, the connections and soul ties— we could call them "transneural pathways"—created between people and groups of people can be holy, nourishing, empowering, and beautiful. We have all experienced the joy of sharing deeply with another living soul. Yet, the intimate relationships, caring communion, authoritative agreements, binding covenants, deep fellowship, and lasting bonds that God meant for human good and His glory have been used by the enemy as tools for enslavement and destruction. Understanding how the enemy does this, the types of ties he uses to bind and defile our souls, and what we can do to break free are all the tools we need to overcome his evil devices. This is how you are able to *"work out your own salvation with fear and trembling"* knowing *"it is God who works in you both to will and to do for His good pleasure"* (Phil. 2:12-13).

Knowledge of God's power at work in you will set you free. As Paul told the Romans, *"What we've learned is this: God does not respond to what we do; we respond to what God does"* (Rom. 3:27-28 MSG). The more we learn about what God is doing in the universe—the universe not only expanding around us, but also within us—the more effectively we will be able to respond it.

Dr. Vilayanur S. Ramachandran, called the "Marco Polo of neuroscience" made the following observation: "There are 100 billion neurons in the adult human brain and each neuron makes 1,000 to 10,000 contacts with other neurons in the brain. The number of permutations and combinations of brain activity exceeds the number of elementary particles in the universe." Think about that for moment. Think of the possibilities—the potential—let alone the sheer creative power of the human imagination.

What might seem miraculous now, will one day become—like so many other discoveries—common knowledge. Quantum physicists are currently studying new dimensions each representing new realms of infinite possibilities. Interestingly, each dimension is called a "degree of freedom" made up of nonphysical, yet measurable, waves of energy that influence everything and of which everything is made. Subatomic particles consisting of plane waves create electromagnetic fields within which electrons oscillate back and forth in an endless exchange, connecting and reconnecting—like the neural synapses within our brains—a dance of ever-present currents much like the interchanges and exchanges we continually have with one another.

Pure energy. Energy patterns we can influence as much as they influence us.

The key to resiliency is stewarding this relational energy for the higher good. It is amazing the dualistic potential and possibility of discovery each exchange offers. Just as the many exchanges in science possess the ability to both create or destroy, so the relational exchanges we engage in daily have the ability to contribute to our personal resiliency as well as keep us ensnared in an endless cycle of bondage.

> There is an internal landscape, a geography of the soul; we search for its outlines in our lives. Those who are lucky enough to find it, ease like water over a stone, on to its fluid contours, and are home. —Josephine Hart

Chapter Four

THE POWER TO CHANGE

Everything is either an opportunity to grow or an obstacle to keep you from growing. You get to choose. —Wayne Dyer

And you shall know the truth, and the truth shall make you free (John 8:32).

Life is characterized by change. Change is all around us. The world changes every three months—we call it seasons. Change is a law of life. Whether you realize it or not, change is happening all of the time, and each one of us consciously, or unconsciously, is a participant.

I have learned that it is not the strongest that survive, nor the most intelligent, but the most adaptable. The same is true for thriving, successful relationships—they must adapt to changing circumstances, needs, and seasons of life. So many people seek to create richer lives and relationships, yet continuously do the same things over and over again—they simply refuse to adapt. Overcoming challenging circumstances and resolving conflicts requires you to be flexible enough to change.

Incredible as it may seem, many people never even contemplate entering into the process of change. Such individuals prefer to continue with their old lifestyles and habits even if they feel miserable, lonely, bored, inadequate, or abused. They aspire to live cautiously within the perceived safety of established patterns and routines. Although they don't feel fulfilled, and never will, they pursue a formula they hope will protect them from failure—desperately trying to "make do" or "make something work"; a marriage that is withering, a dead-end job, or even an addiction.

These individuals, on a daily basis, put their formula into practice. When they get up in the morning they put on the appropriate "mask" for the day, and then go out to merge with the anonymous masses that are also busy putting a similar formula into practice. Everyone then is content to "go along with the crowd," to "people please," and ensure that the "boat is never rocked"—maintaining the status quo, for them, has become the primary aim. Unfortunately, such persons not only lack the motivation to change, they lack the courage to change. Granted, most people are not motivated to do what they are afraid of—yet change requires courage:

- It takes courage to believe change is possible
- It takes courage to trust one's self to change
- It takes courage to move from the familiar to the unfamiliar
- It takes courage to open one's mind to new possibilities
- It takes courage to cooperate with the process of change
- It takes courage to feel vulnerable during times of change
- It takes courage to let go of old habits
- It takes courage to face new, unforeseen challenges
- It takes courage to be the change one wants to see

Could you muster the courage to change if you knew it would lead to greater freedom, fulfillment, and joy? The greatest gift you can give yourself is the gift of change. The greatest skill you can acquire is that of learning to manage change. Could things be the way they are because you are the way you are? What one thing can you change that will change everything? Although you cannot go back in life to restart your beginning, you can start today to create a new ending. How? By harnessing the power to change.

PRACTICE STRETCHING

Change requires tremendous flexibility. It is our inflexibility that prohibits us from benefiting from the ongoing transformational processes taking place all around and within us. Yet these are the processes that enable us to grow. If we are not growing, we are stagnating. And we know nothing good comes from stagnation—in fact, it can lead to both proverbial and literal death, especially when it comes to our relationships.

Change and growth will stretch us, and in the stretching we build our capacity to do and become more. This can feel risky because it requires a certain vulnerability. And yes it takes courage. Courage, however, is not a feeling. Courage is simply a decision to endure feeling vulnerable. That vulnerability is required for you to live more authentically—and is vital to strengthening the health of your relationships. According to vulnerability expert, Dr. Brene Brown, "Vulnerability is the core, the heart, the center, of meaningful human experiences." Brown links vulnerability to wholeness and resiliency. In fact, she writes in her best-selling book, *Daring Greatly*:

> The willingness to be vulnerable emerged as the single clearest value shared by all of the women and men whom I would describe as wholehearted. They attribute everything—from their professional success to their marriages to their proudest parenting moments—to their ability to be vulnerable.[1]

She adds that it is our vulnerability that "determines the depth of our courage and the clarity of our purpose"—and that

71

"the level to which we protect ourselves from being vulnerable is a measure of our fear and disconnection."[2] If you can't muster the courage to be vulnerable when circumstances demand it, how can you demand the same from others? Stay connected, stay engaged, stay in the game by deciding to endure feeling vulnerable. It will stretch you and help you press through to greater resiliency and wholeness in every area.

Managing change is simply embracing that *you* must change. When you change, you will find so does the situation. As Mahatma Gandhi so famously said, "We must be the change we wish to see." Dr. Viktor Frankl, a holocaust survivor, echoed this by stating, "When we are no longer able to change a situation, we are challenged to change ourselves."

So what do *you* need to do to change?

ADD TO YOUR FAITH KNOWLEDGE

We read a great deal about change and transformation in the New Testament. When we accept Christ as our Lord and Savior we become a new creation[3]—we are changed from glory to glory[4]—transformed by the renewing of our mind[5]. We are told in Second Peter that we can change our very nature by adding knowledge to our faith. Knowledge is not only power, but it is the power to change. Discernment and insight enable you to make internal adjustments that allow you to alter your course—to adapt to diverse circumstances and people.

The best way for you to protect yourself in any area of life is through knowledge—and the proper application of it, which is wisdom. The Bible says, "*A wise man is strong and is better than a strong man, and a man of knowledge increases and strengthens his power*"[6]—it also says, "*My people are destroyed for lack of knowledge.*"[7] The more you know about the forces working to diminish the life of your soul—the source of the abundant life Jesus paid for you to have—the more light you can shine on the specific ties and attachments keeping you in bondage. The more you know about how they are formed, the less power they will have over you and the more power you will have to resist and, if necessary, break them.

Our goal is to empower you to live a more resilient life. In order to do this, it is imperative for us to first identify the enemies of resilience, which come in the form of *destructive* soul attachments. The key clarifier here is "destructive."

As we've discussed, not all soul attachments are bad. There are legitimate connections and relationships that are divinely appointed, such as the ties between husbands and wives, parents and children, family and kinship groups, divine friendships, business partnerships, joint ministry ventures, community collaboratives, and institutional liaisons. These can be personally empowering and socially and spiritually edifying. But as we have seen, there are also illegitimate soul ties that can be destructive and plummet a

> *The most evil component of a soul tie is not how it binds, but how it blinds.*

person into cycles of defeat and failure. The most evil component of a soul tie is not how it binds, but how it blinds. What we can see we can take authority over or work to change. It's what we can't see that keeps us held hostage and in bondages we don't even realize we are trapped in. As novelist James Arthur Baldwin observed, "Not everything that is faced can be changed, but nothing can be changed until it is faced."[8]

FORCES OPPOSING A RESILIENT LIFE

There is a wide range and varying degrees of soul ties—and innumerable avenues through which they are created—but the principles and processes for how they are formed and dissolved are fairly simple.

In short, Jesus provided the grace to liberate us from any

soulish entanglement—*"for where the Spirit of the Lord is, there is liberty."*[9] At the same time, our own negligence, sin, or ignorance can keep us returning to the same traps of entanglement. This is why entrapping soul ties are a direct assault to the resilient life. Resilience creates a lifestyle that is completely opposite to what destructive soul ties work in us. Though God has made provision for us to experience freedom from these attachments, it is key that we discover how to maintain this freedom as a way of life rather than pursuing a lifelong series of trips to the altar, continually laying down and picking up what God desires us to walk in victory over. Keep in mind; God desires a victorious, resilient life to be your normal, not the occasional exception.

Proverbs 5:22 notes, *"His own iniquities entrap the wicked man, and he is caught in the cords of his sin."* *"Cords of sin"* bind us to doing what is wrong or from doing what we know is right—they tie and tug at us, and cut us off from the resilient life of God. Reading this passage from The Message drives home the point:

> *Mark well that GOD doesn't miss a move you make; he's aware of every step you take. The shadow of your sin will overtake you; you'll find yourself stumbling all over yourself in the dark. Death is the reward of an undisciplined life; your foolish decisions trap you in a dead end* (Proverbs 5:21-23 MSG).

Have you ever felt as though you are stumbling over yourself in the dark, groping for the light? Could there be something spiritual—something you're not even aware of—hovering like a dark shadow over your life? Or, although you may not think of yourself as being wicked or outright foolish—*maybe only a little undisciplined*—consider that it is a foolish man who thinks that as long as his little indulgences and habits do not hurt others, he has no need to concern himself with eradicating them. Again, "What one thing can you change that would change everything?"

ARE YOU FREE, OR A FREE RADICAL?

If we go back to the biophysical metaphor we introduced in the first chapter, our *soulular* health functions in a similar manner as our cellular health. To our thoughts, intentions, emotions, and desires, sins are the free radicals of our soul, and the Word of God is the ultimate antioxidant. Nutritionists tell us that we need six to eight servings of fruits and vegetables *every day* to get the antioxidants we need to keep us healthy. If you told them, "Well, I eat a big meal of fruit and vegetables every Sunday; sometimes I'll have two servings on a Sunday. I may also add a serving on Wednesday night." They would say that isn't a very healthy meal plan. In the same way, only being nourished from the Word of God on Sunday isn't enough to keep you free of "*the sin which so easily ensnares us.*"[10] That isn't *abiding* in the Word of God.

Living daily with God's Word feeding your heart and mind is the only way to keep the free radicals of lies and deception, that cause the world system to be so toxic, from clinging to your soul and corrupting your life. Praise and worship, prayer, and meditating on the Scriptures block such things from adhering to your innermost being and causing a hardness of heart and aggressive emotional cancers from metastasizing. If you find it important enough to take your vitamins on a daily basis, eat healthy foods, exercise, and brush your teeth—how much more important is a small thing like praying and reading your Bible every day? It's the one thing you can do that can very well change everything!

Don't underestimate "*the little foxes that spoil the vines.*"[11] Those little sins, small deceptions, that little bit of complacency, causes a mildew of the mind, a wasting away of your will, and a putrefaction of your emotions. Temptations are like the free radicals of the soul. When you connect with them they defile your healthy molecules, and if that happens enough, sin will metastasize into a cancer or cause the hardness that leads to cardiovascular disease of the "inner man"—which gives a whole new meaning to *heart* disease. If not treated immediately, *dis-ease* of the soul will not only derail your purpose and enjoyment of life, it *will* kill you.

We are a people to whom the windows of heaven have been thrown open—why then would we want to return to a lifestyle that drags us through hell? When we accept God's liberating grace, nothing around us changes, the change comes from within—but only if we allow it. It only if we rejoice in troubles rather than let them defeat us. Only when we resist selfish temptations and choose instead to walk in unselfish love. Only then can we live the type of life where *"we can't round up enough containers to hold everything God generously pours into our lives through the Holy Spirit!"* (Rom 5:5 MSG). It is the shift we make on the inside of us that will change everything around us.

Overcoming Your Hidden Sins

It's all too easy to persuade yourself that your hidden vices do not sabotage and deprive your soul of virtues or insight. Virtue can only take root in your soul when you are divested of your proclivity for convenience and comfort. Left unchecked, sin will draw to itself like-minded characters who will only reinforce your bad habits and shortcomings. And did you also not know the cords of other wicked and foolish people could ensnare you? David wrote in Psalm 140:5,

The proud have hidden a snare for me, and cords; They have spread a net by the wayside; They have set traps for me.

He prayed God would preserve him from those who *"purposed to make my steps stumble."*[12] He also knew that if he were ever to stumble and become ensnared, he could look to God to set him free. As he wrote in Psalm 129:4 (NLT), "*But the LORD is good; he has cut me free from the ropes of the ungodly.*"

No matter how daunting it seems to identify and under-stand all the ways your soul can be bound—from what you've done in the distant past or what others are doing around you now—if you ask God, He will give you the discernment you need to pray for the correct

> " *Virtue can only take root in your soul when you are divested of your proclivity for convenience and comfort.* "

application of His bondage-breaking grace. As we are told in Isaiah 10:27: "*It shall come to pass in that day that his burden will be taken away . . . and the yoke will be destroyed.*" Whatever has ensnared you is not greater than God's power to set you free. As Paul wrote to the Colossians, "*Stay grounded and steady in that bond of trust.*"[13]

Be encouraged. Faith in God's grace will free you from what-ever cords of sin, addiction, or unhealthy relationships you may now find yourself entangled. As it says in Romans 5:20, "*Where sin abounded, grace abounded much more.*" Yet even if you feel unable to fully embrace that grace, you can rest assured knowing that "*God is able to make all grace abound toward you*"[14] and that it "*is God who works in you both to will and to do for His good pleasure.*"[15] These truths will empower you to keep your mind anchored and fixed on God and bind you to His grace, freeing you from the corruption of sin. Fix your mind's eye on the goodness of God. Remember the words of Isaiah:

> *You will keep him in perfect peace, whose mind is stayed on You, because he trusts in You* (Isaiah 26:3).

Two things will deliver you from the power soul ties can have over you: knowledge and faith. Knowledge of how ungodly attachments form will enable you to effectively pray for deliverance; faith in God will enable you to effectively activate the grace that provides deliverance. You must hook your heart up with your mouth. Praying and speaking in faith are two sides of the same coin—the medium of exchange in the Kingdom of God—the coin you'll need to exchange for your freedom.

THE POWER OF EXCHANGE

Every action results from some kind of an exchange—from the exchange of time, energy, or attention to the exchange of atoms, particles, or molecules. It's simple physics. Newton's Third Law comes to mind: "The Law of Action-Reaction." Everything that exists is in a constant state of interaction—influencing and being influenced by whatever is around it. If the rocks and mountains bear the scars of time and events, then how much more do our souls?

As living, breathing beings, our bodies move through time and space interacting with the atmosphere and exchanging oxygen for carbon dioxide as we inhale and exhale. In the same way, our minds inhale information and exhale ignorance. When we receive Christ, our spirits inhale redemption and exhale condemnation—we exchange death for life enabling our souls to exchange the bondage of sin for the freedom of grace. That's the greatest exchange of all.

Every type of soul tie is also the result of an exchange. When you sin, for example, you exchange a righteous activity for an unrighteous one—or your right standing with God for separation from God. You exchange what is of God for what is of the world: "*The lust of the flesh, the lust of the eyes, and the pride of life.*"[16] You exchange obedience for disobedience, blessing for cursing.

An *exchange* is defined as: "The act of giving or taking one thing in return for another; the act or process of substituting one thing for another."[17] On the atomic level, it is "the transfer of particles."[18] Soul ties are formed through extrinsic and intrinsic exchanges with people, entities, and even ideas. Soul ties result from the exchange of energy at the most basic level, from what you pay attention to, invest your time in, communicate with, or desire, to what you give and receive in terms of money, gifts, services, acts, and symbolic gestures.

A soul attachment can be created through an extrinsic exchange, which represents how you are impacted by your environment, culture, and society—things outside of you. Additionally, soul attachments can be created through intrinsic exchanges, which deal with how you are impacted by your own paradigms, experiences, core values, personality or perceptions—things that are inside of you or inside of others that you are drawn to.

Two Powerful Exchanges: Your Words and Thoughts

Your words and thoughts are powerful mediums of exchange—they are significant carriers of energy, and in some respects, are your most valuable natural resource. They carry limitless potential to create as well as destroy. As Proverbs states, *"Death and life are in the power of the tongue."*[19]

The concept of exchange is more clearly revealed in the verse previous to this passage, *"A man's stomach shall be satisfied from the fruit of his mouth; from the produce of his lips he shall be filled."*[20] To say this another way, the words you speak result in an exchange. As God said through the prophet Isaiah,

> *So shall My word be that goes forth from My mouth; It shall not return to Me void, But it shall accomplish what I please, And it shall prosper in the thing for which I sent it* (Isaiah 55:11).

Your words—especially when they are conductors of God's Word—are a powerful form of currency. They provide a current through which creative energy is conducted—a currency recognized in every realm and dimension. Like any treasure or economic unit of exchange, where you invest it is where your heart will be bound.[21]

This is the soul tie principle in a nutshell. What you invest energy in is what you tie your soul to, both positively and negatively. As currents of electricity create electromagnetic fields connecting positive or negative charges, your thoughts create similar fields. Your positive thoughts attract positive attachments, and your negative thoughts attract negative attachments. Within whatever your soul can conceive there is potential for attachment. As a mother will form attachments to the life conceived within her, so your soul forms attachments to whatever it thinks, feels, desires, or chooses. The seed of a thought, like the seed of a life, when planted, will always result in an exchange of energy and therefore some kind of a connection. Even when aborted or stillborn, an exchange of energy will have still taken place.

> *What you invest energy in is what you tie your soul to, both positively and negatively.*

This is the premise that underlies the Law of Attraction made so popular in recent pop culture. This is not a secular teaching, but a biblical one. The Law of Attraction teaches that we attract into our lives whatever we focus on simply because everything is made of energy and energy tends to either be positively or negatively charged—"like attracts like." The energy created by our thoughts and words that we can't see, either attracts or repels the energy produced by what we can see.[22] It is rooted in the findings of quantum physics, which states that all matter is vibrating energy; therefore nothing is unchangeable. Everything is raw energy that responds to the vibrations of our thoughts and words. This should be nothing new to us because it is how God created the universe. As Hebrews 11:3 tells us, *"By faith we understand that the worlds were framed by the word of God, so that the things which are seen were not made of things which are visible."*

EXCHANGES THAT PRODUCE ATTACHMENTS

Attraction can easily turn to attachment. Soul ties result from spiritual, intellectual, social, emotional, financial, and physical exchanges between you and other individuals, organizations, institutions, ideologies, systems, and spiritual entities—or any type of association or affiliation your spirit, mind, or body might enter into.

An exchange takes place through investments of time, energy, focus, attention, and action in the form of thoughts, deeds, or words. Exchanges can be both intentional and unintentional. Sometimes we can be completely oblivious to what we've attached our souls—something may have taken hold in our mind because we inadvertently paid attention to it for too long, like watching too much television. I believe this is why Isaiah stated, he "*who stops his ears from hearing of bloodshed, and shuts his eyes from seeing evil: He will dwell on high.*"[23]

You have to be careful what you pay attention to—what you spend time and energy thinking about and allow your thoughts to dwell upon—because one of the most powerful and binding things you can invest are your thoughts. Your life will move in the direction of what you contemplate. As it says in Proverbs 4:23 (NLT), "*Guard your heart above all else, for it determines the course of your life.*" The Message makes it especially clear that you need to be careful about everything you say, see, and focus on:

> *Keep vigilant watch over your heart; that's where life starts. Don't talk out of both sides of your mouth; avoid careless banter, white lies, and gossip. Keep your eyes straight ahead; ignore all sideshow distractions. Watch your step, and the road will stretch out smooth before you. Look neither right nor left; leave evil in the dust.*

What consumes your thoughts gives you a good indication of what ties up your soul. This is why family ties are so extremely powerful. Our family experiences shape our lives on many levels—from our DNA and genealogy to the values and beliefs we absorbed growing up. Our families inform how we navigate our surroundings, who we identify with, and how we interact with the world around us—and either nurture or erode the health of our souls from early on. Our family ties will be among the most influential, deeply rooted, and longest lasting—they influence how generations of members think and choose to live.

In fact, it has been documented that both the quantity and quality of relationships a child has growing up determines how prone that child will be as a teenager to engage in risky behaviors. The Search Institute identified what they call "40 Development Assets" that are proven to promote positive behaviors and build resiliency in youth. There are twenty internal and twenty external assets— the more assets a child has, the more resilient he or she will be. Many of the assets are built around issues of identity, integrity, commitment, and compassion in the context of family, community, peers, role models, and mentors.

> " *What consumes your thoughts gives you a good indication of what ties up your soul.* "

In the next section, we will be taking a closer look at the internal and external exchanges that can either empower or disempower us as well as the forty disciplines of a resilient person. So now with a clearer understanding of who God created us to be, the potential we have as multidimensional beings to connect with heaven and with one another, and the power of choice we've been given to live a life of wholeness and abundance, let's begin to examine those relational habits, behaviors, and best practices that will keep us free and victorious.

In the forty days ahead, we will explore the actual mechanics of emotional attachments, how they are formed, and how you can avoid and/or sever them. The keys to breaking, avoiding, and living free from these attachments are summed up in the "40 Disciplines of a Resilient Person."

Remember, God's best for your *soulular* life is resilience. It's time to end the cycle of attachment – deliverance – freedom – attachment – deliverance – freedom. The adult members of the Hebrew nation brought out of captivity never made it to the Promised Land, although it was their destiny. It was not because God did not will it for them, but because they could not shake their attachment to Egypt. How could bondage look better to them than freedom?[24]

The problem was that the Israelites of old lived in a cyclical state. Even though deliverance and freedom are positive, God-willed things, the Hebrew people experienced them only seasonally—not consistently. You and I today, having been set free, tend to launch the whole cycle of bondage over and over— either dealing with a different attachment or the same attachment repeatedly throughout our lifetime. In the same manner that we should prefer divine health to divine healing, we need to prefer a resilient lifestyle to repeated deliverance.

For the next forty days, we will look at very practical steps you can take to put your soul back in the driver's seat. You will learn to apply the Truth of God's Word to your relationships and daily encounters—the Word of Truth that is able to save and restore the health of your soul.[25] The road to greater resiliency is a process of learning how to take back your personal power each and every day.

> So much of life is how we react to what we experience. We cannot control everything that happens to us, but we can control our choices in response. Because we see various perspectives, we also visualize creative solutions. You are now more powerful than ever. —Dr. Kevin Snyder

Part Two

THE ROAD TO RESILIENCY: 40 DISCIPLINES OF A RESILIENT PERSON

Do what God tells you. Walk in the paths he shows you: Follow the life-map absolutely, keep an eye out for the signposts, his course for life set out in the revelation to Moses; then you'll get on well in whatever you do and wherever you go (1 Kings 2:1-4 MSG).

Let us lay aside every weight, and the sin which so easily ensnares us, and let us run with endurance the race that is set before us (Hebrews 12:1).

For all good and evil, whether in the body or in human nature, originates in the soul, and overflows from thence, as from the head into the eyes. —Plato

Emotions are the colors of the soul.
—William Paul Young

YOUR NEXT FORTY DAYS

I know but one freedom, and that is the freedom
of the mind. —Antoine de Saint Exupery

In the forty days ahead, I want to take you on a transformational journey. The goal of the first book in this series, *The 40
Day Soul Fast,* was to help you understand your authentic self and
provide a template for how life would look from that perspective—the position of living aligned with the truest expression of
your unique being.

At its core, *The 40 Day Soul Fast* is a journey of self-discov-
ery—coming to grips with who you are and why you're here.
Understanding your identity is foundational to living an
authentic life. Now that you are
familiar with the characteristics
of an authentic person, I want
to empower you to live out of
that identity on a behavioral
level. This is where we are going
in the next forty days, and the
genesis behind *Reclaim Your Soul: Your Journey to Personal Empowerment.* (For more personal empowerment tools, visit www.your
lifeempowerment.com.)

> *I will be showing you
> day by day how you can
> create the resiliency nec-
> essary to live strong and
> stay true to your identity.*

Over the course of the next eight weeks, we will be addressing
the behaviors and habits essential to living true to your authentic
self and developing a resilient lifestyle. I will be showing you day

by day how you can create the resiliency necessary to live strong and stay true to your identity. What is the secret to sustaining the health of your soul? What is the one thing you can do every day to maintain freedom from unhealthy attachments and soul ties? It has to do with mindfulness. It has to do with self-awareness. It has to do with being intentional and deliberate regarding how you act and react to people and circumstances. In other words, it has to do with discipline.

The Delight of Discipline

The moment someone brings up the term "discipline" in a conversation, a shift in concentration or emotion often takes place. We either tune out or we tense up, expecting that any mention of discipline is synonymous with considerable strain and joyless duty.

For too long, the concept of discipline has made us unnecessarily defensive and prone to "push back." Why? Perhaps we equate discipline with engaging in activities that are incompatible with our sense of normal, convenience, or comfort; we would rather sit and watch television than go to the gym. Our disdain for discipline and preference to cater to our fleshly appetites is the result of a faulty understanding of discipline.

We would do well to embrace a significant paradigm shift here. Connecting with your authentic self will not automatically transform your behavior and make you a resilient person overnight. Simply having a clearer sense of who you are does not mean the fruit of a more authentic lifestyle will spontaneously appear, as if knowledge by itself produces results.

> *The process of setting your knowledge into motion creates a resilient life.*

Information is not kinetic; it only holds the possibility of creating value—of *potential* energy. It is the actual *practice*—of converting that knowledge into an actionable discipline—that makes it kinetic and therefore powerful. It is the process of setting your knowledge into motion that creates a resilient life.

This is the place where the transformed soul will begin to influence your actions, change your behaviors, and build an unshakable resiliency into your life. The authentic self thus emerges and begins its conquest over destructive behavioral patterns that have perhaps plagued you for years, if not an entire lifetime.

The forty disciplines we are going to address in the upcoming forty-day journey are very practical—they will position you to respond to life's challenges with resiliency rather than being reactionary. In the days to come, I encourage you to approach discipline from a new perspective. I invite you to view these forty disciples as forty tools for developing a resilient life. They are not forty ways to make your life more difficult; on the contrary, they are forty best practices that will take you closer to experiencing the life you have always wanted.

> *We must learn how to walk in a whole new realm of freedom.*

The next eight weeks will be divided into two parts. The first four weeks specifically target the different kinds of soulish attachments that need to be broken and types of relationships that need to be healed. We must first confront the sick, hurting, and wounded aspects of our lives if we truly desire to experience transformation.

In the final four weeks, we will highlight the key principles and essential practices of those who desire to live a more resilient life. It is not enough to simply break off harmful attachments and sever destructive soul ties—we must learn how to walk in a whole new realm of freedom.

Could it be that the incredible life God has for you is just on the other side of practicing these forty simple disciplines?

DAILY SEGMENTS

As with *The 40 Day Soul Fast*, the following eight-week study has been structured to be read in five daily segments each week. This gives you the opportunity to implement a Monday through Friday practice, without the challenge of working your daily study into the often "non-routine" joys of the weekend. It is also my hope that the Sabbath remain set apart to focus exclusively on worship and family.

With that in mind, each of the five days offers the corresponding Daily Discipline that will help position you for greater resiliency as it concerns each day's topic.

The reflection segment is your daily Power Point, intended to raise your awareness of the different patterns you will be transforming in your life. Not all of the patterns you will be studying are negative in and of themselves. In fact, most of them have both healthy and unhealthy ramifications. Attachments, for example, become deadly soul ties and thwart our resiliency when they are exchanged incorrectly. This is why discipline is so important. We are not simply going to identify negative exchanges, attachments, and behaviors, but I am going to show you how they can be governed for your greatest good.

Each day concludes with a meditation or Power Thought—a quote, Scripture passage, or statement you can commit to memory and use as a springboard or empowerment tool that will help move you toward the transformation you desire.

THE VISION

The following forty days describe relational behaviors that are common to every human being. While these are common, they are not by any means comprehensive; my goal here is to simply help you develop the necessary daily disciplines to effectively negotiate and master some relational best practices. Some areas will demand that you break a potentially unhealthy soul tie. Perhaps there will be other issues you have not dealt with or even encountered yet. My hope is that your mindfulness and application of these forty daily disciplines will keep it that way!

While the effects of these behaviors have been truly devastating to so many throughout the ages—perhaps even yourself—I want you to become someone who is not only healed, whole, and personally transformed, but my vision is to see a company of people living authentic and resilient lives, bringing transformation to nations.

Sound like an enormous task? It really isn't when we understand that global and societal transformation starts with you and I, each making daily decisions that positively direct the course of our lives. The best thing you can do for the world around you is be the most empowered and resilient "you" possible by harnessing the liberating power of discipline!

For God has not given us a spirit of fear and timidity, but of power, love, and self-discipline (2 Timothy 1:7 NLT).

Let us think of life as a process of choices, one after another. At each point, there is a progression choice and a regression choice. There may be a movement towards defense, towards safety, towards being afraid; but over on the other side, there is the growth choice. To make a growth choice, instead of the fear choice, a dozen times a day is to move a dozen times a day towards self-actualization. —Abraham Maslow

Week One

CONFRONTING NATURAL SOUL TIES

Once conform, once do what others do because they do it, and a kind of lethargy steals over all the finer senses of the soul. —Michel de Montaigne

Do not be conformed to this world, but be transformed by the renewing of your mind, that you may prove what is that good and acceptable and perfect will of God (Romans 12:2).

The first two sets of exchanges we are going to explore on our forty-day journey can lead to either natural or emotional soul ties. To break these ties effectively and press onward toward a life of resiliency, it is key that we evaluate the root and origin of each.

Natural soul ties are the result of extrinsic exchanges (for example giving or receiving gifts, money, services, symbols [such as tattoos], or other physical acts) while emotional soul ties are formed by intrinsic exchanges (what you give attention to, set your intentions upon, associate with, or who you desire to be like). Both types of exchanges require an investment of physical, mental, emotional, and/or spiritual energy.

Over the next two weeks, we will primarily focus on these two types of exchanges that can potentially result in natural and emotional ties or attachments. This is what our disciplined efforts will initially be aimed at, for the behavior is transformed only when we target the root cause.

The following are examples of the various types of attachments and the spheres they fall into. Although the many ways soul attachments are formed can be divided into the following broad categories (with some overlap), I believe that understanding the nature of the exchange—whether as a result of a specific action or a general association—can help us better navigate the kinds of exchanges we choose to make (or unmake):

- Spiritual (religious, demonic/supernatural, dabbling in the dark arts, witchcraft, participation in sin)
- Intellectual (education, philosophies, ideologies, worldviews)
- Professional (business relationships, professional affiliations, memberships, associations)
- Social (culture, media and entertainment, friendships, associates, mentors, coaches)
- Emotional (romantic relationships, marriage and family, traumatic or euphoric experiences)
- Physical (sexual encounters, deviant activities, giving and receiving of gifts, wearing of tattoos or symbols)
- Institutional (marriage, family, education, church, government)

These primary classifications give an overview of some of the differing sources and forces that have the potential to snag your soul and weigh it down. However, to better explain the mechanics of how soul ties are formed, I have divided some of the channels through which attachments are made into the two main categories we talked about: natural and emotional.

In this first week, I want us to deal with the *natural* soul ties that are the result of extrinsic exchanges. In the second week, we will cover the *emotional* ties that are produced by intrinsic exchanges.

For the five days ahead, I've identified some common types of extrinsic exchanges

> " *The purpose of information is transformation.* "

and divided those into five areas involving words, objects, actions, attributes, and allegiances. Remember, the purpose of information is transformation. I want to inform you about these different areas so you can identify what needs to be transformed in your life and begin applying the appropriate discipline in each area.

In the words of John Maxwell, "Motivation gets you going, but discipline keeps you growing."

Day 1

WORDS

Handle them carefully, for words have more power than atom bombs. —Pearl Strachan

DISCIPLINE #1 — USE YOUR WORDS WISELY

Today, we'll be focusing on the first exchange that produces natural soul ties in our lives—something most of us take for granted or don't think much about. What we communicate—through both our spoken and written word—is the most common exchange we engage in on a daily basis, and probably the most critical to the health of our soul!

This is why it is vital for us to use words that build and unite, not destroy, divide, or cause us to enter into damaging agreements.

Let's explore the different ways we use our words that might potentially result in a soul tie.

Spoken Words

What you say has power.[1] What comes out of your mouth and how you behave according to it is one of the best tests of your character. Jesus made this clear when he made the correlation between the words that come out of our mouths and the condition of our hearts. "*A good person produces good things from the treasury of a good heart, and an evil person produces evil things from the treasury of an evil heart. What you say flows from what is in your heart"* (Luke 6:45 NLT). Words are not only powerful because of what they produce and create, but are powerful indicators of our true, authentic self.

> *What we communicate is the most common exchange we engage in on a daily basis, and probably the most critical to the health of our soul!*

Ask yourself: Am I a person who can be trusted, or is what I say determined by who I am with? Is my speech frivolous, negative, condemning, fearful, self-absorbed, fickle, condemning, or is it uplifting, faithful and faith-filled, positive, full of grace, courageous, and edifying? Make certain your words line up with Scripture. Get rid of carnal conversations, negativity, grumbling, and complaining. Your words actually do shape your future. I have concluded from reading Numbers 14:27-34 that there is a 1:365 ratio. For every day you release negative words out of your mouth you potentially take your life into a year's worth of bondage. In the words of Lao Tzu, "Watch your thoughts; they become words. Watch your words; they become actions. Watch your actions; they become habit. Watch your habits; they become character. Watch your character; it becomes your destiny."[2]

Vows

Verbal contracts, or covenants, can both build up and erode the well-being of a person or group of people. The wonderful covenant between David and Jonathan endured for generations after they made a vow to one another.

> *Jonathan made a covenant with the house of David.... Now Jonathan again caused David to vow...for he loved him as he loved his own soul. Then Jonathan said to David, "Go in peace, since we have both sworn in the name of the Lord, saying, 'May the Lord be between you and me, and between your descendants and my descendants, forever'"* (1 Samuel 20:16-17,42).

As a result of that vow, whatever belonged to David now belonged to Jonathan, and vice versa. They bound their strengths and resources together so both became stronger as a result.

Vows are not only made to other people, but can also be made as internal vows to our own selves. One of my coaching clients has given me permission to share a story I believe beautifully illustrates this point. She observed:

> The times that I felt threatened and bullied in any given situation were a reflection of how I felt so many times with my mother. My mom has a very assertive personality and growing up I often felt a lot of anxiety and viewed myself as a victim of her personality. As a result, I have suppressed the assertive part of me in protest to what I experienced with my mother. I made an inner vow that I would never behave that way because I felt that aspect of my mom's personality was hurtful. I absolutely did not want to treat others that way. In making this inner vow, two things have happened:
>
> 1. I suppressed a part of me that could have propelled me forward in a way that the less assertive part of me does not. I became a victim of many abusive situations that assertiveness could have prevented.
>
> 2. I came to a place where I subconsciously judged others who had stronger personalities or acted more aggressively. In judging others, I put myself on a pedestal. This type of self-righteousness kept my inner vow intact, prevented me from seeing my own issue, and held back my success.

We often think of the things people have vowed to us as the only vows that have derailed our lives. Consider the vows you have made—to yourself: "I'll never trust anyone again," "I will

never forgive him," "When I grow up, I'll never let anyone...,"
etc. *What inner vows have you made?*

Agreements

In the book of Joshua, the people of Israel were bound by an
agreement that wasn't so beneficial. Joshua was tricked by the
inhabitants of a neighboring country to enter into a covenant
of peace with them—he did not consult the Lord, but based on
their deception he *"made peace with them, and made a covenant
with them, to let them live"* (Josh. 9:15). The people of Israel were
forced to allow their enemy to dwell among them because of
their mislaid promise. (God has often been forced to do the
same thing in keeping His promises to humanity.)

> *We will let them live, lest wrath be upon us because of the oath
> which we swore to them. Let them live, but let them be woodcutters
> and water carriers for all the congregation, as the rulers had
> promised them* (Joshua 9:20-21).

In the next chapter of Joshua, five kings conspired to attack
the Gibeonites because they had made peace with Israel. Joshua
and his men were forced to defend them because of their treaty.

Later, when David was king and Saul came against the people of Gibeon, the Lord reminded David of Joshua's covenant:

> *Now there was a famine in the days of David for three years,
> year after year; and David inquired of the Lord. And the Lord
> answered, "It is because of Saul and his bloodthirsty house,
> because he killed the Gibeonites." So the king called the Gibeonites
> and spoke to them. Now the Gibeonites were not of the children of
> Israel, but of the remnant of the Amorites; the children of Israel
> had sworn protection to them, but Saul had sought to kill them
> in his zeal for the children of Israel and Judah. Therefore David
> said to the Gibeonites, "What shall I do for you? And with what*

shall I make atonement, that you may bless the inheritance of the Lord?" (2 Samuel 21:1-3)

There was famine in Israel because of a broken treaty. King David sought the Lord and the breach was revealed to him. He asked the Gibeonites what he could do to make amends. The Gibeonites asked for seven sons of Saul's descendants to be delivered to them for public execution. David agreed, but spared the life of Jonathan's son because of the covenant he had made with him. Covenant agreements are powerful and enduring. Covenants between families and nations create ties that last for generations.

Promises

The marriage covenant, or promise, works in much the same way. When you enter into a marriage contract with another person, you are in covenant with that person's entire family. Both ancestries will affect your children and your children's children. I love this quote by Sir Thomas More, also known as Saint Thomas More, who in the early sixteenth century stated:

> Marriage is an authentic weaving together of families, of two souls with their individual fates and destinies, of time and eternity—everyday life married to the timeless mysteries of the soul.

We will talk more about the "timeless mysteries" and the complexity of the ties created within the marriage relationship later, but for now, think about the covenants, promises, or vows you have made with others and the impact those may be having on your life. Think about the covenant you made with Christ and who you are now as a result. How have God's promises affected you? How have your promises affected you?

POWER POINT

Not only do your words impact those you share them with, but your words have the ability to create attachments and solidify harmful soul ties in your own life. This is why it is so important that you are mindful of the words you communicate.

Remember, your words are pure energy filled with power to create or destroy. Words don't disappear because you have forgotten them. The moment you speak, they become a powerful force for good or evil. Albert Einstein confirmed this when he said, "Energy cannot be created or destroyed; it can only be changed from one form to another." Look at Hebrews 11:4, and take note of how powerful words are.

> *You were created in the image and likeness of a God whose words are powerful.*

You were created in the image and likeness of a speaking God—a God whose words are powerful. One of the first things you can do to reclaim your soul is to use words wisely—invest them in creating, building, and encouraging. Your words not only make a world of difference, they have the power to make a difference in this world.

POWER THOUGHT

Let no corrupt word proceed out of your mouth, but what is good for necessary edification, that it may impart grace to the hearers (Ephesians 4:29).

Day 2

OBJECTS

Giving a gift can open doors... (Proverbs 18:16 NLT).

DISCIPLINE #2 — GIVE AND RECEIVE CONSCIENTIOUSLY

The giving and receiving of gifts are symbols of covenant. They forge relationship and establish allegiance. This is why it is essential that we give and receive with great caution and discernment, as the allegiances we create can either produce life or foster bondage through developing a cancerous soul tie.

Today, we are going to explore three different exchanges that all deal with the process of giving and receiving various forms of objects.

Gifts

When the Queen of Sheba wanted to forge an alliance with King Solomon, she presented him with *"one hundred and twenty talents of gold, spices in great quantity, and precious stones"* (1 Kings 10:10). The wise King Solomon understood the covenanting power of giving and receiving gifts. He gave an annual supply of wheat and oil to his servant Hiram in exchange for his loyalty. As a result, *"there was peace between Hiram and Solomon, and the two of them made a treaty together"* (1 Kings 5:12).

In the book of Daniel, you will read that the king entered into league with Daniel by giving him gifts. It was after Daniel interpreted the king's dream that King Nebuchadnezzar *"promoted Daniel and gave him many great gifts; and he made him ruler over the whole province of Babylon"* (Dan. 2:48).

You will find examples of the significance of giving and receiving gifts throughout the Bible. Where a covenant is sought, gifts will be exchanged. God sought to make a covenant with humanity and gave the gift of His Son, and then in exchange for His Son He gave His Holy Spirit. In return, we *"present* [our] *bodies a living sacrifice"* (Rom. 12:1) and *"offer up spiritual sacrifices acceptable to God through Jesus Christ"* (1 Pet. 2:5). It's an ongoing exchange. God continues to give us each spiritual gifts *"differing according to the grace that is given to us"* (Rom. 12:6).

> *God sought to make a covenant with humanity and gave the gift of His Son, and then in exchange for His Son He gave His Holy Spirit.*

Jesus said that if you and I as parents *"know how to give good gifts to your children, how much more will your Father who is in heaven give good things to those who ask Him!"* (Matt. 7:11). Gifts not only create attachments, but also are how we continue to express those attachments. I know of many people who, once a relationship disintegrates, throw away every gift given by that person. I believe it is a demonstration that whatever they had together is "over" once and for all.

Symbols

If promises and gifts have the power to create attachments, how much more do symbols? Symbols are akin to taking a promise and making it visible, such as a tattoo or a ring. Symbols are gestures, vows, insignias, shared objects, a uniform, or something else endued with meaning by those who share it. Symbols represent specific covenants between people—

specific agreements. When a slave chose to remain with his master when he could otherwise go free, he signified his promise to serve him for the rest of his life by piercing his ear: *"His master shall pierce his ear with an awl; and he shall serve him forever"* (Exod. 21:6).

When Pharaoh made Joseph his representative, he *"took his signet ring off his hand and put it on Joseph's hand; and he clothed him in garments of fine linen and put a gold chain around his neck"* (Gen. 41:42). This signified the authority Pharaoh gave Joseph to rule over Egypt as his Prime Minster, answering to no one but Pharaoh himself. When rings are exchanged as a symbol of the marriage covenant, they represent not only the retaining of love, but also the relinquishing of authority— *"The wife gives authority over her body to her husband, and the husband gives authority over his body to his wife"* (1 Cor. 7:4 NLT).

Symbols can also be the giving of significant personal possessions. When Jonathan made a covenant with David, *"Jonathan sealed the pact by taking off his robe and giving it to David, together with his tunic, sword, bow, and belt"* (1 Sam. 18:4 NLT). In the previous chapter, Saul had made a pact with David when he *"gave David his own armor—a bronze helmet and a coat of mail"* (1 Sam. 17:38 NLT).

Money Exchanged for Goods and Services

There is a story in Second Kings about the prophet Elisha who refused to receive payment from a Syrian commander, Naaman, when God healed him of leprosy according to Elisha's instructions. Naaman urged him repeatedly to accept his gifts, but Elisha refused to take anything from him, so Naaman finally left, taking his silver and fine suits of clothing with him. However, Elisha's servant, Gehazi, ran after Naaman and lied, saying two other prophets had come in need of the silver and clothing. Naaman gladly gave the silver and two changes of clothes to Gehazi. After hiding these things, Gehazi returned to Elisha, but learned you can't hide anything from God:

Elisha said to him, "Where have you been, Gehazi?" And he said, "Your servant went nowhere." But he said to him, "Did not my heart go when the man turned from his chariot to meet you? Was it a time to accept money and garments, olive orchards and vineyards, sheep and oxen, male servants and female servants? Therefore the leprosy of Naaman shall cling to you and to your descendants forever." So he went out from his presence a leper, like snow (2 Kings 5:25-27 ESV).

The message here is twofold: Not only did the leprosy of Naaman cling to Gehazi because he received the payment, but Elisha refused to receive payment because he did not want to be in league with Syria. I think that many of us are "leprous," not in the physical sense, but spiritually. We have tarnished our name and have come to undermine our reputation and influence just because of association—receiving bribes or gifts—that require our souls for life. People hold things over us: "After all I have done for you...you owe me." Sometimes it is best to simply wait on the Lord and press into His wisdom and divine strategy rather than taking money and gifts from people.

We read in Matthew that Judas entered into covenant with the Pharisees when he received payment from them. Then, in desperation to redeem himself, he tried to return the money. But it was too late. His greed and subsequent betrayal of Jesus opened a door that led to a place of no return:

*Judas...seeing that He [Jesus] had been condemned, was remorseful and brought back the thirty pieces of silver to the chief priests and elders, saying, "**I have sinned by betraying innocent blood.**" And they said, "What is that to us? You see to it!" Then he threw down the pieces of silver in the temple and departed, and went and hanged himself* (Matthew 27:3-5).

Indeed, what does it profit a man to gain the whole world and lose his soul? (See Matthew 16:26.). We see here why the love of money causes people to err and lose their way in life, ministry, and business. Paul warns Timothy that, *"the love of money is a root of all kinds of evil, for which some have strayed from the faith in their greediness, and pierced themselves through with many sorrows"* (1 Tim. 6:10).

The love of money is in itself a type of soul tie. But worse, it is the love of money that lures people away from obeying God, causing exposure to all types of intensely ensnaring and vicious soul attachments. I don't think there is a more destructive combination than exchanging sex for money. The act of prostitution causes deep and dangerous attachments. Even if the exchange isn't formally called prostitution, someone who is "taken care of" by someone who has sex with them but won't marry them is forming a dangerous tie involving both the lust of the flesh *and* the lust of money.

> *The love of money lures people away from obeying God, causing exposure to all types of intensely ensnaring and vicious soul attachments.*

POWER POINT

Remember, what you give and receive has the ability to form an attachment with another person. This is why it is so important that you are extremely conscientious of what comes into your possession, and what you exchange with someone else. While the objects themselves are not destructive, the underlying motivation or agenda in making the exchange is what is ultimately responsible for creating the soul tie.

POWER THOUGHT

You give but little when you give of your possessions. It is when you give of yourself that you truly give.
—Kahlil Gibran

Day 3

ACTIONS

Throw off your old sinful nature and your former way of life, which is corrupted by lust and deception. Instead, let the Spirit renew your thoughts and attitudes (Ephesians 4:22-23 NLT).

DISCIPLINE #3 —
PURSUE WHOLESOME ACTIVITIES

What we do often reveals who we are. Problems arise for those whose actions and identities are in staunch disagreement. One of the fundamental disciplines for someone who has decided to break harmful soul attachments and live the resilient life is becoming extremely conscientious of the activities they are participating in. Are your actions aligned with who you want to be? Socrates is quoted for having said, "The way to gain a good reputation is to endeavor to be who you desire to appear." That's called "integrity"—and it's one of the essential keys to building resiliency.

There are several different exchanges that result from our actions and activities, which have the power to create strong, destructive soul ties. As you will see, these are the types of ties that erode the integrity, and therefore resiliency, of a person's life.

Sexual Encounters

The Bible is very clear on the dangers of sex outside of marriage. Your body not only becomes one with another, but so does your soul. The act of sex is not limited to your genitals; it involves your entire being. To "know" another person in a biblical sense is to "become one" with them—it is "the act" of marriage, *the two shall become one flesh; so then they are no longer two, but one flesh*" (Mark 10:8). It is when two people intimately reveal themselves—or make themselves fully known to one another. This is how a marriage is consummated—not by any ceremony or legal document—but by engaging in the act of sexual intercourse.

Because of the covenant nature of sex, it is meant to stay within the context of marriage. This is why Paul wrote the Corinthians:

> *Do you not know that your bodies are members of Christ? Shall I then take the members of Christ and make them members of a prostitute? Never! Or do you not know that he who is joined to a prostitute becomes one body with her? For, as it is written, "The two will become one flesh."* (1 Corinthians 6:15-16 ESV).

This oneness principle is a foundational truth and a profound mystery—you become one with someone when you physically engage in acts of *intimacy*. Even as you opened your heart up to Christ, you became one with Him as we are told in First Corinthians 6:17, *"He who is joined to the Lord is one spirit with Him."* So it is when you open yourself to another. Because you are one with Christ, your body is therefore sacred—it is *"the temple of the Holy Spirit who is in you"* (1 Cor. 6:19). This is why it is especially important to *"flee sexual immorality"* (1 Cor. 6:18). Why? Because *"the sexually immoral person sins against his own body* [and therefore against Christ's Body]. *You are not your own, for you were bought with a price. So glorify God in your body"* (1 Cor. 6:18,20 ESV). Or, as The Message explains this passage:

> *There's more to sex than mere skin on skin. Sex is as much spiritual mystery as physical fact. As written in Scripture, "The*

*two become one." There is a sense in which sexual sins are different from all others. In sexual sin we violate the sacredness of our own bodies, these bodies that were made for God-given and God-modeled love, for "becoming one" with another. Or didn't you realize that **your body is a sacred place, the place of the Holy Spirit**? The physical part of you is not some piece of property belonging to the spiritual part of you. God owns the whole works. So let people see God in and through your body* (1 Corinthians 6:18-20 MSG).

When you engage in a physical, sexual relationship with anyone, you actually share a piece of your soul with him or her, as they share a piece of theirs with you as well. Unfortunately today, people are walking away from sexual experiences with more than just a soul tie. They are walking away with communicable diseases that are often incurable.

Euphoric Experiences from Deviant Activities

Euphoric experiences result from an activity or experience that creates a kinesthetic memory, longing, or fantasy such as engaging in pornography, promiscuity, perversion, sexual or physical abuse, drug and alcohol abuse, demonic fascination, or satanic worship. Deviant activities will create experiences and feelings that will consume your thought life—they will take over your mind and tie up your soul.

The men of Sodom were consumed by such thoughts. They couldn't think "straight"—their minds were twisted to the point where they were banging down Lot's door calling out, *"Where are the men who came to you tonight?*

> *Deviant activities create experiences and feelings that consume your thought life, take over your mind, and tie up your soul.*

Bring them out to us that we may know them carnally" (Gen. 19:5). They would have broken down the door if the angels hadn't struck them blind. God's wrath was about to fall upon Sodom, so while Lot lingered,

> *The* [angels] *took hold of his hand, his wife's hand, and the hands of his two daughters, the Lord being merciful to him, and they brought him out and set him outside the city.* **But his wife looked back behind him, and she became a pillar of salt** (Genesis 19:16,26).

You must not allow your mind to even ponder such deviant activities.

In Leviticus, God gave the Israelites very specific instruction about how to conduct themselves: "*Do not act like the people in Egypt, where you used to live, or like the people of Canaan, where I am taking you. You must not imitate their way of life*" (Lev. 18:3 NLT). Then the next eighteen verses each list a sexual perversion to avoid. God follows these explicit instructions with the strict command, "*Do not defile yourselves in any of these ways*" (Lev. 18:24 NLT) and then with the warning,

> *Whoever commits any of these detestable sins will be cut off from the community of Israel. So obey my instructions, and do not defile yourselves by committing any of these detestable practices that were committed by the people who lived in the land before you. I am the Lord your God* (Leviticus 18:29-30 NLT).

Many believers suffer because of this kind of soul tie. But take heart, Christ has redeemed your life from the curse. In the Old Testament, people had to be removed (or executed!) in order to remove sin from the community. Sinful people groups were eliminated in order to keep their influence away from the children of Israel. However, because of what Jesus did, today we have the power to remove the sin—and its influence—not only from *among* the people, but also from *within* the people. The blood of Jesus has made this possible on an individual basis. Yet although the age of grace has changed how we deal with sin, the issue remains the same—sin will keep us from living in all God has for us!

Mutual Participation in Sin

Sin is the free radical that joins to the good things in our souls and corrupts them. When you engage in a physical act or activity that is in direct disobedience to God, you open your soul to heart *dis*-ease and spiritual cancer. Jesus said, *"This is war, and there is no neutral ground. If you're not on my side, you're the enemy; if you're not helping, you're making things worse"* (Luke 11:23 MSG). You can either serve sin or serve God, but not both. Whichever you choose to serve will rule over you.

> *Sin is the free radical that joins to the good things in our souls and corrupts them.*

Paul told the church in Rome, *"Do you not know that to whom you present yourselves slaves to obey, you are that one's slaves whom you obey, whether of sin leading to death, or of obedience leading to righteousness?"* (Rom. 6:16). The good news is that you can choose. You can choose to *"use your whole body as an instrument to do what is right for the glory of God. Sin is no longer your master"* (Rom. 6:13-14 NLT).

However, when you choose to obey sin, and when you do it in league with another person, you compound the attachment. This includes being an accomplice, such as lying on behalf of another to cover up their sin, or any type of mutual deception. Your soul is not only ensnared by the sin, but also by the person with whom you engaged in the sin. It's the power of agreement working against you—the power of the sin to bind you becomes doubly strong. Separate yourself from sin, and from sinful people— *"You must not imitate their way of life"* (Lev. 18:3 NLT).

POWER POINT

Remember, Christ and His Word define your identity. When you truly understand who you are, then you will recognize that certain actions and activities are far below the standard God has assigned to your life—consider them unworthy of your investment.

POWER THOUGHT

The pleasure of sin is soon gone, but the sting remains. — Thomas Watson

Day 4

ATTRIBUTES

Sin will take you farther than you want to go, keep you longer than you want to stay, and cost you more than you want to pay. —Author unknown

DISCIPLINE #4—KEEP YOUR BODY HOLY AND SPIRITUALLY HEALTHY

For too long, we have devalued our bodies, not recognizing that they are the true windows to our souls. What comes out, by definition, is a revelation of what is on the inside. To consider that thought, many of us would surely cringe, mindful of the chasm between who we believe we are and what our bodies say about who we are. Unfortunately, our "body language" is often the result of harmful soul attachments we have made by how we use our bodies.

It bears repeating that information does not inherently contain the power to transform. You may be informed about your true, authentic self and that is step one. But in order to become someone who is both transformed, and a transformer, you need to marry that information with discipline. We need to treat our bodies like Apostle Paul did: "*I discipline my body like an athlete, training it to do what it should. Otherwise, I fear that after preaching to others I myself might be disqualified*" (1 Cor. 9:27 NLT).

Paul was mindful of the conflict between his true authentic

self, and the self that he would occasionally project; as he often did the very things that he did not want to do (see Rom. 7:15). Even in this great apostle's life, we see glimpses of the conflict we are continually engaged in today. You have an enemy who wants you to devalue and defame your body, for he is well aware of what you carry—the Hope of Glory, *Christ in you* (see Col. 1:27).

We must discipline ourselves to not only protect our bodies, but ever be mindful that our bodies do not actually belong to us, and in fact, they are portable sanctuaries for the Holy Spirit. Paul reminds us, *"Or do you not know that your body is the temple of the Holy Spirit who is in you, whom you have from God, and you are not your own? For you were bought at a price; therefore glorify God in your body and in your spirit, which are God's"* (1 Cor. 6:19-20).

In view of this understanding, here are two physical exchanges we can make with our bodies that can produce harmful, if not deadly soul ties and attachments.

Tattooing and Body Piercing

Tattoos and body piercings that are done to commemorate an event or signify a commitment or association with someone or something create soul ties to those events, people, or things. We already talked about how piercing the ear was a symbol of slavery in the Old Testament. Piercings and tattoos are symbols that represent soul attachments. They are indications that you have submitted your body, and therefore your life, to something other than God. They represent a form of worship. They defile your body. This could be why in Leviticus God gave the following command: *"You shall not make any cuttings in your flesh for the dead, nor tattoo any marks on you: I am the Lord"* (Lev. 19:28).

And, yes, believe it or not, many people go on to regret tattooing their bodies. A friend of mine tattooed a sentence on her body and after hearing this message realized why, after many failed attempts to marry, she could not. Her tattoo read,

"Out of your reach. Can't touch this." It was a vow she was having trouble breaking!

Dabbling in the Dark Arts

Another way we devalue our bodies, and actually use them as tools for demonic purposes, is through any engagement with the dark arts. This is strictly forbidden by Scripture, and involves the spiritual prostitution of a body that was created by and for God's purpose. While your body's physical health is important, its spiritual health is beyond crucial.

Participating in any type of witchcraft, astrology, palm reading, occult, voodoo, and so on is not only in direct rebellion to God, but will tie your soul to others who participate in those things and keep you trapped in darkness.[1]

King Saul had a soul tie to the dark arts, and he also rebelled against God. The prophet Samuel chastised him by saying, *"Rebellion is as the sin of witchcraft, and stubbornness is as iniquity and idolatry. Because you have rejected the word of the Lord, He also has rejected you from being king"* (1 Sam. 15:23).

Because of his rebellion and lack of real repentance, Saul could not discern the will of the Lord. After Samuel died, he sought out a witch who could conduct a séance in order to bring Samuel back from the dead to speak to him: *"'Why have you disturbed me by calling me back?' Samuel asked Saul. 'Because I am in deep trouble,' Saul replied. '...God has left me and won't reply by prophets or dreams. So I have called for you to tell me what to do'"* (1 Sam. 28:15 NLT).

When you are in league with evil spirits, you are in darkness, especially if you think what you're doing will give you special insight or knowledge, such as divination or fortune telling. As Matthew 6:23 (NLT) tells us, *"If the light you think you have is actually darkness, how deep that darkness is!"*

You cannot see by conferring with the dark, because in doing so you are conferring with lying spirits. There is a reason it's called the kingdom of darkness—because it will keep you from seeing the truth! Rebellion—such as witchcraft—will keep your soul anchored in darkness. This is what Paul had to say about the rebellious people of Israel,

> *Rebellion—such as witch-craft— will keep your soul anchored in darkness.*

"*God has given them a spirit of stupor, eyes that they should not see and ears that they should not hear*" (Rom. 11:8).

In the book of Acts we read about a sorcerer named Simon. Simon came to a believing faith in Jesus Christ, but his soul was still in the dark. When he saw people receiving the baptism of the Holy Spirit through the laying on of hands, he offered Peter money to show him how it was done. He wanted to buy the power of God, probably because that was how he learned the "magic" he had practiced in the past. Peter's response was not a measured one:

> *May your money be destroyed with you for thinking God's gift can be bought! You can have no part in this, for your heart is not right with God. Repent of your wickedness and pray to the Lord. Perhaps he will forgive your evil thoughts, for I can see that you are full of bitter jealousy and are held captive by sin* (Acts 8:20-23 NLT).

Simon was still held captive by the sin of witchcraft, and he needed to be delivered of it. Only then could he fully follow the God he so desired to know. He needed to be delivered of how he had learned to function in the past and embrace the new ways of living free in Christ.

In Deuteronomy, God makes it clear that we are to completely separate ourselves from these types of strategies because of their power to blind us and tie up our souls in darkness.

> *Do not let your people practice fortune-telling, or use sorcery, or interpret omens, or engage in witchcraft, or cast spells, or*

function as mediums or psychics, or call forth the spirits of the dead. Anyone who does these things is detestable to the Lord (Deuteronomy 18:10-12 NLT).

POWER POINT

As we move closer to living the resilient life, it is vital that we recognize *Whose* we are and start living accordingly—namely, how we treat our physical bodies. If we begin to live like we are actually temples of the Holy Spirit, and God's earthly residence is inside our mortal bodies, what we do to and with these bodies carries deep significance. In fact, what we do with our bodies determines whether we will be enslaved in a binding soul attachment or break free to living resiliently. The choice is ours. How will we steward the body God has given us?

POWER THOUGHT

Do you not know that your bodies are temples of the Holy Spirit, who is in you, whom you have received from God? You are not your own; you were bought at a price. Therefore honor God with your bodies (1 Corinthians 6:19-20 NIV).

Day 5

ALLEGIANCES

If you have trapped yourself by your agreement and are caught by what you said—follow my advice and save yourself, for you have placed yourself at your friend's mercy (Proverbs 6:2-3 NLT).

DISCIPLINE #5 — BE MINDFUL OF YOUR ASSOCIATIONS

Our associations determine our destinies. Who we enter into an allegiance or association with either leads us into binding soul attachments or freedom and resiliency. This is why it is so important for us to carefully scrutinize with whom or what we enter into any type of relationship, as such allegiances can quickly establish soul ties that directly link us to whatever that individual or group is linked to.

Organizations

Membership in organizations such as fraternities, sororities, lodges, the Masons, and so on will create soul ties with the other members of that organization. Memberships or associations with clubs, cults, or ungodly organizations will create crippling attachments that will hold you back if they are not deliberately broken. This is why it is absolutely essential to be careful of the allegiances you make. Make sure you are earnestly seeking membership in the Body of Christ, and in His Body alone.

In Revelation we are warned to *"watch as I take those who call themselves true believers but are nothing of the kind, pretenders whose true membership is in the club of Satan—watch as I strip off their pretensions"* (Rev. 3:9 MSG).

Don't compromise your membership in the club of Christ by what might be an unwitting membership in *"the club of satan."*

Business Partnerships

Entering into a business arrangement with someone, or acting as their guarantor, is another way that soul attachments—or "yokes" that bind you to others—are formed. It is an exchange that can involve agreements and contracts—or simply the borrowing or lending of money—but is especially powerful because of the myriad of exchanges that come along with being connected in a business relationship.

There is a whole body of attachments you become tied to precisely because that is what defines the nature of a business. In other words, ongoing exchanges are what businesses are comprised of—and if that business fails in any one of those exchanges, that failure becomes your failure. As we are told in Proverbs, *"Don't agree to guarantee another person's debt or put up security for someone else. If you can't pay it, even your bed will be snatched from under you"* (Prov. 22:26-27 NLT).

We would also do well to consider what we are told in Deuteronomy 22:10-11, *"You shall not plow with an ox and a donkey together. You shall not wear a garment of different sorts, such as wool and linen mixed together."* When you enter into a business arrangement, or become a guarantor, make sure you know not only whom you are dealing with, but also whom they are dealing with. Too many have gotten mixed up in illegal activities or with criminal entities as an indirect result of having entered into a business relationship. Enron is a prime example. When that company crashed, so did the finances of every innocent stakeholder. Conversely, when you act as a guarantor for anyone, if they renege on loan payments, the debt is passed on to you.

Employment Relationships

The types of exchanges that take place between an employer and employee can create several kinds of attachments. There are verbal agreements that take place, there is an exchange of money in the form of wages and commissions, there is submission to the authority of another, as well as a "co-laboring" toward a common goal. When an individual or an organization employs you, you are bound to them on several levels. You can get caught up in all sorts of ungodly agendas, unethical arrangements, and even illegal activities. Again, look at what happened at Enron. There wasn't a single employee who wasn't negatively affected by what took place there. When you work for a corrupt employer, even in ignorance, that corruption will attach to you and what happens to them can potentially have an impact on your life and finances beyond your wildest imagination.

In the book of Genesis, we read about Jacob who left home as a young man to work for his uncle Laban. Laban agreed to give Jacob his daughter Rachel after he labored for seven years, but through a bit of trickery he was given Leah, Rachel's older sister, instead. When Jacob confronted him about it, he ended up having to work another seven years as a dowry for Rachel. Laban was greedy and corrupt. Jacob had a hard time breaking free from his arrangement, and even after he left, Laban hotly pursued him. Jacob was blessed to have escaped without violence having been done to him or his family.

But there is another lesson we can learn from Jacob's experience as well. Laban had agreed to allow Jacob to have all of his spotted livestock, but that same day had all of the spotted livestock removed from the flock. So Jacob was left tending a spotless flock—animals that genetically should have produced other spotless offspring. Jacob, however, understood that what you give attention to will replicate in your life. Wasting no time, he carved streaks into branches and *"placed these peeled branches in the watering troughs where the flocks came to drink, for that was where they mated. And when they mated in front of the white-streaked branches, they gave birth to young that* were streaked, speckled, and spotted" (Gen. 30:38-39 NLT). He placed the streaky branches in front of the strongest of the flock and didn't place them in view of the weaker ones. So the stronger became spotted and grew in numbers so that Jacob became very wealthy.

> " *You will eventually become like what or who you give most of your attention to.* "

You will eventually become like what or who you give most of your attention to. Since a majority of your waking hours are spent on the job, either working with or for others, make sure that you are focusing your attention on what represents who you ultimately want to be.

POWER POINT

We should not enter into allegiances with people or groups idly. As I said at the beginning, it is absolutely pivotal for us to enter into agreements, allegiances, and associations with those we trust in the Body of Christ.

This is not a call to be insulated or isolated from the world, nor is it a license to disengage from the very people we are called to impact. However, when it comes to the most intimate dealings of your life—dealing with employment, finances, business, etc.—it is a necessity that you carefully weigh your options before entering into an association. If the partnership forms a dangerous attachment or soul tie, you become intertwined with the dealings, involvements, and failures of the individual or organization you have developed an association with. This thwarts your resilience on every level and keeps you enslaved to the one with whom you have entered an allegiance.

Remember, it is important to maintain a steady mindfulness of the people with whom you relate. Such may well mean the difference between a life of forward momentum and blessing or a life of hardship and bondage.

POWER THOUGHT

Be careful the environment you choose for it will shape you; be careful the friends you choose for you will become like them. —W. Clement Stone

Week Two

CONFRONTING
EMOTIONAL SOUL TIES

A sensible man will remember that the eyes may be confused in two ways—by a change from light to darkness or from darkness to light; and he will recognize that the same thing happens to the soul. —Plato

People sitting out their lives in the dark saw a huge light; sitting in that dark, dark country of death, they watched the sun come up (Matthew 4:15-16 MSG).

Soul attachments are not only the result of our interactions in relation to the physical or external world around us; they also happen in relation to the emotional or internal world, consisting of the ideas, philosophies, focus, and other factors that are a result of the world within us. These attachments are created by intrinsic exchanges.

This week, we will review several of the intrinsic exchanges that we should be mindful of. Each of the presented exchanges is a potential catalyst to developing unhealthy emotional soul attachments in our lives, ultimately restraining us from stepping into the God-willed life of resiliency.

These exchanges will be divided up into five different categories that will be explored one day at a time.

Day 6

THOUGHTS

The secret of your future is hidden in your daily routine. —Mike Murdock

DISCIPLINE #6—INVEST TIME IN CREATING A HEALTHY THOUGHT LIFE

We usually don't connect our thought life with how we structure our time. But they are very interconnected. How you manage time is a direct result of how you manage your thoughts. Or you could say, how you invest your thoughts will result in how you invest your time. That said, you must invest time in managing your thought life!

Your thought life is the result of your thought time—how you invest your mental energy throughout the course of the day. I don't think we often consider our thoughts in terms of an investment of time, but the reality is we think a certain way because we have committed the currency of our time into a series of certain thoughts, either healthy or destructive. The time we give to entertaining these thoughts invariably shapes our thought lives, and therefore the course our lives take.

How you manage time is a direct result of how you manage your thoughts.

Your thought life is determined by several exchanges, all

129

resulting from how you spend or invest your time. How you invest your time sets the course for what your mind will spend most of its time thinking about; what you focus on paints the canvas of your thought life.

If we are going to reclaim our souls and live the resilient lives God has made available, we need to be intentional about how we use time. Just as we enter into allegiances and covenants with those we make financial investments with—we can also form ties when we invest the more precious currency of time. The following are some of the different exchanges to be aware of as you seek to develop a healthy thought life.

Spending and Investing Time

You naturally form a bond with whomever or whatever you spend a great deal of time, so pay attention to what you pay attention to! The more time you invest with someone, the more attention you give him or her, the more you will absorb his or her values and views. *"Do not be so deceived and misled! Evil companionships (communion, associations) corrupt and deprave good manners and morals and character"* (1 Cor. 15:33 AMP).

Ben Stein is quoted as saying, "Genuine relationships are the fertile soil from which all advancement...all success...all achievement in real life grows." How true. The less time you associate with some people, the more your life will improve. Any time you tolerate mediocrity in others, it increases your mediocrity. An important attribute in successful people is their impatience with negative thinking and negative people.

> Friends who don't help you climb will keep you crawling.

As you grow, your associations will change. You'll find that friends who don't help you climb will keep you crawling. "Your friends will stretch your vision or choke your dream. Those that don't increase you will eventually decrease you. Find friends that have the capacity to carry you to greater heights in all areas of your life."[1] Remember, you resemble those with whom you assemble!

Extended Association with Un/Non-Believers

Be careful about spending too much time with people who do not share the same values and convictions, or hold God in the same place you do. Nonbelievers are often anti-God, anti-Christ, worldly, or absorbed in gratifying their sensuality. They can tug at your soul, cause you to question your faith, and turn your heart away from God. This is why it is so essential that we associate with people of "like-precious faith." We are urged in Hebrews to *"not neglect our meeting together, as some people do, but encourage one another"* (Heb. 10:25 NLT). The first verses of Psalms tells us:

> *Blessed is the man who **walks not in the counsel of the ungodly, nor stands in the path of sinners,** nor sits in the seat of the scornful; but his delight is in the law of the Lord, and in His law he meditates day and night* (Psalm 1:1-2).

Meanwhile, Proverbs warns:

> *Make no friendship with an angry man, and **with a furious man do not go, lest you learn his ways** and set a snare for your soul* (Proverbs 22:24-25).

In First Samuel, we read about Hannah and Peninnah. Every year when they went to worship and sacrifice at the Tabernacle, *"Peninnah would taunt Hannah and make fun of her because the Lord had kept her from having children. Year after year it was the same.... Each time, Hannah would be reduced to tears and would not even eat"* (1 Sam. 1:6-7 NLT). In her despair, Hannah went to the Temple to pray. She was so beside herself in prayer, Eli the priest thought she must be drunk. He reprimanded her, but she responded, *"I haven't been drinking wine or anything stronger. But I am very discouraged, and I was pouring out my heart to the Lord.*

Don't think I am a wicked woman! For I have been praying out of great anguish and sorrow" (1 Sam. 1:15-16 NLT). Her association with Peninnah had bound her soul to the negative words Peninnah had spoken over her. To break the tie it took a prophetic proclamation by Eli who blessed her saying, *"Go in peace! May the God of Israel grant the request you have asked of him"* (1 Sam. 1:17 NLT). The writer of Hebrews warned about this very thing: *"Make sure there's no evil unbelief lying around that will trip you up and throw you off course, diverting you from the living God"* (Heb. 3:12 MSG).

Living Under the Same Roof

When you live with someone, that person will deeply affect you on levels you might not be aware of—they can affect how you see yourself, your world, and even your destiny. Look at how Sarai was affected by Hagar and vice versa. After not being able to bear children, Sarai finally gave her maid, Hagar, to Abram to bear a child on her behalf. Sarai was tainted by the ways of the world in this decision, and Hagar went willingly. Then, when Sarai felt despised by Hagar, she threw her out. That's when the angel of the Lord found Hagar along the roadside in the wilderness and said to her, *"Return to your mistress, and submit to her authority"* (Gen. 16:9 NLT). He also told her, *"I will give you more descendants than you can count"* (Gen. 16:10 NLT). Because Hagar lived under the same roof as Sarai, she partook of her destiny as the mother of many nations. That is a positive scenario. The opposite holds true as well, as we now see these two nations continually embattled for the legacy of Abraham.

Media and Entertainment

Information feeds the soul—it's "soul food." What you feast your eyes upon will attach to you. Energy follows attention. What you give attention to, and therefore fill your mind with, will certainly tie up your soul.

Media is seductive. Visual images draw your eyes—and music

seduces the ears. Both sight and sound are powerful attractors and channels for overt or covert messages that can fill your heart and mind with ungodly thoughts, ideas, and imaginations. As Matthew 6:22-23 states, *"The lamp of the body is the eye. If therefore your eye is good, your whole body will be full of light. But if your eye is bad, your whole body will be full of darkness."*

Movies, music, and books that are horror-oriented or sexually explicit, as well as clubs or shows that are provocative, create inroads into your soul. Dark, demonic, violent, sexual, or crude programming creates insidious attachments. In this area in particular, it is so important to guard what you put into your mind through what you watch and listen to. It is one of the significant ways you can guard your heart, as Proverbs 4:23 tells us to do, *"Keep your heart with all diligence, for out of it spring the issues of life."* John said it this way:

> *Do not love the world or the things in the world. If anyone loves the world, the love of the Father is not in him. For all that is in the world—the lust of the flesh, the lust of the eyes, and the pride of life—is not of the Father but is of the world* (1 John 2:15-16).

You will tie your soul to whatever you admire and let into your home—be it through the television, video games, music, or the Internet. Even all those subtle forms of "social networking" can open your soul to unhealthy attachments. Whatever you feast your eyes upon has the power to draw you in and bind your soul! This also holds true for advertisements.

Whatever you feast your eyes upon has the power to draw you in and bind your soul!

As I edit this book in London, I am on a forty-day consecration. Today, I left my hotel to go to church. Along the way, there were so many billboards and adverts for food, I almost wanted to ask my driver to turn the car around so I could spend the rest of my holiday locked away in my hotel to avoid the seduction of these advertisements.

I had no desire for any of the delicacies I saw advertised, but the power of suggestion was indeed powerful! The same is true concerning media and entertainment. It's unsettling what unholy and unnatural desires visual images can awaken in the viewing public.

POWER POINT

Our lack of intentionality in guarding our thought lives is satan's great assignment to steal, kill, and destroy. His goal is nothing less than total takeover. By taking control of our thoughts, he can influence mindsets. These mindsets shape our attitudes, which determine our beliefs, and ultimately decide our paradigms.

How you view and interact with everything in life is contingent upon how you invest your "think time."

POWER THOUGHT

For as he thinks in his heart, so is he (Proverbs 23:7).

Day 7

MINDSETS

The evil mindset spread to the leaders and priests and filtered down to the people—it kicked off an epidemic of evil... (2 Chronicles 36:14 MSG).

DISCIPLINE #7—CAREFULLY EVALUATE ALL THOUGHTS THAT COME INTO YOUR MIND

In the context of Second Chronicles 36, we witness the destructive intrinsic exchange that takes place between the leaders and the people. Through the power of association, evil mindsets spread like an epidemic from those in authority to those under authority. In other words, keeping society with those who entertain evil in their minds is like a exposing yourself to a contagious virus.

> *Associating with those who are evil-minded is like a exposing yourself to a contagious virus.*

Today, we will examine some of the intrinsic, emotional-level exchanges that produce harmful soul ties.

Former Coverings and Affiliations

Sometimes there are things that keep us emotionally, spiritually, and psychologically tied to an old season or way of conducting our spiritual affairs. In the book of Acts, we read about a group of itinerant Jewish exorcists who *"took it upon themselves to call the name of the Lord Jesus over those who had evil spirits, saying, 'We exorcise you by the Jesus whom Paul preaches'"* (Acts 19:13). Because of their affiliation with the old Jewish order, still operating under that covering, the evil spirit answered them saying, *"Jesus I know, and Paul I know; but who are you?"* (Acts 19:15). The key is to break all ties with former affiliations, and make sure you are in partnership with Christ alone as you submit to the new.

In his first letter to the Corinthians, Paul warned the church there not to follow after other teachers or their opinions of the truth. They were becoming divided and arguing about who was the greater leader among them. *"Each of you says, 'I am of Paul,' or 'I am of Apollos,' or 'I am of Cephas,' or 'I am of Christ.' Is Christ divided? Was Paul crucified for you? Or were you baptized in the name of Paul?"* (1 Cor. 1:12-13). Paul understood the dangers of submitting to someone or some belief that was not based on the simple message of the Gospel. In his second letter to the Corinthians he wrote, *"I fear, lest somehow, as the serpent deceived Eve by his craftiness, so your minds may be corrupted from the simplicity that is in Christ"* (2 Cor. 11:3).

Everything you have ever heard, tasted, touched, experienced kinesthetically or olfactorily (smelled) is permanently imprinted on your soul. And yet, God is able to cleanse every area by the *"washing of the water by the word"* (Eph. 5:26).

Demonic Inroads

Satan recognizes that the mind is the inroad into your life. This is why Apostle Paul used such combative language in describing the battle over your thought life: *"For the weapons of our warfare are not physical [weapons of flesh and blood], but they are mighty before God for the overthrow and destruction of strongholds"* (2 Cor. 10:4 AMP).

Interestingly enough, Paul is not simply referring to thoughts, as we discussed yesterday. A single thought alone does not give the enemy an inroad into your life. Rather, it is how we respond to these thoughts that determines what kind of territory satan is able to lay claim to in our lives. This is why we must be violent in how we respond to his attempts at laying siege to our minds and establishing demonic mindsets.

Paul continues, "*We destroy every proud obstacle that keeps people from knowing God. We capture their rebellious thoughts and teach them to obey Christ*" (2 Cor. 10:5 NLT). These mindsets do not simply keep worldly people blinded to the Gospel message, but they have the ability to prevent you and me from *knowing God*.

By giving the enemy any inroad into your thoughts, you embrace his mindset; you start thinking less like an ambassador of Christ, and more like a citizen of this fallen world. This is why the enemy works so hard at establishing false mindsets in Kingdom citizens—and one of the main ways he does this is by getting you to associate with those who foster mindsets dominated by darkness. He knows how dangerous the people of light are to his dark kingdom when they acknowledge Who God is, and when they embrace an identity based on what He has said about them. Such people refuse to yield to demonic associations that produce mindsets of darkness in their lives.

I reiterate, the enemy is thoroughly interested in crafting your mindset, or how your mind is set. He does not want you thinking according to the Word of God and thereby adopting a Kingdom mindset.

We are living in enemy-occupied territory. That enemy is actively seeking to enslave you. He can't enslave your spirit,

> *The enemy is thoroughly interested in crafting your mindset.*

but he can enslave your soul, and thus your mind, will, and emotions. He builds inroads into your mind, unleashing his spirits of deception, perversion, addiction, manipulation, and every imaginable (and unimaginable) thing he can devise to keep you from the freedom that is in Christ.[1] David wrote in Psalm 143:3:

For the enemy has persecuted my soul; he has crushed my life to the ground; he has made me dwell in darkness, like those who have long been dead.

Peter warned us to *"be vigilant and cautious at all times; for that enemy of yours, the devil, roams around like a lion roaring [in fierce hunger], seeking someone to seize upon and devour"* (1 Pet. 5:8 AMP).

The enemy and his cohorts look for those they can deceive, seduce, and captivate. *"God's Spirit clearly says that in the last days many people will turn from their faith. They will be fooled by evil spirits and by teachings that come from demons"* (1 Tim. 4:1 CEV). Believers will be led astray and fooled into partnering with evil spirits. In more cases than not, this door is opened through an association or affiliation with one who is given to darkness. In the book of Revelation, John warns the church in Thyatira about this:

I have this against you, that you tolerate that woman Jezebel, who calls herself a prophetess and is teaching and seducing my servants to practice sexual immorality...I will strike her children dead. And all the churches will know that I am he who searches mind and heart, and I will give to each of you according to your works (Revelation 2:20,23 ESV).

Revelation 2:22 in The Message reads, *"I'm about to lay her low, along with her partners."*

In the Old Testament, Jezebel was a cruel, immoral queen who fostered the worship of Baal and aggressively sought to murder the prophets of God. She was the queen of Israel, the wife of Ahab, and the daughter of Ethbaal. She was a seductress and manipulator. According to the *Enhanced Strong's Lexicon*, the name *Jezebel* is defined as "Baal exalts" or "Baal is husband to" or "unchaste." She aims to lead God's servants astray in order to promote Baal's agenda, or the agenda of Beelzebub, who is the ruler of demons—satan. We are told in First John, *"Do not believe every spirit, but test the spirits, whether they are of God"* (1 John 4:1).

God still had more to say to the church in Thyatira:

But I also have a message for the rest of you in Thyatira who have not followed this false teaching ("deeper truths," as they call them—depths of Satan, actually). I will ask nothing more of you except that you hold tightly to what you have until I come. To all who are victorious, who obey me to the very end, to them I will give authority over all the nations. **They will rule the nations with an iron rod and smash them like clay pots.** *They will have the same authority I received from my Father, and I will also give them the morning star!* (Revelation 2:24-28 NLT)

Hold tightly to the truth that you know. Stay strong in the measure of faith you've been given. Don't complicate the message of the Gospel. Remember the love God has for you and how you first came to love God in response, and continue in that love *"lest somehow, as the serpent deceived Eve by his craftiness, so your minds may be corrupted from the simplicity that is in Christ"* (2 Cor. 11:3).

POWER POINT

In conclusion, this is not a call for radical separatism. Those dwelling in darkness desperately need the light you carry. There is a difference, though, between interacting with such people and entering into dangerous soul attachments by embracing their mindsets.

POWER THOUGHT

The less you associate with some people, the more your life will improve. The simple but true fact of life is that you become like those with whom you closely associate—for the good and the bad. —Colin Powell

ATTITUDES

The more you reaffirm who you are in Christ, the more your behavior will begin to reflect your true identity. —Neil T. Anderson

DISCIPLINE #8—EMBRACE WHO GOD SAYS YOU ARE IN CHRIST

The way we respond to stimuli is absolutely important, as our responses reveal what we believe. Our mindsets determine our methods of response, and our methods of response would be classified as our attitudes.

Since we are called to be representatives of Jesus Christ, we must discipline ourselves to build our attitudes on our true identity—as new creations in Christ.

As we are dealing in the realm of intrinsic—or emotional—exchanges, we are going to be covering several significant factors that are extremely formational when it comes to shaping attitudes. Though there are undoubtedly others, the following exchanges must be carefully monitored if we are to avoid the soul ties that produce unhealthy attitudes in our lives.

> *Our mindsets determine our methods of response—our methods of response are our attitudes.*

Entitlement

We've talked a lot about the affects of negative words, abusive relationships, or unfortunate circumstances on the health of our souls. However, there are also some soul-health issues when it comes to status or privilege. Those who are born with a silver spoon can become as entangled in their sense of entitlement as those who are born with no spoon can become enslaved to a mentality of lack. Presuming you have a right to be served, lavished with luxury, or provided with whatever you desire with no effort or reciprocity on your part, can not only be debilitating, but also toxic to everyone around you. It can cause you to become pretentious, if not manipulative.

Feeling entitled is an obstacle to progress—it keeps you from growing and building your capacity to do and become more. It can even become a type of handicap and limitation to fulfilling your potential and experiencing true freedom and abundance. A sense of entitlement makes you more susceptible to discontentment, disappointment, and discouragement. It is in direct opposition to an attitude of gratitude.

Acts of Kindness

There are certain acts of kindness that produce a sense of obligation or produce feelings of indebtedness. Sometimes as a recipient of someone's kindness you will feel a tugging in the heart that you owe them—that they own part of you because of what they have done for you. This creates an attitude that can color everything you do as long as you are around the person who extended a particular kindness to you. Sometimes this can be healthy and positive—but there are times it can become oppressive.

In the case of Jonathan showing kindness to David, David felt he owed it to show kindness to Jonathan's descendants. In Second Samuel 9:1 he asks, *"Is there still anyone who is left of the*

house of Saul, that I may show him kindness for Jonathan's sake?"
Here is where David is introduced to Mephibosheth, Jonathan's
son, who eventually fell on his face before David and cried, *"Here
is your servant!"* (2 Sam. 9:6). David said to Mephibosheth, *"Do
not fear, for I will surely show you kindness for Jonathan your father's
sake"* (2 Sam. 9:7).

In other cases, acts of kindness can create bonds that develop
an unhealthy attitude toward another person, and therefore
produce a type of soul attachment. People who extend kindness from a heart that is not pure will often request a return
favor: "After all I've done for you!"—and its underlying implication, "You owe it to me."

Traumatic Experiences

Traumatic experiences can lead to Post Traumatic Stress
Disorder (PTSD), which connects a person on a deep emotional level to an experience causing them to relive the past
through painful memories, dreams, nightmares, and ongoing
emotional trauma.

Rather than being defined as someone redeemed by Christ,
the traumatic experience becomes the primary driver of definition and purpose. Sadly, many arrive at a point where they are
so intrinsically linked with their past trauma, they are unable
to recognize who they are apart from their unfortunate experience. Their pain sadly defines their present.

Old heart wounds, war wounds, and perceptions of being
wounded can tie a person to a past experience. When the people of Israel left Egypt, they could not get beyond the wound-
ing, the memories, or the shame of their past lives. In the book
of Exodus we are told:

*The whole congregation of the children of Israel complained
against Moses and Aaron in the wilderness. And the children
of Israel said to them, "Oh, that we had died by the hand of*

143

*the Lord in the land of Egypt.... For you have brought us out
into this wilderness to kill this whole assembly with hunger"*
(Exodus 16:2-3).

They could not hope in the future because of the despair
of their past. They could not have faith in the present because
they were haunted by former fears. War veterans and people
who have lived in fear in war-ravished parts of the world commonly suffer from this, as well as those with a past filled with
oppression and abuse.

POWER POINT

Your attitude is everything when it comes to living a resilient
lifestyle. Recognize that you play an integral role in determining the type of attitudes you exhibit toward people and stimuli.
Don't allow these exchanges to produce soul attachments that
restrain you from the life you've always wanted.

POWER THOUGHT

For you died, and your life is now hidden with Christ in God
(Colossians 3:3 NIV).

Day 9

BELIEFS

In religion and politics people's beliefs and convictions are in almost every case gotten at second-hand, and without examination, from authorities who have not themselves examined the questions at issue but have taken them at second-hand from other non-examiners, whose opinions about them were not worth a brass farthing. —Mark Twain

DISCIPLINE #9 — DELIBERATELY FORM YOUR BELIEF SYSTEM

We all maintain a certain set of beliefs. As much as many of us would like to claim that we hold to an accurate biblical worldview that is defined by a Scripture-based belief system, often this could not be further from the truth.

A belief is not merely a spoken confession or intellectual assent to certain denominational doctrines or theological concepts. Your beliefs are the very things fundamentally that shape how you perceive, and in turn, respond to reality. This is why it is vital that you practice the discipline of forming your beliefs according to the Word of God.

Remember, this is a discipline, which means it will not come to you naturally. You will not develop healthy, balanced, and solid belief systems through osmosis; it demands intentionality on your part.

145

In addition to studying Scripture, this discipline requires the confrontation of false and destructive belief systems—many of which are developed through soul attachments. This will require some deep thought and self-reflection, as many of us often do not even recognize the dangerous doctrines we carry around as our own, subconsciously building our lives upon these erroneous belief systems. In fact, we may be convinced we believe one thing, but in reality, we believe something that is contrary to the very thing we say we believe.

> *Your beliefs are the very things fundamentally that shape how you perceive, and in turn, respond to reality.*

For example, people can proclaim, shout, sing, and even preach that God "is good" from now until the moment they exit the planet, but if the view of God they carry deep within their hearts is one of an austere, angry, and distant deity, that is how they will ultimately respond to Him—regardless of how vehemently they disagree.

Beliefs are deeper than words, thoughts, and even mindsets. Beliefs are a step beyond attitudes, for what we believe determines what type of attitudes we adopt and express.

Often, we do not think of beliefs in conjunction with soul ties or attachments. The truth is, we do not always consciously form our belief systems. They are a composite of many different factors and influences, some of the most significant stemming from soul ties we have developed over our lives. Let's look at a type of exchange that contributes to the building and fortifying of our belief systems.

Mentors, Coaches, Spiritual Directors

Mentors and coaches have many positive gifts and insights to impart to those who seek their direction. They may also have sins and negative attributes that can be imparted as well.

Think about this example from Scripture. Although Samuel received good instruction from Eli and grew up to become a great prophet, he also carried with him the effects of Eli's failures. God told Samuel, *"I have warned* [Eli] *that judgment is coming upon his family forever, because his sons are blaspheming God and he hasn't disciplined them"* (1 Sam. 3:13 NLT).

Eli did not raise his sons to fear the Lord, and neither did Samuel: *"But* [Samuel's] *sons did not walk in his ways; they turned aside after dishonest gain, took bribes, and perverted justice"* (1 Sam. 8:3). When you submit yourself as an apprentice to someone, they will impart to you both their strengths and their weaknesses. This is why it is absolutely imperative for you to personally build your belief systems on the written Word of God rather the opinions of people.

Though leaders have much to offer and impart, keep in mind that they are indeed human and prone to error. The only teacher we can trust completely is the Holy Spirit. He is the only One worthy of our unquestionable allegiance and wholehearted *attachment.*

As we form our beliefs based on the Truth of God's Word, shaping them after what God says, not the thoughts and opinions of people, we position ourselves to experience a life of resiliency.

The problem with putting all of our metaphorical eggs in one teacher's "belief basket" is that we forget that, like you and I, that individual is also growing. That means continuous change. Therefore, if the person after whom we are modeling our entire belief system is in flux, that does not make for a reliable compass as we attempt to navigate a forward-moving, empowered lifestyle.

By default, because of the attachment we have made with his or her belief system, we too are constantly changing. Stability becomes a foreign concept, for everything is built upon the shifting sand of a person susceptible to error, transition, and change. Be it positive transition, which produces maturity, or negative change resulting from compromise, it is completely unhealthy for us to develop an attachment or soul tie to someone else's belief system.

> *We must pursue Truth and establish our own beliefs based on the Word of God.*

This is why we must pursue Truth for ourselves and establish our own beliefs, based on the sure Word of God. There is but one Compass, one true Coach, one ultimate Teacher and Master Mentor.

POWER POINT

Perhaps the most belief-shaping exchange that we need to be mindful of, particularly in the day in which we live, is that which takes place between us and our leaders—spiritual and otherwise.

We cannot idly entrust our personal belief systems to others. While our leaders have much grace and truth to impart to us in effectively building our belief systems, we cannot become overly dependent. The only One we should be attached or tied to is the Holy Spirit, as it is impossible for Him to lead us astray. Stay in the Word of God. Allow the Holy Spirit to build your beliefs according to the ironclad, eternal Truth contained within its precious pages.

POWER THOUGHT

No prolonged infancies among us, please. We'll not tolerate babes in the woods, small children who are an easy mark for impostors. God wants us to grow up, to know the whole truth and tell it in love—like Christ in everything (Ephesians 4:14-15 MSG).

Day 10

PARADIGMS

We see the world, not as it is, but as we are—or, as
we are conditioned to see it. —Stephen R. Covey

DISCIPLINE #10—
MAINTAIN A KINGDOM PERSPECTIVE

Some might wonder if there is a step beyond belief systems.
After all, how could there be anything more important than
what we believe?

Actually, there is. Remember, as integral as your beliefs are,
they change. You grow and mature, and with that, your beliefs
follow suit. If you are on the road to maturity, then your beliefs
are constantly challenged and redirected by Truth, which is
defined by God's Word.

Just because you hold to a certain belief does not mean your
entire life is bound and thereby defined by it. Again, there will
always be unhealthy beliefs we need to adjust that are the product of unhealthy soul attachments. Even the most mature person is still developing in his or her personal beliefs.

What actually defines who you are and how you respond
to your beliefs is your personal paradigm. This is the lens or
perspective through which you see and interact with the world.
This is why it is vital for you to embrace the discipline of maintaining God's Kingdom perspective in all things.

Our beliefs are certainly formative factors in helping us establish our paradigms, but ultimately, our paradigms determine what beliefs we embrace and apply to our lives.

For example, two foundational paradigms would be Kingdom-centric or self-centric. If we recognize that everything is built upon and revolves around the Kingdom of God—that Jesus Christ is truly the center of our lives and we are committed to advancing His cause in the earth—then we will believe and build accordingly. If self is our paradigm, then likewise, everything we believe and everything we build will be devoted to promoting ourselves.

> *Our paradigms determine what beliefs we embrace and apply to our lives.*

A Kingdom paradigm is the resilient life personified. When we see from the King's perspective and manifest our Kingdom citizenship, we recognize that *"No weapon formed against you shall prosper"* (Isa. 54:17). We understand that we are part of something that is unshakable (see Heb. 12:28), undefeatable (see Matt. 16:18-19), and ever increasing in government, territory, and rule (see Isa. 9:7).

While every believer should ascribe to this paradigm, there are a series of deep attachments that shape our lives and define the lens through which we see life. Though we cannot always change the circumstances of our birth, upbringing, or culture, we can challenge the incorrect paradigms we were raised in, evaluate them by the standard of God's Kingdom paradigm, and rid our lives of attachments that keep us ensnared in destructive, unbiblical paradigms.

Cultural Attachments

Culture shapes and molds how we view the world. Culture is influenced by how a people group defines—or identifies—itself. Culture is defined as shared attitudes, values, goals, and practices—shared tastes in art, food, entertainment, and behavior; it is the beliefs and customs that are characteristic of a particular social group or organization. Every person has a cultural identity shaped by the community in which they live. A culture is influenced by its educational, political, and economic systems, religious institutions, technology, sports, media, diversity of ethnicities, group thinking, core values, wealth, entertainment, geography, climate, and so on. All of these factors determine the values, perceptions, mindsets, and paradigms that form strongholds. For example, you have probably heard of the term "ghetto fabulous." This phrase describes a culture defined by deviant dress codes, language, and morals, and often produces what some call "hood rats" who engage in gang-related and criminal activities. I am not making a disparaging statement here, because this is the term used by many individuals themselves. This is simply an example of a strong soul tie to culture, where people use adjectives that are less than complimentary to describe themselves.

The ties created by a culture are so strong they reach across generations. In First Kings, we read about Ahaziah, the son of Ahab, who became king and reigned over Israel for two years. *"He did evil in the sight of the Lord, and walked in the way of his father and in the way of his mother and in the way of Jeroboam the son of Nebat, who had made Israel sin"* (1 Kings 22:52). Ahaziah was a product of the environment he grew up in and was unable to break the cycle of wickedness that had become his cultural norm. These cultural ties can become strongholds in our lives. Paul's letter to the Corinthians gives clear instructions on how to tear down worldly strongholds, *"We use God's mighty weapons, not worldly weapons, to knock down the strongholds of human reasoning and to destroy false arguments. We destroy every proud obstacle that keeps people from knowing God"* (2 Cor. 10:4-5 NLT).

In his letter to the Romans, Paul wrote:

Don't become so well-adjusted to your culture that you fit into it without even thinking. Instead, fix your attention on God. You'll be changed from the inside out. Readily recognize what he wants from you, and quickly respond to it. Unlike the culture around you, always dragging you down to its level of immaturity, God brings the best out of you, develops well-formed maturity in you (Romans 12:2 MSG).

Institutional Ties

Institutional attachments are profound and far-reaching. They are concealed below the surface of everyday life. Unlike cultural ties that you can actually see and observe, institutional ties can be almost imperceptible.

The Matrix movie comes to mind. The main character, Neo, had to work hard to actually "see" the framework in which he existed. While becoming "unplugged" nearly killed him, it also enabled him to really live. In the same way, if we are to really live "unplugged"—free from invisible attachments that keep our souls bound to the world's systems—we will need to understand the institutions that govern our lives.

Institutions exist to promote a specific purpose, agenda, or cause. They are instrumental in creating the paradigms in which we live—the world's systems. Godly institutions, such as the institution of marriage, are healthy and hold the family and society together in righteousness. Ungodly institutions, such as the institution of slavery, are demonic. The god of this world seeks to enslave humankind and has successfully kept the institution of slavery alive and well in the earth to this day. Remember, *"we do not wrestle against flesh and blood, but against principalities, against powers, against the rulers of the darkness of this age, against spiritual hosts of wickedness in the heavenly places"* (Eph. 6:12). Because the role of institutions is so far-reaching—their presence in our society so pervasive—their effect on our minds and in our everyday lives is hard to discern. You must diligently *"seek the Kingdom of God above all else"* (Matt. 6:33 NLT) and continually *"Be transformed by the renewing of your mind"* (Rom. 12:2). You don't have to be a product of your environment or remain a prisoner of culture.

National Ties

Whatever takes place in a nation and among its leaders affects the souls of its people. The soul of a nation is tied to its leaders. We can see examples of how national leaders around the world have kept the souls of their people bound. The Duvalier family of Haiti reigned as dictators for thirty years turning the country into an isolationist kingdom with a personality cult. Less obvious than national dictators, are the leaders who compromise and allow sin and corruption to reign supreme. Jeroboam, Ahab, Ahaziah, and Jehu on down the line are the kings who all led Israel to sin. They allowed pagan worship, perversion, and moral decay to take over the nation.

We see what transpires when you sell your soul to be prostituted by the world system in Luke 15. This is what happened in the story

> *Whatever takes place in a nation and among its leaders affects the soul of its people.*

of the prodigal son. He left home to "get in bed" with the world, and the world used him up and spit him out. Finally, *"when he came to himself, he said, 'How many of my father's hired servants have bread enough and to spare, and I perish with hunger!'"* (Luke 15:17). Although the son was heir to his father's kingdom, he was still held captive by the world.

> *"For all the nations have fallen because of the wine of her passionate immorality. The kings of the world have committed adultery with her. Because of her desires for extravagant luxury, the merchants of the world have grown rich." Then I heard another voice calling from heaven, "Come away from her, my*

people. Do not take part in her sins, or you will be punished with her" (Revelation 18:3-4 NLT).

You may have given your heart to Jesus, but satan can still hold sway over your mind. He can keep you in a stupor if you let him. Paul wrote the Ephesians,

"Awake, you who sleep, arise from the dead, and Christ will give you light." See then that you walk circumspectly, not as fools but as wise (Ephesians 5:14-15).

Apostle Paul made this urgent plea:

I insist—and God backs me up on this—that there be no going along with the crowd, the empty-headed, mindless crowd. They've refused for so long to deal with God that they've lost touch not only with God but with reality itself. They can't think straight anymore. Feeling no pain, they let themselves go in sexual obsession, addicted to every sort of perversion (Ephesians 4:17-19 MSG).

Paul wrote the Corinthians, *"So, come out from among [unbelievers], and separate (sever) yourselves from them, says the Lord, and touch not [any] unclean thing; then I will receive you kindly and treat you with favor"* (2 Cor. 6:17 AMP).

POWER POINT

Don't be "double-minded," as James wrote, *"Such people should not expect to receive anything from the Lord. Their loyalty is divided between God and the world, and they are unstable in everything they do"* (James 1:7-8 NLT). Jesus made clear, *"You cannot serve both God and money"* (Matt. 6:24 NLT). You must *"choose for yourselves this day whom you will serve"* (Josh. 24:15).

You can either tether your soul to God's Kingdom or to the world's—which do you choose?

POWER THOUGHT

Don't become so well-adjusted to your culture that you fit into it without even thinking. Instead, fix your attention on God. You'll be changed from the inside out (Romans 12:2 MSG).

Week Three

CONFRONTING RELATIONAL SOUL TIES

You can kiss your family and friends goodbye and put miles between you, but at the same time you carry them with you in your heart, your mind, your stomach, because you do not just live in a world but a world lives in you. —Frederick Buechner

So we, being many, are one body in Christ, and individually members of one another (Romans 12:5).

Relationship is at the center of all God does. God's Kingdom is made manifest in our relationship with Him and with one another. *"All this comes from the God who settled the relationship between us and him, and then called us to settle our relationships with each other"* (2 Cor. 5:18 MSG). God created humanity to enjoy intimate fellowship with Him even as we pursue that closeness with each other—that we, with Christ, would become one, unified whole.

The New Testament is riddled with references about conducting ourselves as "one body: *"for we are all parts of one body and members one of another"* (Eph. 4:25 AMP), *"closely joined and firmly knit together"* (Eph. 4:16 AMP), *"that their hearts may be encouraged, being knit together in love"* (Col. 2:2).

We are also told, on the other hand, that *"Where envy and self-seeking exist, confusion and every evil thing are there"* (James 3:16).

> *God created humanity to enjoy intimate fellowship with Him so we all together, with Christ, would become one, unified whole.*

The enemy of our soul takes what God meant to liberate us, twists it just a little, and then uses it to enslave us instead. What God meant to knit our souls together in the liberating bonds of love and truth, satan uses to tie up our souls with the yokes of selfishness and deception. Our souls are entrapped in life-draining, codependent relationships rather than life-giving and mutually supportive partnerships. I concur with the following sentiment offered by retired US General Colin Powell:

> The less you associate with some people, the more your life will improve. Any time you tolerate mediocrity in others, it increases your mediocrity. An important attribute in successful people is their impatience with negative thinking and negative acting people. As you grow, your associates will change. Some of your friends will not want you to go on. They will want you to stay where they are. Friends that don't help you climb will want you to crawl. Your friends will stretch your vision or choke your dream. Those that don't increase you will eventually decrease you.

Nothing about our human experience seems to be completely perfect—especially when it comes to relationships. We are challenged to develop and grow as a result of the inherent complexities of even our most treasured relationships. Those to whom we attach ourselves are an integral part of our quest to find a mirrored image of who we really are. No man is an island; we were created for community. Overcoming relational difficulties and the emotional pain associated with the disappointments of past relationships demands that we face our present challenges with insight and resolve.

Life is a kaleidoscopic contradiction. Our relationships with friends, spouses, colleagues, and family members can be wonderfully rewarding. Conversely, they can also produce some of the deepest pain, heartache, frustration, and disappointment. There are those who make us feel open, authentic, and at ease—while others cause us to become guarded, defensive, and awkward; they leave us feeling emotionally depleted and diminished, if not powerless. It is a conundrum why we choose to remain in such dysfunctional relationships. How do we break these unhealthy relational cycles, or even muster the courage and strength to walk away from relationships that are toxic?

Healthy, loving, and mutually beneficial relationships take work to cultivate and maintain. Why? For starters, we are each dynamic beings who change from day to day. Secondly, we come into relationships from different backgrounds bringing the life scripts we are most accustomed to with us—scripts that have been reinforced by our socialization, education, and cultural experiences. Add to that all of the repressed emotional anchors and psychological triggers garnered from our childhood experiences, and you have a recipe for complexity!

For example, each of us experienced and interpreted love as a child differently. If you experienced constant fighting, yelling, and belittlement in your family, you might conclude that family relationships bring suffering and unhappiness. You might have seen one of your parents dominated and controlled by the other. Thus, in your own relationships, you either dominate or become dominated. You might have experienced love shown in the form of lavish gifts rather than emotional connection or physical affection. We have a tendency to repeat what we are familiar with. Indeed, as Shakespeare intimated, "all the world is a stage." In other words, we all have our scripts. If you ever find the inner strength to drill down below the psychological surface of your conscious mind, you will discover a well spring of clues as to how to change your life scripts. In so doing, you will have discovered how to break unhealthy cycles and to cultivate beautiful, mutually beneficial relationships.

There are also those who may have developed a negative internal dialogue as a result of being bullied, teased, isolated, rejected, or ignored. The scripts we replay internally are as debilitating as those we play out in our relationships. Knowing that life is so much fuller and richer when we are free from toxic thoughts and relationship patterns, why don't we do more to take control of them? A major reason is because we have not been offered an alternative pattern, strategy, or model to follow.

The most important relationship lesson I have learned is that the relationships we have with other people are projections of the relationship we have with ourselves. We do not draw to ourselves whom we want, but who we are. It is an issue of like attracting like. Our external relationships are simply an extension of our internal relationship. When we establish relationships with others, we are actually searching for a mirrored image of ourselves—often causing us to search for love in all the wrong places. This is why when we find something in common with another person, we get excited because that person is mirroring for us who we really are and validating our sense of identity. Even many of the things we reject in others, we actually secretly harbor or struggle with on a subconscious level. Conversely, when we learn how to authentically love ourselves, we will attract people who will mirror that love. This is another area where knowledge of the truth will set you free!

With this in mind, we will begin delving into the heart of our study. For the next four weeks, we will be going deeper into the realm of relational dynamics, take a look at some of the most destructive types of relational attachments, and begin practicing the corresponding disciplines that will empower you to press toward experiencing the resilient life that God always intended for you.

Life doesn't get easier or more forgiving, we get stronger and more resilient. —Jodi Picoult

Day 11

WE VERSUS ME

Coming together is a beginning; keeping together
is progress; working together is success.
—Henry Ford

DISCIPLINE #11 — BE "WE-MINDED"
INSTEAD OF "ME-MINDED"

As we explored in the previous two weeks, everything that
exists is in a constant state of interaction and exchange—influencing and being influenced by whatever is around it. There
is nothing more influential than the relationships you enter
into with other people. As I also stated, the electromagnetic
exchange that takes place between two living souls is dynamic
and powerful. That exchange—or interaction—can either be
life giving or life depleting. Soul ties influence the trajectory and
limitations of your existence.

If your relationships are   *Nothing is more influen-*
motivated by selfishness, envy,   *tial than the relationships*
pride, or fear, these ties will   *you enter into with other*
split the soul so that they result   *people.*
in an "I" and "you" rather than
a "we" and "me" dynamic. When such a split takes place, there
is division, conflict, and strife—a disconnect with Christ and
the members of His Body that leads to *"every evil thing."* Paul

told the Corinthians, *"there should be no schism in the body, but that the members should have the same care for one another"* (1 Cor. 12:25). Our interactions determine the health of our souls—whether they will be tied and yoked in the bondage of darkness, or *"bathed in sunlight…free to enjoy God!"* (Isa. 58:10,14 MSG).

In a very powerful passage of Scripture, the prophet Isaiah outlines the will of God in this area. He makes clear that how we choose to relate to others will determine how God chooses to relate to us.

> *Is this not the fast that I have chosen: to loose the bonds of wickedness, to undo the heavy burdens, to let the oppressed go free, and that you break every yoke? Is it not to share your bread with the hungry, and that you bring to your house the poor who are cast out; when you see the naked, that you cover him, and not hide yourself from your own flesh? If you take away the yoke from your midst, the pointing of the finger, and speaking wickedness, if you extend your soul to the hungry and satisfy the afflicted soul, then your light shall dawn in the darkness, and your darkness shall be as the noonday* (Isaiah 58:6-7,9-10).

Learning to treat others with love, honor, and respect will unfold the Kingdom of God before us. This is what defines holiness, more than what we wear, eat, or drink—more than what we watch on TV, listen to on the radio, or pump into our souls through our MP3 players. Love is how we take up residence in the Kingdom of God, walk in constant fellowship with Him, and always remain in His presence, because *"God is love, and he who abides in love abides in God, and God in him"* (1 John 4:16)—*"By this all will know that you are My disciples, if you have love for one another"* (John 13:35).

The greatest training ground to modeling God and revealing our Kingdom citizenship is by being we-minded when it comes to our relationships instead of being self-consumed. Being self-centric is the exact opposite of God's nature—when we become me-focused instead of we-focused, we are actually walking outside of a place of true intimacy with God.

POWER POINT

Our relationships with other people tend to mirror our personal relationships with God. If we are walking in communion with Him, we will represent Him accurately in our lives. Time after time, Scripture upholds the value of being we-minded instead of me-minded. In fact, the Great Commandment issued by Jesus was two-fold, involving a love for God *and* a love for people. In other words, the Great Commandment is a divine call for all of us to be we-minded!

POWER THOUGHT

That there may be no division in the body, but that the members may have the same care for one another (1 Corinthians 12:25 ESV).

Day 12

JUST VERSUS UNJUST

Walk straight, act right, tell the truth. Don't hurt your friend, don't blame your neighbor; despise the despicable (Psalm 15:2-4 MSG).

DISCIPLINE #12 — VALUE SERVICE OVER SELFISHNESS

There are four types of relationships that create soul ties. Of these four types of relationships, only one is healthy—or *just* (defined as "honest, honorable, righteous, moral, and truthful").

The other three are a result of what has been commonly called "dysfunctional" relations. We will explore these in more depth later. For now, I would like to start by discussing what a healthy relationship looks like, and then take you through the dynamics, symptoms, and effects of dysfunctional relationships in more general terms.

If there is any doubt that "God's Chosen Fast" (as presented in Isaiah 58) is defined by how we choose to relate with other people, Ezekiel makes it even plainer. Read the following verse in light of what you've already learned about how soul ties and entanglements are created, and what you can do to avoid them:

Imagine a person who lives well, treating others fairly, keeping good relationships...doesn't seduce a neighbor's spouse, doesn't indulge in casual sex, doesn't bully anyone, doesn't pile up bad debts, doesn't steal, doesn't refuse food to the hungry, doesn't refuse clothing to the ill-clad, doesn't exploit the poor, doesn't live by impulse and greed, doesn't treat one person better than another, but lives by my statutes and faithfully honors and obeys my laws. This person who lives upright and well shall live a full and true life (Ezekiel 18:5-9 MSG).

This is how David lived until he threw much of it away with Bathsheba—and how he lived after he repented of those sins. This is why God was so *"extravagantly generous in love"* (1 Kings 3:6 MSG) with him and why He said of him, *"I have found David...a man after My own heart"* (Acts 13:22). What is God's heart? How can we align our hearts with the heart of God?

In First Kings we read where Solomon speaks to God saying, *"You were extravagantly generous in love with David my father, and he lived faithfully in your presence, his relationships were just and his heart right"* (1 Kings 3:6 MSG).

A "right heart"—or an upright heart—and "just relationships" go hand in hand. What is a *just* relationship versus an *unjust* one? How can you be sure you are honoring God in all of your interactions and associations? What can you do to cultivate healthy relationships, and therefore a healthy soul? Let us start by briefly identifying what a "just relationship" looks like before exploring those birthed out of dysfunction.

A Symbiotic Relationship

Divinely ordained or "destined" soul mates form a kind of *synergetic* or *symbiotic* relationship. This type of relationship is a mature, healthy, mutually beneficial one, comprised of healthy individuals whose personal lives are built on integrity and authenticity, with each contributing to the other's success, destiny, vision, prosperity, growth, development, and enjoyment in life.

Someone once said, "Soul mates are people who bring out

the best in you. They are not perfect, but are always perfect for you." Soul mates can be two people who are joined together in marriage, or they can be lifelong friends or business partners, or brothers and sisters in the Lord. You might discover a soul mate in a person of a different generation or gender that you might not naturally be attracted to or comfortable with, such as David and Jonathan, Ruth and Naomi, or Paul and Timothy. The encounter of soul mates is often analogous to the collision of matter and antimatter: A violent explosive reaction that, if held through to completion, will result in pure energy and harmony.

This is a picture of the type of relationship God hoped to create between Himself and humanity when He exchanged the life of His Son—His own flesh and blood—for the life of every human being. God made the ultimate sacrifice so that we could experience a symbiotic relationship with Him and each other *in Him*—an interdependent, mutually abiding, grafting in of heart, soul, and mind of one living being with the heart, soul, and mind of another.

Our relationship with Christ has been likened to a marriage covenant. It is symbiotic in that it is capacity building, stretching, strengthening, and value adding. A healthy marriage relationship is purposeful and functional. Although every marriage relationship will result in a soul tie, not all are symbiotic.

Marriages of convenience (such as for immigration purposes), shotgun marriages, same-sex marriages, or where the parties are unequally yoked, will result in dysfunctional, unhealthy soul ties. God warned Solomon about entering into such a marriage knowing that "becoming one" means just that—taking on another's characteristics, history, and values. *"You shall not intermarry with them, nor they with you. Surely they will turn away your hearts after their gods"* (1 Kings 11:2). In losing his heart, Solomon lost his kingdom—the Kingdom God had foreordained that he and his descendants would rule.

For it was so, when Solomon was old, that his wives turned his heart after other gods; and his heart was not loyal to the Lord his God.... Therefore the Lord said to Solomon, "Because you have done this...I will surely tear the kingdom away from you and give it to your servant" (1 Kings 11:4,11).

The same tragedy happens today. It is your legacy to enforce the rule of God's Kingdom in the earth, but when you marry yourself to worldly people, you marry yourself to the world and become absorbed by its systems instead of absolved of them—bound by them instead of freed from them.

So to keep your soul healthy and your heart right before God, keep your relationships just. There is nothing more empowering and energizing than a symbiotic relationship when expressed appropriately. Cherish those precious soul mates God has given you for the purpose of making you more than you would be otherwise. As the French novelist, Marcel Proust, so wisely stated, "Let us be grateful to people who make us happy, they are the charming gardeners who make our souls blossom."

> *Jesus wants to be more than your Friend—He wants to be your Soul Mate.*

Remember, Jesus intends to be more than your Friend; He wants to be your Soul Mate—eternal souls, joined together for eternal purposes. This is why the Church is referred to as His Bride. That is the model for the kind of soul connection we are to have with other members of His Body, as well as the members of our own families.

POWER POINT

The following is a checklist of things that identify a healthy and just relationship. Consider whether your relationships have the following characteristics:

- Committed to spiritual health and growth
- Empowering
- Authentic and transparent
- Lead to increased maturity, problem-solving skills, and a sharpening of focus
- Clear expectations and responsible follow-through
- Clear and healthy boundaries
- Personal responsibility for actions and thoughts
- Loyal
- Reliable
- Thoughtful
- Respect for personhood, opinions, ideas, personal space, privacy, and confidentiality
- Personal convictions are never violated
- An allowance for differing temperaments, personalities, preferences, and habits
- Mutually beneficial

Are you able to identify relationships that meet these criteria? Take time to thank God for them. In fact, I would encourage you to go the extra mile and take time to thank each person individually, whether it is face to face, on the phone, in an email or ecard, or even in an old fashioned, handwritten letter.

POWER THOUGHT

Words are easy, like the wind; faithful friends are hard to find. —William Shakespeare

Day 13

INTERDEPENDENCE VERSUS INDEPENDENCE

The strength of the team is each individual member. The strength of each member is the team. —Phil Jackson

DISCIPLINE #13—PURSUE INTEGRATION OVER ISOLATION

We must learn to value interdependence rather than independence—to see ourselves as an interconnected whole rather than a sum of disconnected parts:

For because of [Jesus] *the whole body (the church, in all its various parts), closely joined and firmly knit together by the joints and ligaments with which it is supplied, when each part [with power adapted to its need] is working properly [in all its functions], grows to full maturity, building itself up in love* (Ephesians 4:16 AMP).

This begins with loving our neighbor as we do ourselves—*"For the whole Law [concerning human relationships] is complied with in the one precept, You shall love your neighbor as [you do] yourself"* (Gal. 5:14 AMP). An expression of love is service.

*Do nothing out of selfish ambition or vain conceit. Rather, in
humility value others above yourselves, not looking to your own
interests but each of you to the interests of the others. In your
relationships with one another, have the same mindset as Christ
Jesus* (Philippians 2:3-5 NIV).

When we value others as we do ourselves and are able to
lay down our own preferences to serve someone else, that is
the start of having a Christ-like relationship. This should not be
one-sided however. The people with whom you are in relationship should also lay down their preferences and want the best
for you. Of course, there must also be boundaries in these relationships. We will discuss the topic of building healthy boundaries in Week Six.

In Western society we are taught to believe that it is our number one job to look out for ourselves. The concept of being part
of something bigger where we can provide and receive nourishment is nearly alien to most people. When we gave our lives
to Jesus, we became part of a bigger family called the Body of
Christ. A divine assimilation took place, adopting us into a system of relationships designed to function in spiritual harmony
with one another. This is not simply a nice group of people to
have coffee with on Sunday mornings, but a unified body of
interconnected souls with whom we experience life and depend
on when needed.

Serving one another in love is one important component of
being an interdependent family. The other component of interdependence is the ability to receive what other people have to
offer. Some people find giving much easier than receiving. It takes
some measure of vulnerability to say "yes" to someone's offer of
help, let alone to ask for help. There is beauty in vulnerability—
and in not always being the one doing the giving. When was the
last time you gratefully received assistance or asked for help?

The wonderful thing about the Body of Christ is that just like the parts of our natural bodies, we each have important, but different, functions to play. We fool ourselves thinking that we can do everything all by ourselves. It is this independent spirit that says you don't need anyone else to be happy or get the job done.

> *The wonderful thing about the Body of Christ is that we each have important functions.*

When dealing with a spirit of independence, usually, there is an unhealthy soul tie at the root. Some type of relational catalyst took place in our lives through betrayal, hurt, abuse, or some other type of exchange, causing us to make the decision to withdraw from interdependence and pursue independence. This does not justify any of the hurtful actions that you experienced, but we cannot let such things become catalysts for isolationism.

Functioning Together

The Message translation of Romans 12:4-6 says:

In this way we are like the various parts of a human body. Each part gets its meaning from the body as a whole, not the other way around. The body we're talking about is Christ's body of chosen people. Each of us finds our meaning and function as a part of his body. But as a chopped-off finger or cut-off toe we wouldn't amount to much, would we? So since we find ourselves fashioned into all these excellently formed and marvelously functioning parts in Christ's body, let's just go ahead and be what we were made to be, without enviously or pridefully comparing ourselves with each other, or trying to be something we aren't.

Immediately following this passage about being members of one body and one another, Paul talks about different gifts or strengths each brings to the table.

Having then gifts differing according to the grace that is given to us, let us use them: if prophecy, let us prophesy in proportion to our faith; or ministry, let us use it in our ministering; he who teaches, in teaching; he who exhorts, in exhortation; he who gives, with liberality; he who leads, with diligence; he who shows mercy, with cheerfulness (Romans 12:6-8).

Why waste time and energy trying to do something you are not particularly gifted in? You will build resiliency into your life when you draw from other people's strengths. Selfishness restrains divine activity and productivity. In the just-cited passages, we notice that when we operate interdependently, effective ministry is accomplished and our fellow man is served.

> *Receiving someone's strength gives them the opportunity to use their gift and, in turn, be blessed.*

Jesus said, *"It is more blessed to give than to receive"* (Acts 20:35). If you find yourself thinking that you do not want to inconvenience someone by either receiving or asking for help, remember this verse. When you receive from someone's strength, you are giving them the opportunity to use their gift and, in turn, be blessed. Ultimately, you are empowering them to take their strategic place and flourish in their unique graces and giftings.

POWER POINT

Ask the Lord if there is a spirit of independence in your life and what you can do to break it. Next time you find yourself in a situation that is a struggle for you to face alone, intentionally ask someone for help. Chances are, there is a person close by who would be glad to lend you their strength.

At first glance, independence might seem like the ideal way

to live because of the messages we receive from society—as well as this deceptive idea of not wanting to inconvenience someone by receiving or asking for help. But when we choose interdependence by allowing other people to use their gifts and strengths instead of trying to do everything ourselves, the Body of Christ functions more efficiently and effectively.

POWER THOUGHT

But now indeed there are many members, yet one body. And the eye cannot say to the hand, "I have no need of you"; nor again the head to the feet, "I have no need of you" (1 Corinthians 12:20-21).

CONTENDING FOR VERSUS COMPETING WITH

Agree with each other, love each other, be deep-spirited friends. Don't push your way to the front; don't sweet-talk your way to the top. Put yourself aside, and help others get ahead. Don't be obsessed with getting your own advantage (Philippians 2:2-4 MSG).

DISCIPLINE #14 — CONTEND FOR RATHER THAN COMPETE WITH OTHERS

Instead of competing with one another, we should be contending for one another—"*Put yourself aside, and help others get ahead,*" Paul wrote to the Philippians. "*Don't be obsessed with getting your own advantage. Forget yourselves long enough to lend a helping hand*" (Phil. 2:3-4 MSG).

Worse still, those who we love most usually feel our fiercest wrath. Competition thrives in family dynamics—particularly with *sibling rivalry*. We tend to take for granted those we hold dearest. We must not only learn to love our neighbor as ourselves, but also our closest family members. We should be especially grateful for and highly esteem those within our most enduring and closest spheres.

I believe this poem by 19th century American poet Ella Wheeler Wilcox best sums up this timeless principle:

There's one sad truth in life I've found
while journeying east and west—
The only folks we really wound
are those we love the best.

We flatter those we scarcely know—
we please the fleeting guest,
and deal many a thoughtless blow
to those who love us best.

To contend for one another and lay our lives down for service instead of competition is the lifestyle Jesus Christ modeled for us. Right after Paul's exhortation for believers to be selfless servants, he describes Jesus' selfless attitude:

In your relationships with one another, have the same mindset as Christ Jesus: Who, being in very nature God, did not consider equality with God something to be used to his own advantage; rather, he made himself nothing by taking the very nature of a servant, being made in human likeness. And being found in appearance as a man, he humbled himself by becoming obedient to death—even death on a cross! (Philippians 2:5-8 NIV)

The first thing that may come to mind when discussing the topic of selflessness is acts of service. However, physically serving someone is not the epitome of stepping into Christ-likeness.

> *We should be especially grateful for and highly esteem those within our most enduring and closest spheres.*

One of the most expressive ways we can display Christ-like character is when we genuinely celebrate the successes of others and refuse to display a hint of jealousy when they prosper. Competition is one of the ultimate by-products of independence.

When we see ourselves as part of a collective whole, our

neighbor's success is really our success, and vice versa. We are family. Sadly, as I alluded to earlier, the family context is absolutely riddled with competition. Siblings, spouses, in-laws, and even entire generations can exist in a state of competitive tension. Such a climate of competition proves that someone somewhere entered into a destructive soul attachment and ushered in a climate of independence. Remember, a soul attachment is not always caused by a person. We studied several exchanges that are responsible for creating soul ties with people, systems, groups, and other such things. Independence is the fruit of some type of soul tie that very well may have been formed by one of the attachments we reviewed in the first two weeks. Either way, for competition to cease, the attachment needs to be broken.

One of the key strategies to breaking these ties is to start declaring and practicing what the Word of God says concerning the very things we are struggling with. For example, we should *"Rejoice with those who rejoice; mourn with those who mourn"* (Rom. 12:15 NIV). This is what it looks like to love well and in turn, defeat those competitive tendencies.

When someone has the opportunity to succeed in some way and asks for prayer, would your first reaction be to pray for their success, or would it be to secretly hope for their failure? And if they do succeed, would your first reaction be to rejoice with them? How about if someone does poorly? Would your heart feel empathy toward them? These are good questions to check your heart to see if you are truly contending for your brothers and sisters out of love.

Here is a partial description of what love is in the famous love chapter of the Bible:

> *Love never gives up. Love cares more for others than for self. Love doesn't want what it doesn't have. Love doesn't strut, doesn't have a swelled head, doesn't force itself on others, isn't always "me first..."* (1 Corinthians 13:4-5 MSG).

Although this definition is the polar opposite of what we see modeled in society, it is the way of the Kingdom. Caring for others, celebrating them, and proactively thinking of ways to help them succeed, are expressions of genuine love. This is how the world will be attracted to Christ in us.

It can be easy to celebrate with those whose victories are not in any way related to us, but let's bring this closer to home. What if your brother or sister gets the promotion at work that you have been wanting? Or what if someone gets healed of the very thing you need healing in? Or what if someone gets to do the thing or take the vacation that is on your bucket list? Would you genuinely be happy and excited for them, or would you be jealous? *"Let us not become conceited, provoking and envying each other"* (Gal. 5:26 NIV).

POWER POINT

Loving and serving our brothers and sisters like Christ means contending for their success as well as celebrating when it manifests. Having jealousy in our hearts is an indication of competition, and does not promote unity and love in the family of God. It binds our souls and keeps us from living more resiliently—if not individually, then as a community of believers.

Tomorrow, we are going to discuss a very practical way that we can start celebrating our brothers and sisters by believing their victory is our victory.

POWER THOUGHT

Love each other with genuine affection, and take delight in honoring each other (Romans 12:10 NLT).

Day 15

WIN-WIN
VERSUS WIN-LOSE

Win-win sees life as a cooperative arena, not a competitive one. Win-win is a frame of mind and heart that constantly seeks mutual benefit in all human interactions. Win-win means agreements or solutions are mutually beneficial and satisfying. We both get to eat the pie, and it tastes pretty darn good!—Stephen Covey

DISCIPLINE #15—CHOOSE TO ADD VALUE TO EVERY RELATIONSHIP

Earlier this week, I introduced you to the concept of a symbiotic relationship. I want to conclude this week by emphasizing the value that such relationships add to each participating party.

A symbiotic relationship is evidenced by a mutual commitment to spiritual health, growth, and accelerated development. It is mutually valuable, empowering, trusting, authentic, transparent, and genuine. There are clear and responsible expectations, clear and healthy boundaries, personal responsibility for actions, behaviors, and thoughts; there is an undercurrent of loyalty, reliability, thoughtfulness, and respect for personhood, opinions, ideas, personal space, privacy, and confidentiality. Personal convictions are never violated; there is an allowance for differing temperaments, personalities, preferences, and habits.

Symbiotic relationships are purpose-driven and pose challenges that lead to increased maturity, problem-solving skills, and a sharpening of focus. Developing a symbiotic relationship takes intentional effort and work.

> What greater thing is there for two human souls than to feel that they are joined for life—to strengthen each other in all labor, to rest on each other in all sorrow, to minister to each other in all pain, to be one with each other in silent, unspeakable memories at the moment of the last parting? —George Eliot

When Jesus walked the earth, He demonstrated the power of that kind of relationship. He chose twelve men to walk by His side for the duration of His earthbound life. He offered all that He had been prepared to do from the beginning of time in exchange for their commitment. In other words, in exchange for their loyalty, He would dedicate Himself to not only their eternal salvation, but also their growth, development, destiny, purpose, and lifetime mission. Simply put, He was prepared to add value to their lives. A healthy relationship starts with the intent of adding quality to that person's life. It creates a transformative, mutually beneficial association.

> *A healthy relationship starts with adding quality to a person's life.*

A key to maintaining these types of relationships is viewing situations where other people succeed as win-win instead of win-lose for us. Jesus did not observe the successes of His disciples as a loss for Him or distraction from His spotlight. Quite the opposite, He poured into the disciples so that they could, in turn, become everything they were destined to be. Jesus is the ultimate example of One who prized adding value to others.

Think about the attitude of players on an athletic team. When one person scores for the team, the whole team rejoices. The individual breakthrough becomes a corporate or community-wide breakthrough. This is how we should think—we are all members of the same team whether it be the Church, a community, a corporation, or a country.

Some people seem naturally inclined to compete to win. This is not necessarily a bad thing, but the question is whether they believe in order to win others must lose. That indicates a mentality of lack—an attitude of scarcity that embraces the belief there is not enough to go around. The truth is that God, the Almighty Father, possesses all the resources in the world, and these resources are enough for all of us.

Imagine all of the resources of heaven being at your disposal. That is not fantasy; it is reality for every Kingdom citizen. In addition to the resources of heaven being readily available, God's heart is for you and He wants to lavish you with His love and kindness. His love extends toward you just as much as it does the next person. When someone else experiences a profound breakthrough or life-changing miracle, it does not indicate that God loves that person any more than you. Take time to ask the Lord what His heart is toward you the next time you feel a twinge of jealousy over someone else's victory or accomplishment.

What about when you sense other people might be jealous toward *you* because of *your* success? Does this mean you should restrain your strength and not shine? No. While you may not enjoy being envied instead of celebrated, this does not mean you should willfully "lose" so that others can feel better about themselves. That would be a perverted lose-win situation where you choose to lose to someone who struggles with envy or jealousy. The problem with this scenario is that such a person will feel they have won because someone else has lost. This is not an attitude anyone should legally encourage others to perpetuate in their lives. While you cannot change another person's response to your success, you can transform your beliefs and behaviors to celebrate and add value to every relationship.

Another way to add value to your relationships is by giving. Paul talks about giving in the following passage from Second Corinthians:

> *At the present time your plenty will supply what they need, so that in turn their plenty will supply what you need. The goal is equality, as it is written: "The one who gathered much did not have too much, and the one who gathered little did not have too little" (2 Corinthians 8:14-15 NIV).*

You can see that the goal is not to be in a lose-win or win-lose situation. It is to create a win-win situation where everyone has enough. Paul is talking about monetary resources or material goods here, but we can apply it beyond that realm to include giving of our time, talents, and energy. Consider what you can give next time you are in a conversation and someone mentions a need or desire. Your soul will be refreshed by helping your team member!

> *Transform your beliefs and behaviors to celebrate and add value to every relationship.*

POWER POINT

Can you imagine living in a world where everyone is secure in who they are, rooted in how much they are valued by God—and are therefore able to fully celebrate who other people are, and how much God honors them and their successes? While you cannot change how other people think, you can shift your own mindset. Once your mindset changes, your behavior will follow. This is the fundamental key to reclaiming your soul and practicing a more resilient lifestyle. As you've heard me say so many times, "Think for a change!" Change your thoughts; change your world!

Next week is the final segment where we review the relationship dynamics and behaviors that produce destructive soul attachments.

POWER THOUGHT

And if one member suffers, all the members suffer with it; or if one member is honored, all the members rejoice with it (1 Corinthians 12:26).

Week Four

CONFRONTING DYSFUNCTIONAL RELATIONSHIPS

Our souls sit close and silently within,
And their own webs from their own entrails spin;
And when eyes meet far off, our sense is such,
That, spider-like, we feel the tenderest touch.
—John Dryden

As each one has received a gift, minister it to one another,
as good stewards of the manifold grace of God
(1 Peter 4:10).

What isn't a healthy relationship is a dysfunctional one. And it's not only marriage relationships that can be unhealthy, but relationships with friends, coworkers, sometimes even acquaintances, and most definitely your family members. As you have heard it said, "You can choose your friends, but you can't choose your family!"

Ideally, everyone should be raised in a healthy and stable family environment, however the idyllic family scenario is more often the exception than the rule—you would be hard pressed to find a family void of any dysfunctional characteristics at all.

This week, we are going to look at five different dimensions of dysfunctional relationships, trace some of their roots back to unhealthy soul attachments, and embrace the liberating truth that no matter what environment you grew up in, you don't have to continue the dysfunction—the buck can stop with you. The manifold grace of God is readily available to help propel you into a better, healthier existence.

Day 16

THE DYNAMICS OF DYSFUNCTION

Even now the axe is laid to the root of the trees (Matthew 3:10 ESV).

DISCIPLINE #16—DEAL WITH THE ROOT TO CHANGE THE FRUIT

If you saw this week's title and immediately thought, "This is for me!" I want to encourage you that instead of offering you some type of quick fix where you simply modify the problem at hand, God might be inviting you to do some deeper reflection and examination. Why? He wants you to understand the dynamics of dysfunction so that you are armed with knowledge that empowers you to sever the soul attachments that brought you to this place. Remember, your life does not happen accidently. In the same way, dysfunctional relationships do not just appear in our lives without a reason.

> *Everything begins with a root.*

Everything begins with a root. John the Baptist recognized this in Matthew 3:10 when he used the word picture of examining a tree's fruit. If the tree was not bearing good fruit, then it needed to be cut down at its root using an axe. The same is true for the roots of dysfunctional relationships in our lives. In our case, the "roots" are what I am calling the dynamics of dysfunction.

There are all sorts of family dynamics that lead to dysfunctional relationships, but primarily, the dysfunction begins in the marriage relationship and influences how a couple will engage in parenting.

Dysfunctional parenting is characterized by enmeshment and inordinate attachments—including addictions and unhealthy habits and behaviors of all kinds. Dysfunctional relationship patterns in families perpetuate the development of dysfunctional grown-ups. Dysfunctional people have a tendency to gravitate to other dysfunctional people.

This is why it is so important for us to resist the temptation of quick fixes. We can try and deal with the addictions and unhealthy behaviors, but if they are simply the result or fruit of a dysfunctional root system, dysfunctional patterns will continue to emerge—just in different ways.

The common root for all of us is childhood. This is where most of the dysfunction is birthed, and this is the place where we need to commence self-reflection.

Ideally, children ought to grow up in a healthy family environment that helps them feel worthwhile and valued. In this type of environment they learn that their feelings and needs are important, their identity is distinct and treasured, and that their personal characteristics are praiseworthy. However, when the family unit fails to provide for the emotional and physical needs of their children, these youngsters acquire poor life skills, with weaknesses in communication, problem solving, resource management, and social competence that will affect future relationships if not corrected somewhere along the way.

Addictive behavior, emotional instability, domestic violence, abuse, molestation, incest, and infidelity create deviant, perverted soul ties. The black sheep syndrome among children, issues of rejection, the failure to bond, sibling rivalry, role reversal, gender confusion, and premature or inappropriate sexual activity are manifestations of an unhealthy family environment.

Most dysfunction is multigenerational. One or both parents will have been exposed to physical and domestic violence, have been abandoned physically or emotionally, and experienced parental detachment or rigidity, or the strict enforcement of inflexible roles and rules. Their parents will have failed to provide for their physical, emotional, financial, educational, or social needs. Growing up they will have experienced parent-child role reversals—or surrogate parenting, such as protecting another parent from abuse, negotiating on behalf of a parent, or lying on behalf of one parent to alleviate further abuse or conflict from the other.

If you have been raised in an unhealthy family environment, you will have been deeply affected by that atmosphere. This will be evidenced by excessive attention-seeking behavior, lying, misrepresentation and exaggeration of the truth, constant power struggles, a fear of rejection, indifference, escapism, patterns of substance abuse, mistrust, failure to connect in relationships, sexual dysfunctions, difficulty in loving and accepting self and body, abandonment issues, boundary issues, emotional numbing, panic attacks, flashbacks, anxiety attacks, feelings of losing it, feelings of worthlessness, poor self-image, feeling dirty, ashamed, or oppressed—or the use of manipulative or controlling behaviors, such as witchcraft or other occult tactics. Other symptoms include not being able to trust others, openly share feelings, or follow through with commitments, as well as continual blame shifting, not wanting to talk about things that are unpleasant, general apathy and dissatisfaction with life, feelings of unhappiness, resentment, frustration, and despair.

There are six primary roles assumed by members of a dysfunctional family.

1. The *surrogate parent* assumes responsibility for the welfare of siblings as well as parents.

2. The *comedian* assumes responsibility for the emotional climate of the home by using comic relief.

3. The *hero* is an overachiever who assumes the role of making sure the family looks "normal" by being academically and financially successful.

4. The *black sheep* rebels by engaging in self-destructive behaviors, such as abusing drugs or alcohol, sexual promiscuity, stealing, and so on.

5. The *scapegoat* copes by taking the blame for whatever is wrong.

6. The *patient* distracts the family from crisis situations by "requiring" compassionate care for their psychosomatic illnesses, mishaps, and accidents.

Sadly, children who deal with these issues and create unhealthy soul attachments are completely insulated in a culture of dysfunction. It is unfortunate that it takes most people many years, if not decades, to identify the dysfunction, evaluate its inappropriateness, assess the damage, and move forward in breaking the attachments that were created during those formative years.

POWER POINT

The dynamics of relational dysfunction begin in childhood. This is undeniably the reason that most counselors, therapists, and psychiatrists begin with talking about the past rather than immediately addressing the present. They recognize the power of dysfunctional root systems that are, in some way, responsible for the present condition.

For our study, we need to identify some of the malignant soul attachments that are created—most often, in our youth—and that must be broken for us to experience freedom and resiliency in life.

POWER THOUGHT

Your vision will become clear only when you can look into your own heart. Who looks outside dreams; who looks inside awakens. —Carl Jung

Day 17

THE DE-MOTIVATOR
OF SHAME

Because the Sovereign Lord helps me, I will not be disgraced. Therefore, I have set my face like a stone, determined to do his will. And I know that I will not be put to shame (Isaiah 50:7 NLT).

DISCIPLINE #17—FOCUS ON ISSUES, NOT INDIVIDUALS

Dysfunctional families resist positive or strength-based change in family members because they want to avoid psychological disequilibrium. They use blame, fear, manipulation, shunning, threatening, and isolation to control behavior. Rather than pinpointing and dealing with the problem, one person might make others feel as though they *are* the problem. This is the breeding ground for shame, and the continued enabling of dysfunctional relational behavior.

> *Shame is such a strong emotion, that we tend to cut ourselves off from whatever has caused it.*

Interactions within these types of families are shame based—and shame is such a strong emotion, that we tend to cut ourselves off from whatever has caused it. This is why memories that bring shame are often repressed or we unconsciously avoid them without even realizing it. Our shame continues as we refuse to acknowledge it, because we are unwilling to actually confront the memory which created the shameful soul attachment to begin with.

The problem with shame is that it creates significant division in our relationships—particularly family units. Those who use shame to manipulate other family members are effectively isolating themselves from those they claim to love. In the same way that we repress memories that have shame attached to them, we distance ourselves from people who released shame into our lives. Ultimately, this leads to strained relationships across the board.

Shame is actually the result of an unhealthy soul attachment. How? When shame is used as a tool to motivate change, it does not end up producing lasting positive effects. It may provide for some temporary adjustment, but ultimately, the words, actions, and attitudes that carry shame create harmful soul attachments in our lives. Shame is released into our lives through these catalysts, and just as positive affirmation and encouragement become pillars of strength for us, shame becomes a tool of destruction that eats away at our very souls. It enslaves and destroys if not dealt with. If we do not identify and reject it for what it is, we will embrace it, and commence a long road of living with a vicious parasite of the soul.

> *Just as positive affirmation and encouragement become pillars of strength for, shame is a tool of destruction that eats away at our souls.*

Atmospheres in the home where shame is used as the primary source of motivation are a result of dysfunctional parents who suffer with their own shame. They are emotionally unhealthy and imbalanced, and therefore, have no sound insight on how to actually deal with the issues of life outside of tearing others down. In many cases, we use shame because we think that by disgracing the other person, we will motivate them to fix the issue. We link the person to the issue, and this communicates—loud and clear—that *"you* are the issue. You *are* the problem."* This is why shame is a de-motivator, producing the exact opposite of its intention. People use shame in vain hope that it will illicit change in someone else, when in fact, it de-motivates and destroys.

Often, parents such as those listed above suffer from some kind of addiction disorder; addiction to drugs, alcohol, food, pornography, promiscuity, gambling, shopping, media, sports, entertainment, overworking or "workaholism," and so on can cause them to be socially handicapped, financially irresponsible, and psychologically impaired.

Parents whose souls are bound by various types of addictions are prone to exhibit emotional outbursts; they are unreliable and unpredictable; they are out of touch with themselves, their feelings, and their impact on others, not recognizing what their responses release. Their senses are dulled to the dysfunctional patterns in which they were raised, and how their own attitudes and behaviors contribute to continuing that legacy.

Dysfunctional relationships destroy the true value of self, lower self-esteem, and distort self-image. These types of relationships are shallow, shaming, unsanctified, self-centered, self-protective, spiteful, and carnal.

Example of King Saul and David

Saul was addicted to approval, which ultimately was responsible for destroying his relationship with David. Hearing the celebratory songs that announced *"Saul has slain his thousands, and David his ten thousands!"* (1 Sam. 18:7) pushed him over the edge. Think of all that transpired between Saul and David. Saul was overtaken with a consuming desire to shame and destroy a boy he once loved and who had grown up in his home, who was now a man married to his daughter, and who was like a brother

199

to his son, Jonathan. Saul even turned on his own son because of it:

> *Saul boiled with rage at Jonathan. "You stupid son of a whore!"*
> *he swore at him. "Do you think I don't know that you want him*
> *to be king in your place, shaming yourself and your mother? As*
> *long as that son of Jesse is alive, you'll never be king. Now go*
> *and get him so I can kill him!" "But why should he be put to*
> *death?" Jonathan asked his father. "What has he done?" Then*
> *Saul hurled his spear at Jonathan, intending to kill him*
> (1 Samuel 20:30-33 NLT).

Beyond his approval addiction, Saul exhibited many of the classic symptoms of having been raised in a dysfunctional family. Because of his own insecurities, he wanted to suppress the success of anyone around him. His sense of personal power came from disempowering others, regardless of how much they loved him or were devoted to serving him. David always acted in Saul's behalf, to honor him and bring him glory, yet Saul continued to lash out at him and be abusive. David was forced to run for his life, though at the same time he refused to do anything other than honor his king. David's soul was tied to Saul's as much as it was tied to Jonathan's, only it was an unhealthy soul tie based in Saul's fear and shame rather than David's love and respect.

POWER POINT

Shame is a deadly tool of manipulation. As we have just read, when shame is released upon someone through words or actions, it knits itself to their soul like a parasite. As long as it is not addressed, it continues to feed on emotion, self-esteem, worth, value, identity, etc. The problem is, the cycle of shame

continues to be enabled, as most children are not able to identify this root of dysfunction, let alone call it out in those who are
practicing this behavior. The next generation continues to fall
prey to dysfunctional parents who never addressed their personal, shame-producing soul attachments. These ties must be
broken—if not for our sakes, for the sake of our children and
future generations.

Of all the causes and symptoms of dysfunctional relationships, there are three main types that cause unhealthy soul ties.
In the days to come, I will briefly introduce the unhealthy ties
that result from a broad spectrum of dysfunctional relationships.

POWER THOUGHT

What you repress will make you regress.
—Michael H. Ballard

Day 18

WHEN HELPING YOU IS HURTING ME

The righteous should choose his friends carefully, for the way of the wicked leads them astray (Proverbs 12:26).

DISCIPLINE #18 — RESIST YIELDING TO THE CONTROL OF OTHERS

When helping you is hurting me sums up the type of relationship we'll be addressing today. It is observed in two different relational expressions—codependence and parasitic.

These relationships typically have one person who relates to the other primarily by making demands, while the other relates primarily by meeting those demands. The person making the demands is benefitted, while the person satisfying these demands on a consistent basis is being imprisoned in a ruthless cycle of soul attachment. This is the essence of codependence.

Codependent Relationships

Codependent relationships are made up of emotionally, socially, or psychologically handicapped individuals. Codependence is commonly defined as a "set of maladaptive compulsive behaviors learned by family members in order to survive within a family unit that is experiencing great emotional pain and stress."[1]

Codependence was a term originally coined when psychologists were studying the effects of alcoholics on their families. It was discovered that patterns of codependence developed where the "crisis manager" or caregiver was as dependent upon being needed and providing care as the alcoholic was on receiving that care. In some cases, the victim learns to need the victimizer in order to feel validated.

According to the National Mental Health Association, "Codependency is a learned behavior that can be passed down from one generation to another. It is an emotional and behavioral condition that affects an individual's ability to have a healthy, mutually-satisfying relationship."

Interestingly, this also represents what is known as *relationship addiction* because "people with codependency often form or maintain relationships that are one-sided, emotionally destructive, and/or abusive."[2] It was discovered that wherever there was an imbalance in relationship (for example where one person exerted excess control over another, made excessive demands, or demonstrated excessive needs—from domestic abuse to drug addiction), there were patterns of codependency.

> *Codependency keeps one person in the role of victim or sufferer and the other as problem solver or relief provider.*

You could say codependent relationships appear wherever there is obvious disparity in dependency. As opposed to interdependent relationships, in which each individual is fully independent while at the same time mutually reliant—codependency keeps one person in the role of victim or sufferer and the other as problem solver or relief provider. Codependent people have a greater tendency to get involved in relationships with people who are unreliable, emotionally unavailable, needy, or who set themselves up for continued failure. They are unlikely to get involved with people who have healthy boundaries, coping skills, and behaviors. This is why it is so common to see abused children grow up and marry abusers, or children of alcoholics grow up to marry people with addictions. The multigenerational relationship patterns—and subsequent soul attachments—are tremendously difficult to break without divine intervention.

Parasitic Relationships

Biologically speaking, a parasite is an organism that grows, feeds, and is sheltered on or within a different organism while contributing nothing to the survival of its host. Socially speaking, these are individuals who take advantage of the generosity of others without offering anything useful in return. We would call such a person a *sycophant*; one who flatters the rich—or those who they perceive as being prosperous, powerful, and influential—in the hope of gaining something from them.

Parasitic relationships are only beneficial to the one who acts as a "leech" or a "parasite," living off of the other person's resources—from their money and intellect to their emotional and spiritual energy. They bring nothing to the relationship except their needs, wants, and selfish ambitions. Like vampires, they suck the very life out of their victims. Like pariah, they prey off those they are in relationship with—they are predatory, cunning, and deceptive.

Parasitic people focus solely on their own wants and desires. They are not needy as much as they are greedy. They do not have the will or self-respect to adjust to the demands of interpersonal relationships and the stress involved in daily living. They live off other people's strengths, reputations, money, vision, goals, family, resources, time, and brainpower. Parasitic relationships result in soul attachments because the "host" is drawn into the parasite's life by the sad stories they tell, the needs they feign, and the mind games they play—completely unaware they are being used and manipulated. Parasitic relationships are characterized by hidden agendas, obscure motives, blame shifting (parasite), unclear boundaries (host), lack of personal responsibility (parasite), violation of convictions and values (host), under/unemployment (parasite), emotional bankruptcy (host), chronic complaining (parasite), debt (host), crisis (parasite), and spiritual depletion (host).

> *Parasitic people focus solely on their own wants and desires. They are not needy as much as they are greedy.*

Whether the relationship is codependent or parasitic, there is commonality between the two. In both cases, there is someone who is exercising control, and there is another person who is yielding to the control. The reason people yield to these types of unhealthy relationships is because, somewhere along the line, an unhealthy soul tie was created between the victim and the controller—between the host and the parasite.

Relationships like these take years, even decades to develop, so I do not want to suggest an overly simplified quick fix. That said, the goal of this study is to help you move toward a resilient lifestyle. However, to live in that place of freedom and victory, it is essential to identify and break the cycles that have imprisoned you. This is a critical step to experiencing sustained breakthrough in your life.

POWER POINT

Remember, I am not interested in seeing you enjoy only a measure of seasonal freedom, joy, and blessing. The goal is not for you to reclaim your soul only to lose it again four weeks down the road by developing some other harmful soul tie. We are after a new way of living—*resilient living*—that is the product of confronting some hard issues and making choices to deal with them head-on. God's will is for you to live a lifestyle of freedom that ultimately releases this same freedom to others.

POWER THOUGHT

Nobody can hurt me without my permission.
—Mahatma Gandhi

SPIRITUAL DIMENSIONS OF RELATIONSHIPS

The thief comes only to steal and kill and destroy (John 10:10 ESV).

DISCIPLINE #19—DISCERN THE SPIRITUAL RAMIFICATIONS OF ALL YOUR RELATIONSHIPS

Even though the third type of soul tie we are discussing is not particularly popular in this day and age, it is nevertheless real and highly relevant to our everyday lives.

Diabolical soul ties cause enmeshment of emotions, will, thoughts, perceptions, intentions, and attitudes between people, things, entities, etc. Look what happened to Adam and Eve in the Garden. A short encounter with satan—a brief interaction and momentary acquiescence to a demonic suggestion—pulled them out of the idyllic state of peace and prosperity into sin and survival by the sweat of their brows. Cain was drawn out of the presence of the Lord because of an attachment with an envious spirit. The result? He became the first murderer.

Other biblical examples include Solomon's association with foreign gods through the women he married—he went as far as building them altars:

Solomon built a high place for Chemosh the abomination of Moab, on the hill that is east of Jerusalem, and for Molech the

*abomination of the people of Ammon. And he did likewise for
all his foreign wives, who burned incense and sacrificed to their
gods* (1 Kings 11:7-8).

And look at what happened to mighty Sampson when he
tied his soul to Delilah—he lost his strength, his sight, and
finally his life. Sampson must have cried out as David did:

*For the enemy has persecuted my soul; he has crushed my life to
the ground; he has made me dwell in darkness, like those who
have long been dead* (Psalm 143:3).

Satan, the enemy of your soul, *"does not come except to steal, and
to kill, and to destroy"* (John 10:10). He is the author of death—
the spirit of abortion.

A diabolical relationship will cause you to abort the plans and
purposes God has put in your heart and mind. As the enemy did
with Adam and Eve, so will he try to do with you—he will seduce
you away from God's best intention for your life—away from the
realm of life to the realm of death. When you enter a relationship where the spirit of death is present, you create soul ties with
that spirit—likewise, when you participate in abortion, you create soul ties with the spirit of death. It is perpetuated through
all types of abortive activities, such as uncompleted assignments,
unfulfilled dreams, and unrealized potential. You open yourself
up to other types of murderous activities such as character assas-
sination, financial famine, and professional suicide.

It is even possible to experience these types of relationships
with family members. If our families have given themselves over
to darkness, we do not have to consent to their choices. We need
to be discerning in how close we become with such people who
have granted satan right of passage in their lives. Remember,
the enemy is on a mission to steal, kill, and destroy. His agenda
is the absolute abortion of everything God wants to birth into
the planet—and into your life.

The Bible is very clear about how God views abortion and

the activities that surround it. In the book of Genesis, a woman named Tamar was married to a firstborn son who *"was wicked in the sight of the Lord, and the Lord killed him"* (Gen. 38:7). As was Jewish custom, she was given as a wife to the younger brother to bear an heir for the older brother. However, the brother *"knew that the heir would not be his; and it came to pass, when he went in to his brother's wife, that he emitted on the ground, lest he should give an heir to his brother. And the thing which he did displeased the Lord; therefore He killed him also"* (Gen. 38:9-10). Every seed is precious in the sight of the Lord. Wasted seed deprives future generations of great leaders, doctors, lawyers, artists, spouses, parents, and so on.

In Exodus, God rewarded the midwives who saved the male babies from being drowned at birth per Pharaoh's orders: *"But the midwives feared God, and did not do as the king of Egypt commanded them, but saved the male children alive. And so it was, because the midwives feared God, that He provided households for them"* (Exod. 1:17,21). If it weren't for a brave mother preserving the life of her son, Moses, there may never have been a deliverer born to the children of Israel.

Even here, we witness a diabolical plot to destroy life—to terminate the unborn. Satan is terrified of the unborn, from people to potential. He recognizes the potential that exists for every unborn human being, along with every unborn plan, purpose, and promise in your life.

This is the overarching purpose for diabolical relationships. They are plans of the evil one to infiltrate and destroy your life. We cannot permit this if we are going to birth the plans and purposes God has ordained for us.

> *Birth and fulfillment are a direct assault upon the advancement of darkness in the earth.*

Birth and fulfillment are a direct assault upon the advancement of darkness in the earth. Think about it. As new life is birthed, that new soul brims with the potential to change history.

Even in your life, there is so much within you just waiting to be birthed. The potential is absolutely enormous.

Remember, you have the ability to say "Yes" or "No" to the enemy. Too many of us say "Yes," not because we actually want to give him a place in our lives, but because we do not recognize how dangerous diabolical soul attachments are. We are not discerning when it comes to evaluating whether or not a relationship has the potential to bring us into the captivity of darkness or produce spiritual edification.

POWER POINT

Diabolical attachments have one assignment for your life— *death.* Abortion is not just performed upon unborn children—it takes place every day as we give satan the opportunity to invade our lives and terminate the dreams, plans, and futures that God ordained from the very beginning.

Even though it does not involve a physical death, satan's strategy is to get you enmeshed in these diabolical soul ties so that he is able to gain some type of legal access or entry into your life. He cannot break your door down, so he has mastered the art of deception. You can, however, discern these types of relationships, move toward breaking these attachments, and live a life that declares a "No" to the assaults of the enemy.

POWER THOUGHT

Yell a loud no to the devil and watch him scamper
(James 4:7 MSG).

KEEP WATCH!

Stay alert! Watch out for your great enemy, the devil. He prowls around like a roaring lion, looking for someone to devour (1 Peter 5:8 NLT).

DISCIPLINE #20—NEVER LET YOUR GUARD DOWN

Today represents an important shift in our study. It is the last day we will be focusing on some of the identifying factors of soul ties and attachments. For the last twenty days, we have been looking at the various exchanges and relationships that produce soul attachments. I have given you daily disciplines and strategies for how to identify and confront some of these factors; but today, we are getting ready to take an important turn in our journey—from identifying soul ties to focusing on how to break them.

Yesterday, we examined what is perhaps the most sinister of all soul attachments—relationships that open the door to demonic infiltration in your life. Now that we have described what these types of relationships look like, and what the enemy's purpose for them is, it is important that we learn how to *keep watch* for such things.

I ended yesterday exhorting those who have experienced, or are experiencing, these types of soul ties to say "No" to the enemy and cancel the attachment. Just because you have carried a relationship with you for a season or even a lifetime, does not mean you need to move forward into your next season of life beaten down, hindered, and spiritually assaulted by a diabolical attachment. You can move forward free and never go back.

Today, I am addressing a different audience. I want to encourage the free. Whether you just prayed to get free from these attachments, or have been free for a while, on this monumental day I want to leave you with a word of caution—keep a diligent eye open, as the enemy will do anything he can to start the cycle all over again. Even if you have never experienced a deeply dysfunctional relationship, he is ever looking for a house that is swept, clean, and put in order.

In Matthew 12:43-44, Jesus describes this phenomena.

When an unclean spirit goes out of a man, he goes through dry places, seeking rest, and finds none. Then he says, 'I will return to my house from which I came.' And when he comes, he finds it empty, swept, and put in order.

The unclean spirit identified a potential residence in the house that was "put in order"—the very place from which the spirit was expelled proved to be a potential house of habitation in the future. How is this possible? It all depends on what the person does who is set free from the spirit in the first place.

In the Amplified Bible, the word "unoccupied" is added to the list of terms used to describe the type of house the evil spirit was looking to repossess. It is not good enough for us to get free—the key is staying free by replacing unhealthy soul attachments with the tools and disciplines we have been learning about. After all, you may have never truly dealt with a toxic soul attachment—or

> *We must keep our spiritual eyes open.*

you have an unoccupied house that your soul's enemy wants to take up residence in. All of us need to keep our spiritual eyes open. This takes place through discernment, which I will return to in a moment.

I do not want to simply arm you to receive victory in a season or for a moment; I want you to destroy the cycles in your life that the enemy has perpetuated. Over the next twenty days, you will identify several essential keys that will help you guard the house of your soul from every attachment and tie that would attempt to work its way into your life and wreak havoc. The first step, however, is keeping a sharp lookout for all of the exchanges and relationships that would threaten to recapture and ensnare your soul. This comes through developing discernment—particularly in regard to people and the relationships you engage in.

Nehemiah discerned the motives of Sanballat and Tobiah who wanted to keep him from rebuilding the wall around Jerusalem. Their intent was to cause him to abort the project and kill him in the process. Nehemiah did not allow them to intimidate or deter him. Even after the wall had been finished, Nehemiah wasted no time clearing away any who would seek to create soul attachments with those allied with the spirit of death. When the son of the high priest married a daughter of Sanballat, Nehemiah banished him from his presence (see Neh. 13:28).

> *Keep diligent watch over your soul by keeping diligent watch over your relationships.*

Keep diligent watch over your soul by keeping diligent watch over your relationships. Ralph Waldo Emerson is famous for having said, "A man is known by the company he keeps," but it was William Law, who a century earlier wrote in his famous book *Christian Perfection* (1726), "A man is known by his companions."

Perhaps this is why Paul warned the Corinthians *"not to keep company with anyone named a brother, who is sexually immoral, or covetous, or an idolater, or a reviler, or a drunkard, or an extortioner—not even to eat with such a person"* (1 Cor. 5:11).

Yet even before the birth of Christ, wisdom as eternal as this was spoken when in the 5th century B.C. the ancient philosopher, Euripides, stated, "Every man is like the company he is wont to keep." Words we would do well to live by.

POWER POINT

Your life is defined by the nature of your associations and attachments. When it comes down to it, the health of your soul is determined by the health of your relationships. Guarding your heart, from which *"flow the springs of life"* (Prov. 4:23 ESV), is largely a process of keeping watch over your personal relations—making sure you are clear from any codependent, parasitic, or diabolic relationships by staying alert and diligent to those who are trying to keep you from rebuilding *"the deserted ruins of your cities"* so that you would *"be known as a rebuilder of walls and a restorer of homes"* (Isa. 58:12 NLT).

POWER THOUGHT

The key is to keep company only with people who uplift you, whose presence calls forth your best. —Epictetus

Week Five

BREAKING
THE CYCLE

In everyone's life, at some time, our inner fire goes out. It is then burst into flame by an encounter with another human being. We should all be thankful for those people who rekindle the inner spirit. —Albert Schweitzer

God's Spirit is on me; he's chosen me to preach the Message of good news to the poor, sent me to announce pardon to prisoners and recovery of sight to the blind, to set the burdened and battered free... (Luke 4:18 MSG).

Now that we have identified many of the inroads that make you vulnerable to destructive types of soul ties, we are positioned to focus attention on becoming free and setting up some roadblocks for the future. This week we will cover practical steps you can take for building resiliency into your life.

Remember, the quick-fix route is not our desired travel plan. I do not want to set you up to achieve temporary victory in one area, only for you to find yourself bound and oppressed in another. Our objective here is to completely break the cycles that keep you from moving forward into a life of freedom and fulfillment.

Once these destructive patterns are reversed, you will need to intentionally replace old ways of thinking and behaving with new ones, as well as build some new, positive relationships. Over the next five days, I will describe five *pursuits* that you must embrace if you want to move beyond temporary deliverance into a lifestyle of stability and resiliency. Rather than call these keys, secrets, tips, or strategies, I believe the term pursuits more clearly indicates the concept; the implication is that you will experience transformation not to the degree that you *want* or *desire* it, but to the degree that you intentionally *go after* it.

> *You will experience transformation not to the degree that you want or desire it, but to the degree that you intentionally go after it.*

The next five days are critical, as they represent a significant transition point in our study. We are moving from information to transformation. The first four weeks were purposed to inform you about the different inroads that soul attachments use to pollute our lives and relationships. We became acquainted with some of the different soul ties—we learned how they manifest and caught a glimpse of the emotional chaos they bring into every arena they contaminate.

Now it is time we took that information and used it as a weapon to break the cycle. We are informed. Ignorance has been confronted. Light has been cast upon dark areas. Let's take the next five days and move toward a complete soul overhaul. We will discuss the five pursuits that are designed to help you cultivate a lifestyle of freedom from former soul ties and attachments. It is not enough to acknowledge them or even to systematically sever them; we are identifying and discussing this next series of pursuits in order to *reinvent* your life once it becomes void of these entanglements.

Remember, the enemy is looking for a vacant house. This is why so many people experience measures or seasons of freedom, but ultimately become enslaved again to destructive soul attachments. They legitimately tasted freedom, but did not take the necessary steps to develop a lifestyle that supports continued victory in every area.

Let the journey continue!

Day 21

PURSUE DESTINY-DEFINING MOMENTS

God has already lined up the right breaks, the right people, the answers you need. —Joel Osteen

DISCIPLINE #21—SEEK LIFE-GIVING RELATIONSHIPS

Destiny-defining moments are those liberating interactions birthed out of relationships with other people, and also through personal encounters with Christ. As we discussed back in Week 3, God did not design you and me to be independent, but rather, interdependent with the Body of Christ. Our relationships are critical to fulfilling our destinies, and this is why it is absolutely essential for our relationships to be healthy.

Although relationships are one of the primary vehicles through which soul ties are formed, they are also a dynamic catalyst through which those ties can be broken. One meeting, conversation, or encounter can launch your life on a completely different trajectory.

Author Jill Koenig describes destiny encounters as "specific life-defining moments" when a transformation or "radical shift occurs inside a person" to such an extent that they are never the same again. "Your defining moments may occur upon meeting a pivotal person," writes Koenig—"such as a mentor or when you lock eyes with your soul mate or your spouse for the first time."

One touch from God through another person can transform destructive mindsets you didn't even know you had. So how can we set ourselves up for truly meaningful destiny-defining moments?

The first way is to pray and ask God to lead you. *"Ask and it will be given to you"* (Matt. 7:7 NIV). It is God's pleasure to connect you with people who can take you deeper in your relationship with Him, and as a result, push you further toward fulfilling your destiny. Actively listen to hear His voice in your day-to-day activities. Ask the Holy Spirit to direct where you should go and at what time. This involves an intersection of innate, God-given wisdom, as well as sensitivity to the supernatural direction of the Spirit. We cannot simply "float around on a cloud" waiting for God to tell us where and when to brush our teeth or tie our shoes. There are choices that require practical wisdom. However, to engage a destiny-defining moment, it is vital for you to be in continuous communion with the Holy Spirit, always listening to those inward "nudges." This is what the Apostle Paul meant when he wrote, *"Pray without ceasing"* (1 Thess. 5:17).

> *One touch from God through another person can transform destructive mindsets you didn't even know you had.*

There is a point of intersection between both the practical and supernatural. God does not simply want to set you free and break a cycle in your life, but He wants to position you to fulfill your destiny. He also wants to use you to help launch other people into their destinies. You very well could be the divine encounter that someone else needs to propel him or her forward. God might place people in your path to be that collision of destiny they desperately need. At the same time, those people may in fact be integral to God launching *you* into your destiny. Though this knowledge is veiled to us, we do have the Holy Spirit living within us, who gives us wisdom, direction, and clarity.

In addition to being sensitive to God's leading in your home city, be open to going to new places. For example, go to a conference or meeting not in your home church or city. Visit somewhere that specializes in what you want to do or who you want to become. As you position yourself to be in the right place at the right time, look to see who stands out to you. *"Seek and you will find"* (Matt. 7:7 NIV). Ask yourself who you feel drawn to—be open to cultivating new relationships that could possibly shift everything in your life. Breaking the cycle is not simply a matter of getting *out* of the old and leaving behind the damaging relationships of your past. Rather, it involves pursuing life-giving relationships that will set you up to fulfill your destiny.

Power Point

Pray with intentionality for God to set you up with destiny-defining moments. Keep your senses open to the Holy Spirit's guidance in your schedule, see who you feel drawn to, introduce yourself to new people, and ask to meet with potential mentors and friends. When you live surrendered to God's leading, and pursue life-giving relationships, destiny-defining moments will start to take place on a regular basis.

Power Thought

For everyone who asks receives; the one who seeks finds; and to the one who knocks, the door will be opened (Matthew 7:8 NIV).

Day 22

PURSUE
A RENEWED MIND

Be renewed in the spirit of your mind (Ephesians 4:23).

DISCIPLINE #22—REPLACE NEGATIVE
MINDSETS WITH GOD'S TRUTH

A destiny moment is always a *redefining* moment—an experience or decision that transforms you because it causes you to re-evaluate and redirect your mindset and expectations; it compels you to renew your mind. As we break free from former soul ties that have had an adverse impact on our mindsets and perspectives, we need to become intentional about filling our minds with something new and transformative. This is the secret to stewarding your transformation and successfully living life beyond the broken cycle— no longer to return to the slavery of an old paradigm.

> *Studying, fellowshipping, and learning from others facilitates the renovation of your soul.*

Paul told the Romans to *"be transformed by the renewing of your mind"* (Rom. 12:2). Transformation comes by renewing your mind. This begs the question, *what does renewing your mind look like?*

There are many ways of renewing your mind, foremost is studying what the Bible says about how God sees you in Christ. Studying, fellowshipping, and learning from the experiences of others will also facilitate the renovation of your soul. In fact, I pray that reading this book will contribute to that renovation— that as a result of our meeting here in these pages you will be able to understand what has plagued your soul and the series of unfortunate meetings and associations that have kept you from moving forward and maximizing your fullest potential. Above all, I hope to direct you to an encounter with the One whose presence will sever every encumbrance and free you from every defiling attachment.

Today we will focus on specific ways you can renew your mind. As alluded to earlier, the first step is studying what the Scripture says about how God sees you in Christ. This can be a struggle for those who approach Scripture from a natural perspective. Renewing your mind is anything but natural. In fact, the alignment of your thought processes and mindsets with Scripture's revelation of "Christ in you," and "you in Christ" is nothing short of supernatural. You need to work with the Holy Spirit in this process, as some of the concepts you will study in Scripture—with natural eyes and natural logic—will not immediately register or make sense.

Our tendency is to move on to the next concept or idea that we can quickly understand, when in fact, there is life-changing Truth waiting for you just behind the veil. I want to encourage you to pause in places where your mind becomes frustrated. This is where meditation is crucial to the mind-renewing process. Scriptural meditation is different from Eastern mediation; where Eastern meditation involves the emptying of the mind, Scriptural meditation is a *filling* of your mind. As you fill your mind with God's Word, you are undergoing what Scripture describes as *"the washing of water by the word"* (Eph. 5:26). This is why Scripture meditation is an integral part of breaking the cycle caused by soul attachments. By living yoked in a soul attachment for so long, that relationship or exchange contaminates the way you think. We studied earlier how soul ties form alien mindsets, beliefs, and even paradigms that must be reprogrammed. They are "alien" because they are foreign to God's good plan and purpose for your life.

While experiencing this "mind cleansing" through your encounter with Scripture, you may discover that some of the truths presented are difficult to believe about yourself. This is evidence that the process is working, for you are confronting false mindsets. It comes down to a choice, really. You must choose to believe God's Word, even if past mindsets are trying to tell you otherwise. These mindsets are subject to the final authority of Scripture and you must bring them into agreement with what God says about you.

> *You must choose to believe God's Word, even if past mindsets are trying to tell you otherwise.*

Another method of renewing your mind is found in cultivating the life-giving relationships we discussed yesterday. We all need someone to keep us accountable and tell us when our thinking is not lining up with Truth. Renewing your mind can also look like learning from people who are thinking and living like you would like to be. It could be a minister in your area or someone who speaks to audiences around the world. You can follow them online, read their books, or download their messages. When you listen to people who make your heart come alive because they speak words of life, follow that inclination and receive as much as you can from them.

Similarly, researching and studying a certain topic can be mind renewing. When you feel a strong desire to discover more about a topic or issue, pursue it with vigor. There may be many different people writing or speaking on that topic from unique angles—by learning from a variety of sources, you will find yourself making new connections that offer revelatory insights that you would not have discovered by learning from one teacher alone. As we all know, knowledge is extraordinarily empowering.

Music is another way you can fill your mind with truth. There is something about music that speaks to our souls so that the messages eventually transform our minds, whether we are paying attention to the lyrics or not. Once you identify a truth you would like to fill your mind with, listen to songs with messages that declare that truth. There is no better way to get a concept down into your heart than to continually sing about it. We are instructed by Paul in his letter to the Ephesians to speak out *"in psalms and hymns and spiritual songs, singing and making melody in your heart to the Lord"* (Eph. 5:19).

The last way to renew your mind is by guarding what goes into your eye gates. What we see on TV, in movies, and in magazines influences us, whether we realize it or not. It taints our souls. *"Summing it all up, friends, I'd say you'll do best by filling your minds and meditating on things true, noble, reputable, authentic, compelling, gracious—the best, not the worst; the beautiful, not the ugly; things to praise, not things to curse"* (Phil. 4:8 MSG). If you find yourself doing all of these suggestions while still filling your mind with messages opposed to the Kingdom, everything else will not have staying power. For this reason, seek to watch and read only what is going to foster abundant spiritual life. Do it for the sake of your mind and personal transformation.

POWER POINT

In summary, renewing your mind can look like:

- Reading and meditating on what the Bible says about who you are in Christ

- Enlisting friends and mentors to encourage you
- Listening to messages and reading books by people who have renewed minds
- Filling your soul with music that reinforces positive messages about who God is and who you are
- Taking in media that will not taint your soul

POWER THOUGHT

You cannot have a positive life and a negative mind.
—Joyce Meyer

Day 23

PURSUE JOY

Joy is the serious business of Heaven. —C.S. Lewis

DISCIPLINE #23 — SEEK ACTIVITIES AND PEOPLE WHO MAKE YOU COME ALIVE

Joy is a fruit of the Spirit (see Gal. 5:22) and is part of the definition of the Kingdom of God. *"For the kingdom of God is not eating and drinking, but righteousness and peace and joy in the Holy Spirit"* (Rom.14:17). Jesus was anointed with the oil of joy, and so should we be: *"God, your God, has set you above your companions by anointing you with the oil of joy"* (Heb. 1:9 NIV).

To be filled to overflowing with joy is a testament to the Holy Spirit's indwelling presence. Joy is something that everybody wants to experience. It goes without saying that when we are joyful we will become attractive to the world and they will be curious to discover why we are so happy.

> *To be filled to overflowing with joy is a testament to the Holy Spirit's indwelling presence.*

What are some practical ways we can pursue and experience joy? Refreshing ourselves by reading the Word, praying, meditating on God's love, and worshiping are just a few. We are told in Psalm 16:11 that *"fullness of joy"* is found in God's presence. We will talk more about pursuing God's presence on Day 25.

Today I want to give you a few practical truths about joy and how to experience it in your life. As we understand what joy is, what it looks like, and the benefits it releases in our lives, we will intentionally pursue activities and relationships that convey this Kingdom characteristic.

"The joy of the Lord is your strength and stronghold" (Neh. 8:10 AMP). Joy makes us strong and protects us from despair and hopeless thinking. Not only is joy a protective stronghold, but it is also a bondage-breaking force. Did you know people can be set free from emotional and physical issues simply by laughing? Try laughing out loud the next time a difficult situation arises. Recognize when the enemy is attempting to get you down and choose joy instead. Likewise, be mindful to engage in relationships with those who are always willing to choose joy over defeat and discouragement. It is only a matter of time before the attitudes of your associations rub off on you.

> *Joy, praise, and thanksgiving create supernatural inroads for God's Spirit and His Kingdom to manifest. Self-pity, pride, and bitterness open the door to the enemy to wreak havoc upon your soul.*

"Be happy [in your faith] and rejoice and be glad-hearted continually (always)" (1 Thess. 5:16 AMP). It is important for us to maintain *continual* joy. Often, this involves a proactive decision to rejoice. Joy, praise, and thanksgiving create supernatural inroads for God's Spirit and His Kingdom to manifest—while self-pity, pride, and bitterness open the door to the enemy to wreak havoc upon your soul. This is why Paul admonishes believers to rejoice and be thankful *continually* (see Phil. 4:4).

"I'm thanking you, God, from a full heart, I'm writing the book on your wonders. I'm whistling, laughing, and jumping for joy; I'm

singing your song, High God" (Ps. 9:1-2 MSG). Being thankful to God and counting our blessings is a powerful way to gain an appropriate perspective on our situations, remain humble, and position our hearts to receive more joy. Practice writing down things you are thankful for on a consistent basis (perhaps before bed) and proactively praise God for those things. This creates a climate of thanksgiving that begins to define your life and the personal presence you carry. Ensure that your relationships consist of those who are more blessing-minded than disappointment-driven. Our joy is stirred by being surrounded by people who continuously focus on what God is doing and how He is releasing blessing—rather than those who are always disappointed at what they perceive is not happening in their lives.

"I came that they may have and enjoy life, and have it in abundance (to the full, till it overflows)" (John 10:10 AMP). Another way to pursue joy is by simply making the decision to enjoy your life. God is not a killjoy. On the contrary, He is the author of true enjoyment. He instituted festivals for the Hebrew people to celebrate Him in the Old Testament. Scripture does not mention God revoking our license to enjoy life. If anything, Jesus came to make available a whole new dimension of joy and abundant living. Unfortunately, in our time-crunched schedules, we don't always make enjoying life a priority. Depending on the culture we live in and our personality type, we may even

> *Seek activities that make us come alive and be assured that the pursuit of joy is ordained by God.*

feel guilty for doing enjoyable things. To maintain a joyful attitude in life, we need to seek activities that make us come alive and be assured that the pursuit of joy is ordained by God.

Ask yourself what brings you joy and then make time in your schedule to do it. It does not need to cost a lot of money. There are many activities you can do for free that can help foster joy.

Here are some ideas to help you start your own list of what makes you come alive:

- Sing or play an instrument
- Dance
- Explore the outdoors
- Make art
- Cook or bake
- Play games or sports
- Watch a funny movie
- Listen to joyful music
- Go to a concert

Use this list as a springboard to start thinking about the activities in your life that bring you joy. Maybe it has been a long time since you believed it was okay to enjoy yourself. As mentioned earlier, some of us live with soul attachments for so long—many since childhood—that we actually need to *learn* how to enjoy ourselves. What comes naturally to some is a real strain for others because of the soul slavery they previously experienced. That said, it is time to take full advantage of your freedom. This is not a license to become irresponsible. It is a summons, however, to start living again.

"To everything there is a season, a time for every purpose under heaven. A time to weep, and a time to laugh; a time to mourn, and a time to dance" (Eccles. 3:1,4). Our last key to pursuing joy is seeking and intentionally spending time with people who are joyful. There is certainly a time to buckle down and be responsible, but likewise, there is a time for enjoyment and fun. There is a time to comfort those who are mourning, and there is also a time to find people with whom you can rejoice.

POWER POINT

Intentionally and proactively pursue joy in every area of your life! Two of the main ways you can cultivate joy is by first cultivating healthy relationships with those who are also pursuing joy, and second, by engaging in activities that cause your heart to come alive. Both require choices. An attitude of joy will not automatically overtake your life—you must pursue joy intentionally. You may experience moments of happiness, but if you are intent about pursuing a lifestyle defined by joy, you must recognize its worth and go after it as something precious.

POWER THOUGHT

Rejoice in the Lord always. I will say it again: Rejoice!
(Philippians 4:4)

Day 24

PURSUE PURPOSE

Look carefully then how you walk! Live purposefully and worthily and accurately, not as the unwise and witless, but as wise (sensible, intelligent people) (Ephesians 5:15, AMP).

DISCIPLINE #24 — LIVE INTENTIONALLY

Once we break soul ties and get out of destructive relationships and cycles, we must be purposeful about how we steward our lives. Remember, the enemy's ideal target is the house that has been left "clean and swept." He is looking for empty, inhabitable space. In other words, to break the cycle, not only do you pursue freedom from soul attachments, but you must also deliberately move forward by pursuing a lifestyle of mindfulness and intentionality. Be aware that if you don't intentionally direct your life, your life will be directed by your circumstances, and before you know it five, ten, or twenty years will have passed by. You will reflect back on your life and recognize that you had

> *If you don't intentionally direct your life, your life will be directed by your circumstances.*

little say about what happened—you complacently allowed circumstances, situations, and the "tyranny of the urgent" to define who you became and what you accomplished. Thankfully, you can always reverse this process.

Today I want us to examine the pursuit of purpose from a spiritual foundation, and then we'll review some practical keys to unlocking purpose in your life.

First, let's study Ephesians 5:13-20. Paul gives five prescriptive steps you can take that act as an antidote to the soul tranquilizer of sin and sorrow—the enemies of purpose. He begins by making this urgent command:

*Awake, you who sleep, **arise from the dead**, and Christ will give you light* (Ephesians 5:14).

Make note, he is talking to believing Christians here. He is talking to the Church. Paul also wrote to the Romans, *"Now it is high time to **awake out of sleep**; for now our salvation is nearer than when we first believed"* (Rom. 13:11). So how do we, who have accepted Christ and are eternally saved, wake up and *"arise from the dead"*? What does that mean exactly? Can a believer be sleepwalking through life, never knowing his or her divine purpose? Absolutely.

Let's break down the verses that follow in Ephesians chapter 5 beginning with the last in the series. Working backward, you will see that the genesis of life-imbuing transformation begins with being thankful. How do you revive from the dead and walk in abundant, purpose-*full* life? By first, *"Giving thanks always for all things to God the Father in the name of our Lord Jesus Christ"* (Eph. 5:20). How do you begin to do that? By *"singing and making melody in your heart to the Lord"* (Eph. 5:19). But what if you don't feel like it? You practice *"singing psalms and hymns and spiritual songs"* (Eph. 5:19 NLT)—because this is how you *"let the Spirit fill your life"* (Eph. 5:18 CEV). Once again, these practices demand a decision. They will not come about casually. We must be like David, who actually directed his very will to bless the Lord at all times (see Ps. 34:1).

As a result, you will be equipped to *"understand what the will of the Lord is"* (Eph. 5:17)—and when you understand that, you will be able to *"make every minute count"* (Eph. 5:16 CEV); *"making the very most of the time"* (Eph. 5:16 AMP) and *"every opportunity"* (Eph. 5:16 NLT). That alone makes it worth having an attitude of gratitude, but it doesn't end there. The inner joy that comes from being thankful will enable you to *"live purposefully and worthily and accurately, not as the unwise and witless, but as wise (sensible, intelligent people)"* (Eph. 5:15 AMP)—you will be *"like those who are wise"* (Eph. 5:15 NLT). You will be *"dead to the power of sin and alive to God through Christ Jesus"* (Rom. 6:11 NLT). And, as Revelation says, *"God will bless you, if you are awake and ready"* (Rev. 16:15 CEV).

This is the very place you want to live from. I don't simply want to see you free; I want to see you *dead* to the sins, entanglements, and ties that held you back and restrained you from experiencing your true purpose in life. We end where we began—becoming *awake.* Soul ties keep us in a state of slumber when it comes to discovering our purpose. As long as we are focused on the attachment that is draining our time, life, and energy, it is very difficult to become plugged into our purpose. Now that we are breaking the cycle and inaugurating a lifestyle of freedom, it is time for us to pursue activities that actually contribute to discovering and stewarding our life purpose. It all begins with intentionality.

> Soul ties keep us in a state of slumber when it comes to discovering our purpose.

The Practical Side

God gives us everything that we have, and it is up to us to steward it well. This not only includes our time, treasure, and talent, but also our purpose and destiny. The principle is all encompassing. How we spend our time, where we direct our emotional energy, what we do with our finances—all of these factors contribute to us unlocking purpose in our lives. We can and should consult God on matters of how we are stewarding these assets, but ultimately, it is our decision. Will our stewardship of life's resources propel us toward our highest calling, or will we continue to position ourselves for cycles of continuous bondage?

Consider what the book of Proverbs has to say regarding living purposefully and paying attention to wisdom:

> *So, my dear friends, listen carefully; those who embrace these my ways are most blessed. Mark a life of discipline and live wisely; don't squander your precious life. Blessed the man, blessed the woman, who listens to me, awake and ready for me each morning, alert and responsive as I start my day's work. When you find me, you find life, real life,* **to say nothing of God's good pleasure** (Proverbs 8:32-35 MSG).

Here are some simple starting places to live wisely and pursue purpose in different areas of your life:

- Finances: Make a budget. Save for the future. Tithe to your local church.
- Time: Make a schedule and allocate time with God, people, for self-improvement, professional development, and to have fun.
- Health: Take care of your "temple" by eating healthy and exercising.
- Sleep: Don't deprive yourself of needed rest. Invite God to speak to your spirit even as you sleep. Steward your dreams by recording them.
- Possessions: Regularly maintain what you own by cleaning, organizing, and fixing things when necessary.

Take time to seriously consider how you can best use the time and resources God has entrusted to you and make a plan to invest them wisely. We do not step into purpose by accident.

The very nature of the word *purpose* is one of intentionality. To discover our individual purpose in life, we must pursue purpose by living intentionally.

POWER POINT

Many are waiting around to "receive their purpose" through a vision, dream or some ecstatic experience. This is the opposite of how we are called to live. Remember the admonition of Apostle Paul to the church in Ephesus: "*So be careful how you live. Don't live like fools, but like those who are wise. Make the most of every opportunity in these evil days. Don't act thoughtlessly, but understand what the Lord wants you to do*" (Eph. 5:15-17 NLT).

We escape foolishness, access wisdom, steward opportunity, and discern the will of God by being *careful* with how we live. By living purposefully, we are—in essence—beginning to fulfill our very purpose.

POWER THOUGHT

If you have felt hopeless, hold on! Wonderful changes are going to happen in your life as you begin to live it on purpose. —Rick Warren

PURSUE GOD'S PRESENCE

Now the Lord is the Spirit, and where the Spirit of the Lord is, there is liberty (emancipation from bondage, freedom) (2 Corinthians 3:17 AMP).

DISCIPLINE #25 — CREATE AN ATMOSPHERE CHARGED BY GOD'S PRESENCE

I believe that today's pursuit will empower you to not only break cycles of bondage in your life, but also prove to be a dynamic key to unlocking freedom as a lifestyle, not merely an experience.

It all begins with our awareness and experience of God's powerful presence.

Too many of us are waiting around for something that we already possess. The Spirit of God lives inside you! You do not need to wait for some type of spiritually charged atmosphere before experiencing the freedom that comes by abiding in His presence. Rather, you have the ability to charge your own atmosphere and live in that presence 24/7. The One who lives inside you is the very Agent who empowers you to live a lifestyle of freedom, rather than experience only fleeting seasons of it. Review today's Scripture. Paul defines the type of atmosphere that the Spirit of God creates in our lives as one of freedom.

Paul's very language communicates a position rather than a temporary feeling. He identifies that *"where the Spirit of the Lord is, there is liberty"* (2 Cor. 3:17 AMP). Where is the Spirit of the Lord? He is *not* in a temple made of stone. He is not *upon* you for a season or a time, as He was upon the judges, prophets, and kings under the Old Covenant. Jesus' blood purchased your access to a lifestyle of being indwelt and inhabited by the Holy Spirit. This is your reality and His position. Since God's Spirit lives inside you—the Spirit who brings freedom and liberty—you carry the ability to not only walk in consistent freedom, but also to release it to others by charging the atmosphere with God's powerful presence.

In God's presence is fullness of joy, freedom, truth, love, peace, healing, hope, faith, and so much more. If we live void of consistent awareness of God's indwelling presence, what do we really have? A life of struggle and continuous striving for freedom externally, when we actually possess it internally in the Person of the Holy Spirit. Remember, *"where the Spirit of the Lord is there is liberty"* (2 Cor. 3:17 AMP). The key word here is "is." Paul did not say *where the Spirit of the Lord* "visits" or *where the Spirit of the Lord comes* "upon." The word "is" denotes a resting place—a remaining. If this is true, then just as the Person of the Spirit abides and remains in you, so you should reap the benefits of His habitation. Such rewards include freedom and liberty.

> *You carry the ability to walk in consistent freedom and to release it to others by charging the atmosphere with God's powerful presence.*

So what does it mean to create an atmosphere charged with God's presence?

Where God's Spirit is present, strongholds surrender their grip—and every type of bondage loses its power. Where God is present, His Kingdom reigns. Romans 14:17 states that the Kingdom of God is marked by *"righteousness and peace and joy in the Holy Spirit.*" The Kingdom and reign of God are actually released *in* the Person of the Holy Spirit.

Where there is unrighteousness, disharmony, distress, and despair, *"there you will find disorder and evil of every kind"* (James 3:16 NLT). These are the very things that God's Kingdom dispels through the release of His presence. Where the light of God is *not* present, you will find the fruit of darkness abounding, such as deception, hatred, greed, strife:

> *Sexual immorality, impurity, lustful pleasures, idolatry, sorcery, hostility, quarreling, jealousy, outbursts of anger, selfish ambition, dissension, division, envy, drunkenness, wild parties, and other sins like these* (Galatians 5:19-21 NLT).

Paul goes on to remind the Galatians, *"Let me tell you again, as I have before, that anyone living that sort of life will not inherit the Kingdom of God"* (Gal. 5:21 NLT).

On the other hand, where the Spirit of God is present, there you will find *"love, joy, peace, patience, kindness, goodness, faithfulness, gentleness, and self-control"* (Gal. 5:22-23 NLT). You will find what Jesus called *"life...more abundantly"* (John 10:10).

The key to liberating your soul from the death grip of a fallen world is living in the presence of God. James wrote that humanity's sinful nature leads to death—*"Each one is tempted when he is drawn away by his own desires and enticed. Then, when desire has conceived, it gives birth to sin; and sin, when it is full-grown, brings forth death"* (James 1:14-15)—but James went on to say that if you *"humble yourselves before God"* (James 4:7 NLT), you will be able to *"resist the devil, and he will flee from you"* (James 4:7 NLT). The Message puts it this way: *"Let God work his will in you. Yell a loud no to the Devil and watch him scamper. Say a quiet yes to God and he'll be there in no time. Quit dabbling in sin. Purify your inner life"* (James 4:7 MSG). Peter stated simply, *"abstain from fleshly lusts which war against the soul"* (1 Pet. 2:11).

The Cycle-Breaking Power of God's Presence

Soul ties are broken by both an act of the will and by the power of the Spirit—you must choose to *"walk in the Spirit"* so that you *"shall not fulfill the lust of the flesh"* (Gal. 5:16). The Spirit of God working in your life will give you victory over every stronghold, but you must choose to walk in the presence of that Spirit. It is God's power that tears down strongholds, but it is your power of choice to access it. Paul made clear that you and I must *"use God's power that can destroy fortresses"* (2 Cor. 10:4 CEV). He explained that:

> *The weapons of our warfare are not carnal but mighty in God for pulling down strongholds, casting down arguments and every high thing that exalts itself against the knowledge of God, bringing every thought into captivity to the obedience of Christ* (2 Corinthians 10:4-5).

You must allow Christ to captivate your thoughts. Only by focusing on Him can you guard your heart and mind with the peace of God. As Isaiah 26:3 tells us, *"You will keep him in perfect peace, whose mind is stayed on You."* One of the foundational messages of the Bible is God simply saying, *"Be still, and know that I am God"* (Ps. 46:10).

What does it look like to live in God's presence, and in turn, enjoy the freedom His Spirit makes available? Spending one-on-one time with Him—as well as enjoying His company wherever you are, in whatever you're doing. At all times, you can be God-conscious and mindful of His abiding presence. At other times, it is valuable to pull away and focus on God alone. Make time in your daily schedule—perhaps at the beginning and/or end of each day—to quiet your spirit and rest in your awareness

> One of the foundational messages of the Bible is God simply saying, "Be still, and know that I am God."

of Him. Better still, take a retreat once or twice a year by yourself. Ask God where you should go to be away with Him.

Once you have scheduled your time with God, here are some tips for what you can do to more fully experience His presence:

- Listen to praise and worship music.
- Thank God for who His is and what He has given you (see Ps. 100:4).
- Focus your mind on what you know of the Father, His Son, or His Spirit.
- Ask God what He thinks about you and receive His love.
- Read Psalms (try different Bible versions) to help you pray and praise Him.
- Make up your own spiritual songs and write them down or record them.

Spending time with God in His presence is the only way to live a free and resilient life. The more you spend time with Him, the more time you will *want* to spend with Him. The beautiful thing is that He loves to spend time with His children and is always available.

POWER POINT

Get into the presence of God where you will find His healing love, peace, and joy—that is where His Kingdom is found. You can charge any atmosphere with the bondage-breaking power of His love and power.

POWER THOUGHT

We experience the measure of presence we are willing to jealously guard. —Bill Johnson

Week Six

BUILDING
NEW BOUNDARIES

God, who made the world and everything in it...
He gives to all life, breath, and all things. And...has
determined...the boundaries of their dwellings (Acts
17:24-26).

Personal relationships are the fertile soil from
which all advancement, all success, all achievement in real life grows. —Ben Stein

Throughout the first four weeks we identified the exchanges
and relationships that lead to ensnaring soul attachments.
Last week we talked about five essential practices—or disciplines—you must pursue to break these cycles and continually
reclaim your soul. However, to solidly position you to move forward in the healing and reclamation process, we must address
the issue of boundaries.

I want to help you understand the importance of establishing new boundaries in your life. This will be essential in safe-
guarding your soul from falling prey to the same old attachments and cycles as before.

Healthy boundaries are important because they help to protect you mentally, socially, emotionally, and spiritually—as well as psychologically. Healthy boundaries are clearly defined limits within which you are free to be yourself with no restrictions placed on you by others as to how to think, feel, or act. Healthy boundaries also help you create a quality of life defined by love happiness, peace, and joy—without limiting pleasure or the pursuit of purpose. People who suffer from unhealthy soul ties tend to have unhealthy boundaries as well.

I have had the distinct privilege of traveling the world. Whenever I cross a national boundary or border, I have to be granted permission. Often there is a welcome sign if there is not a border protection agency located on the border site. When people enter your life, they must do so only after you grant them permission. This is how you should conduct all of your relational affairs. Do not allow just anyone into your personhood. Life is a journey and you will be given an opportunity to have many traveling companions. You must choose your companions wisely, and when you deem someone suitable, grant them permission with the necessary restrictions to travel with you.

You *must* establish healthy boundaries.

Day 26

VALUE BOUNDARIES

But let your "Yes" be "Yes," and your "No," "No"
(Matthew 5:37).

DISCIPLINE #26—MAKE YOUR BOUNDARIES CLEAR AND KNOWN

Having clear boundaries allows you to say "No" when something inappropriate makes you feel uncomfortable or vulnerable. It enables you to say "No" to giving something you shouldn't, "No" to behaving in a certain way, "No" to being treated in a way that will hurt your heart, bruise your soul, strip you of your individuality, harm your body, lose control of your self or property, undermine your uniqueness or your rights as a human being, "No" to being devalued, misused, or abused. It is having the mental and emotional fortitude to say, "Back off, you are violating my personal space—you are trespassing on my purpose."

> *Boundaries are essential for loving and looking after your own self.*

Boundaries are essential for loving and looking after your own self. They not only help you gain self-worth and dignity, they help others to respect and value you as well. Boundaries enable you to move out of potentially harmful relationships—

to tell an over-burdening friend with unrealistic expectations "No," to fight for your rights, to voice your opinion, to express your individuality, to take "me-moments" and not feel guilty, to know when enough is enough, to ask for what you need, to demand respect, and to stand up for what you believe.

Defining Boundaries

With all that said, let's establish what a boundary is. A boundary is:

- The setting of balanced emotional and physical limits when interacting with others so that an interdependent relationship of mutually beneficial growth, support, love, and celebration can be achieved.
- Establishing emotional, psychological, and physical "space" between you and another person, which denotes where "you" begin and where the other person ends, and vice versa.
- Having clear expectations of others and limits for yourself (what you will and will not do, give, become, allow, tolerate).
- That invisible "line of demarcation" which you will not allow anyone to cross regarding your emotions, intellect, property, body, finances, psyche, spirit, etc.
- The setting of limitations over what you will and will not do for others.
- Establishing goals and expectations for your physical, spiritual, and emotional well-being which you expect others to respect in relating to you.
- Understanding the emotional and physical space you need in order to live authentically.
- Creating a healthy emotional, psychological, social, and physical distance between you and another so that you do not become overly enmeshed and/or dependent.

- Conversely, maintaining the necessary emotional and physical closeness you need so that you and another do not become too detached and/or overly independent.

Let Your "Yes" be Yes

In the context of Matthew 5, Jesus is specifically discussing oaths. The principle, however, is absolutely applicable when it comes to setting boundaries for our lives. They must be clear and well-defined. It is interesting that after clarifying the importance of our "Yes" being yes and "No" being no, Jesus adds the following statement—*"For whatever is more than these is from the evil one"* (Matt. 5:37).

If we are not sticking to a simple "Yes" or "No," we are actually playing right into the enemy's agenda for our lives. He delights in our compromise, for when we slide in our convictions concerning boundaries, we open a door to him. In the context we have been studying, I believe that when we are inappropriately flexible with our boundaries, we allow issues and individuals into our lives that set us up for unhealthy soul attachments.

We have already identified the various dimensions of such soul ties; my goal here is not to restate the dangerous possibilities that limited or no boundaries open us up to—but to arm you with a revelation concerning the power of clarity when it comes to making your boundaries and restrictions known. Within the context of these Scriptures, and Jesus' words, one can conclude that by sticking to the simple and clear, we actually deny the evil one a place in our lives.

The Power of Defined Boundaries

By refusing to compromise your boundaries, you deny potential attachments your agreement, and thereby forbid them a place in your life. I cannot overstate the power of clear, defined boundaries. Regardless of what area you are establishing the boundary in, remember—it is a clear line of demarcation that declares, "Do not cross."

The reason many of us have dealt with soul ties is far from mysterious. One of the main ways they take root in our lives is through undefined boundaries. Basically, there is very little that we actually say "No" to. We may want to say "No." We may believe deep down in our heart of hearts that "No" is the appropriate decision in a particular situation or when dealing with a certain person. However, belief without application does not produce results. Scripture puts it this way: *"Thus also faith by itself, if it does not have works, is dead"* (James 2:17).

There are many people who have a strong, sincere faith in something—or at least, think they do—but yet, that faith does not practically impact or shape their lives in any way. Faith remains relegated to the heart or mind, but never makes an impact on lifestyle. In the same way, many of us believe that boundaries are appropriate, but continue to go through life without setting them, and thus perpetuating a cycle that God wants to completely break in our lives. However, God will not come down and override your will. He will not set the boundaries for you. This is something that you must do for yourself in every area of your life.

While the Word of God and the Holy Spirit will provide necessary direction in terms of what types of boundaries you need to establish, it is your job to enforce them. This all begins with valuing boundaries and recognizing how essential they are for you to reclaim your soul and experience a more resilient life.

POWER POINT

It is time to transition from the defensive to the offensive. By establishing clear, defined boundaries, you are not simply moving away from the harmful soul attachments of the past, you are moving toward a lifestyle of blessing, victory, and freedom.

The first step to building new boundaries in your life is actually valuing boundaries. To value boundaries, you must begin by valuing yourself. Do you value yourself enough to break agreement with the people, situations, circumstances and attachments that seek to destroy you—and then raise up a new standard of living? I believe you do.

> *Do you value yourself enough to break agreement with the people, situations, circumstances and attachments that seek to destroy you?*

POWER THOUGHT

Boundaries define us. They define what is me and what is not me. A boundary shows me where I end and someone else begins, leading me to a sense of ownership. Knowing what I am to own and take responsibility for gives me freedom. —Henry Cloud

Day 27

HEED THE WARNING SIGNS

Be sober, be vigilant; because your adversary the devil walks about like a roaring lion, seeking whom he may devour (1 Peter 5:8).

DISCIPLINE #27 — RECOGNIZE WHEN YOUR BOUNDARIES ARE BEING CHALLENGED OR VIOLATED

The enemy and his influences usually come *with* warning. The problem is, many of us are not trained to identify the warning signs. This is why Peter encouraged us to be vigilant. To be vigilant is to adopt a posture of acute awareness—to be watchful, particularly in regard to danger.

Today I am going to give you a few warning signs to look out for when it comes to the issue of boundaries. These are behaviors and tendencies you can watch for in other people, as well as *yourself*. By identifying these red flags, you will be empowered to take action as soon as you notice someone trying to push your limits, or think that you are personally becoming susceptible to weakened boundaries.

Over Enmeshment

In many dysfunctional families and unhealthy relationships, people become overly involved in the details of each other's life, marriage, and personal relationships. Often there is an unstated rule that everyone should think the same, feel the same, and do everything together. There is a lack of privacy and nothing you think, feel, or do is your personal business alone, but everyone's business. You begin to feel that nothing you experience can be kept in the privacy of your own domain.

Emotional Detachment

This state occurs when neither you nor anyone else in the group or family is able to establish any fusion of healthy emotional attachment, affinity, or affiliation of feelings. Everyone is an island unto him or herself—totally independent from everyone else—so there is no emotional "glue" that holds you and the others together in healthy union.

Victimhood or Martyrdom

Those suffering from this symptom identify themselves as a violated victim and become defensive to ward off further violation. They are overly sensitive, protective, or clingy. They do not hesitate to tell everyone of their victimization by "everybody" else. They feel "nobody" can be trusted and that "they"—as in other people—are always out to get them, undermine them, sabotage them, and don't like or don't appreciate them.

Black Sheep

These are people who refuse to submit to authority figures—they are determined to do their own thing regardless of who they hurt. They seek attention by being the "bad" one. Once the attention is secured, they may continue to act out in an "in your face" manner letting you know who really is the "boss"—they live "large and in charge."

Chip-on-the-Shoulder

These are the individuals who have the most turbulent relationships and create the most toxic environments within the workplace and within their personal and social constellations. Arguments and confrontational situations are commonplace because they are driven by feelings of victimization, offense, and anger; they convey their rage by bullying, making threats, and being verbally abusive.

Yes-Man

I recently read somewhere that a sign of weakness is perpetually saying "Yes" to unreasonable demands, while a sign of strength is the ability to say "No" regardless how it makes the other person feel. My mother used to describe this kind of person as having no "backbone." "Yes people" have trouble acknowledging their own needs or right to have an opinion—or that saying

> *A sign of strength is the ability to say "No" regardless how it makes the other person feel.*

"No" often results in a new level of respect from those who struggle managing their own time and commitments.

Invisibility

These are the social *wallflowers*—they "see no evil, hear no evil, do no evil." Their goal is not to be noticed so that their boundaries are never violated. They may dress down or take a "vow of silence" refusing to speak up, give their opinion, or confront issues. They feel more comfortable as part of the background scenery and never step near center stage. They seem happy to live in a state of social malnutrition rather than risk being misunderstood, rejected, or disliked.

Aloofness or Shyness

This symptom is a result of insecurity from real or perceived experiences of being ignored, hurt, abused, or rejected in the past. These people quietly demonstrate that others are not invited into their space by habitually crossing their arms and/ or legs. This is a defensive posture of self-protection used as a kind of psychological fence—like a sign that clearly reads, "No trespassing."

Cold and Distant

Being cold and distant is a mental posture of indifference that builds walls or barriers rather than bridges—ensuring that others do not permeate, penetrate, violate, or invade their emotional or physical space. These individuals have mastered the art of maintaining physical, emotional, and psychological "real estate" between themselves and others. Boundaries aren't just important, they are everything! In this way an overdeveloped boundary can sometimes be worse than an underdeveloped one.

Smothering

This person assumes the role of the parent or becomes an unwelcome authority figure. This scenario might involve an overly intrusive friend, the parent of adult children, or a companion who constantly gives unsolicited advice, help, or directives. They "fear" for your safety out of "concern" for your well-being, and don't leave you any space to think for yourself.

Disassociation

This symptom involves psychological detachment or blanking out during a stressful emotional event. Disassociation will cause an individual to try and think of something other than what is happening in an effort to separate him or her from the feelings about what is taking place. Disassociation may result in one's inability to remember events as a way to keep from hurting.

POWER POINT

In this section, we are focusing on taking back your personal power in order to live more resiliently. Heeding these warning signs will save you from forming a destructive soul attachment *To be vigilant, you must* through compromised boundar- *be self-aware.* ies. Knowledge is power! When
someone exhibits any of these behaviors toward you, it is a clear indication your boundaries are being tested.

Also, don't be afraid of rigorous self-reflection. If you iden-tify any of these behaviors, attitudes, or tendencies in your own life, it is absolutely essential for you to acknowledge and adjust them. To be vigilant, you must be self-aware. Remain firm and forbid your lines to be compromised.

POWER THOUGHT

"No" is a complete sentence. —Anne Lamott

Day 28

LIVE ETHICALLY

But for this book [the Bible] we could not know right from wrong. —Abraham Lincoln

DISCIPLINE #28—LIVE ACCORDING TO GOD'S STANDARDS

The next three days are specifically committed to helping you establish new boundaries in your life.

Remember, boundaries help you to say "No" when it is easier to say "Yes." They help you to say "No" when your convictions, beliefs, and values might be compromised. Boundaries help you to say "No" when you, your loved ones, friends, or people in general could be inconvenienced or harmed, or when your character, reputation, personal stability, security, or safety is jeopardized. Boundaries do not merely restrict, they enhance your overall quality of life.

As Christians, we often think we must say "Yes" to everyone because it is a sign of generosity and compassion. However, this can also be a *The pathway to resiliency is carved out by your willingness to yield to God's commandments.* sign of weakness, fear, and laziness. The only One who deserves your unqualified, continuous "Yes" is God. By saying "Yes" to

263

His standards and directives for living, you will establish a powerful boundary in your life. The pathway to resiliency is carved out by your willingness to yield to God's commandments—and your desire to pursue the extraordinary rewards that submitting to His will produces.

Here is the first part of my three-fold challenge to you—*live ethically.*

Live Ethically—What Does It Look Like?

At first glance, this may sound somewhat vague. If I were to ask you, "What comes to mind when I use the phrase, *live ethically*," you might think of a businessperson who conducts their affairs above reproach. Perhaps an image comes to mind of a certain man or woman who is committed to a life of moral excellence. Maybe there are specific behaviors that you would attach to an "ethical lifestyle."

Here is the problem with this thought process. It tends to sound dull, not because the behaviors or actions are incorrect, but because there is no ultimate vision for the benefits that ethical standards are designed to produce.

Allow me to elaborate on what it means to truly live ethically. It is not a matter of simply adhering to a set of rules—but a matter of delighting in them. King David wrote, *"I will delight myself in Your commandments"* (Ps. 119:47). God's commandments are not burdensome (see 1 John 5:3). His standards were not designed to make life tolerable at best, and miserable at worst. This paradigm needs to be boldly confronted, as there is a significant disconnect between a contemporary culture that observes God's commands as restrictive or hostile toward living a fun, full life, and the perspective of King David.

> *Living ethically transcends mere rules and regulations when there is a solid foundation and clear purpose for their implementation.*

I realize that we live in a culture where many people observe commandments as burdensome—even those in the Christian community. The problem has little to do with the commandments in and of themselves, but this negative perspective of what it means to adhere to a standard of holiness. Living ethically transcends mere rules and regulations when there is a solid foundation and clear purpose for their implementation.

Maintaining the Balance

In his timeless *Sermon on the Mount,* Jesus gives numerous instructions and directives on how to conduct one's daily life, but He also offers several corresponding blessings for the described behaviors. Even Jesus endured the cross, motivated by the joy that His sacrifice would release to the entire world, from generation to generation (see Heb. 12:2). Although the pain He endured was excruciating, He was able to bear it with some measure of joy, having a clear vision for what His actions would produce in humanity. He saw reconciliation take place between God and man—a relationship that had been estranged because of sin and rebellion. He saw all of humanity being given the opportunity to be filled with the Holy Spirit—a reality that was only experienced in measure under the Old Covenant. In short, Jesus maintained a clear vision of the benefits that His commitment to God's command would produce.

We need to follow Jesus' model in our lives, knowing that God's motives are pure and in our best interest. Remember, Scripture tells us that God's thoughts and ways are higher than ours (see Isa. 55:9). He is able to look out for your best interest, even when you are unable to effectively do so for yourself. He has provided you with clear instructions for staying in that supernatural sweet spot while walking through the mire and minutia of daily life. By doing what God has outlined in His commandments and through the instruction of His Word, you are building boundaries that keep you aligned with His plan and purpose for your life.

Keeping the Vision

When you understand that living ethically means building boundaries that do not restrict you, but actually propel you forward, your motivation for embracing such a lifestyle changes. The problem happens when you lose clarity. You may understand all of the rules, but not what they are intended to do for you. Vision enhances value. If you can see that divine perimeters protect and enhance your quality of life, your understanding of what it looks like to live ethically shifts. It is no longer a drag, but a delight as you acknowledge the benefits of living in agreement with God's standard of "right living."

POWER POINT

Living ethically *does* restrict you—it restricts you from entering into soul ties and attachments that can utterly ruin your life and derail your destiny. This type of restriction is a very positive thing, as it keeps you walking along God's designated pathway.

Remember, God's commandments are not burdensome to the one who desires to walk in true freedom and liberty, as His regulations are not restrictive, but cautionary. They are prescribed boundaries to help you maintain a steady course on the path to abundant life, helping you bypass the snare of soul ties.

POWER THOUGHT

For this is the love of God, that we keep His commandments. And His commandments are not burdensome (1 John 5:3).

Day 29

CLEARLY
SET YOUR LIMITS

*Blessed is the man who walks not in the counsel of the
ungodly, nor stands in the path of sinners, nor sits in
the seat of the scornful; but his delight is in the law of
the Lord, and in His law he meditates day and night*
(Psalm 1:1-2).

DISCIPLINE #29—PLAY TO AN AUDIENCE OF ONE—THE ONE

It is so important for us to live ethically, as this very foundation will either make or break us in our relationships with other people. The choice to pursue the ethical life is, as we discovered yesterday, a boundary that restricts us only in the greatest of ways. It keeps us on God's path, and prevents us from veering off into alien, dangerous territory.

Remember, your continuous "Yes" belongs exclusively to God—*not* to other people. You do not owe everyone and everything your "Yes." This type of over commitment will render you useless when it comes to fulfilling your personal destiny. Keep in mind, this is not a call to selfishness, but of good stewardship. Our consecrated "Yes" to God actually empowers us to say "Yes" or "No" in the context of our relationships. If a person or situation is tempting you to compromise your "Yes" to God, then that clearly demands a resounding "No." Simple.

I want to further explore this principle—specifically outlined in Psalm 1:1-2—as it provides an essential key to setting clear limits in our relationships.

Part 1 - Avoid the Bait

In the first part of Psalm 1, we see that there is a blessing promised to those who do *not* engage in sin, wickedness, and ungodliness (see Ps. 1:1). Yet the psalmist does not simply deliver us a warning, outlining a bunch of negatives that we are told to avoid. He actually provides the solution in the following verse, giving us the secret of setting clear limits in every single area of our lives.

Predominantly, the enemy will use people to bait us—to get us into the place defined in Psalm 1:1, where we receive ungodly counsel, model ungodly habits, and ultimately, live an ungodly lifestyle. For most of us, the last thing we want to become involved with is the sinful behavior that can ultimately lead to bondage, pain, and even death. However, if the enemy can package sin in the form of a person—perhaps even a close friend, family member, or loved one—he can lure us into his trap and thus launch us into a gradual, diabolical process of moral deprogramming and compromise.

Part 2—The Secret to Setting Clear Limits

This is why our discipline of always saying "Yes" to God is so important. What does this look like in the context of setting clear limits in relationships? Psalm 1 verse 2 says:

But his delight is in the law of the Lord, and in His law he meditates day and night.

You avoid taking the enemy's bait—and thereby stepping into his snare—when your "delight is in the law of the Lord." In other words, this means your "Yes" belongs to God—a delighted "Yes" at that! This is your secret to setting clear limits.

Everything God invites you to say "Yes" to, in terms of His principles, precepts, and commandments, is not only intended to preserve and enhance your life, but is also purposed to protect you from compromise in relationships. God is not vague when it comes to His instructions on what are acceptable and inappropriate behaviors, decisions, and activities.

In addition, you have the Holy Spirit providing insight and direction to your conscience. He will often "flag" something that is not right—something you should not be participating in, or allowing in your life. Such a warning might be difficult for you to embrace and heed, especially when the person attempting to cross your boundary lines is someone close to you.

> *Soul attachments are produced by gradually lowering your guard, compromising your standards, and dismissing the gentle tug of the Holy Spirit.*

Nevertheless, you must recognize that obedience to the Holy Spirit produces life. He will not lead you toward situations or relationships that are ripe with the potential of producing unhealthy soul ties. This is more often a by-product of gradually compromising your personal boundary lines.

This is how dangerous soul attachments are birthed. Rarely, if ever, are they the result of one instantaneous and dynamic encounter with another person that in a moment turns your life around. Though this can and does happen, such is the exception and not the norm. By and large, soul attachments are produced by a lengthy process of lowering your guard and compromising your relationship standards, while dismissing the gentle tug of the Holy Spirit in your heart.

Set your relationship limits on principles outlined in the Word of God. Remember, your "Yes" to Him is not out of obligation or mechanical duty, but is a yieldedness out of delight because you have a clear vision of what obedience produces.

Relationship boundaries tend to fall into five basic categories:

1. The amount of time you are willing to spare

2. The amount of personal space you are willing to share

3. The amount of money you are willing to spend

4. The amount of emotional energy you are willing to invest

5. The degree of access to your personal property you are willing to give

Recognize your limits in all five areas and verbalize them. No one is a mind reader, so you must establish clear rules and limitations at the beginning of all new relationships and take courage in renegotiating the old ones. Learn to say "No" and mean it. Stand firm against manipulation, emotional blackmail, physical or mental violations, abuses, or hurts. If any of these happen, get help.

To set these boundaries, you must get in touch with who you really are, what you want, as well as what you need from others. Certain things will not be spelled out plainly in Scripture. This is where you'll need to rely on the Holy Spirit as well as the guiding principles of God's Word, and ultimately, the principle of being a good steward of *you* and your soul.

Power Point

Know what you do *not* want and need from others. Learn how to articulate what those things are. Get to know when your expectations and limitations are being violated and speak up. Set clear standards for yourself and stick to them. Every relationship involves a certain amount of compromise, but you should never give up fundamental parts of who you are just to be with someone or please someone, especially if your core values and convictions, personhood, or property are being violated.

The more you know about yourself, the easier it will be to communicate who you are with others and set clearly defined boundaries.

POWER THOUGHT

Your personal boundaries protect the inner core
of your identity and your right to make choices.
—Gerard Manley Hopkins

Day 30

RESPECT OTHERS' BOUNDARIES

Respect begins with this attitude: "I acknowledge that you are a creature of extreme worth. God has endowed you with certain abilities and emotions. Therefore I respect you as a person. I will seek to understand you and grant you the freedom to think differently from the way I think and to experience emotions that I may not experience."

Respect means that you give the other person the freedom to be an individual. —Gary Chapman

DISCIPLINE #30—HONOR THE BOUNDARIES OF OTHERS

Honoring the boundaries of other people is a direct expression of your love for them and the fulfillment of one of Jesus' two main commandments.

Today we will look at the relevance of "The Golden Rule" when it comes to respecting others' boundaries. Jesus said, *"You shall love your neighbor as yourself"* (Matt. 22:39). One of the ways we reflect this love toward our neighbors, or fellow human being, is by demonstrating honor and respect for their personal boundary lines.

Respecting the boundaries of others is a two-fold process:

It begins with loving yourself enough to establish your own boundary lines. Only then are you poised to channel this same love toward other people in honoring their boundaries.

It Begins with Loving Yourself

Setting clear boundaries in your life demonstrates that you love yourself. Some look upon the phrase "love yourself" as being vain or selfish, denoting narcissism. This is false humility. I hope by now that you recognize your worth and importance—to God, to creation, to this hour in history, and to your fellow human beings. Your birth was not accidental; it was intentional. You were designed for this moment. There is no one like you—there never has been in the whole of history, and never will be. You are here by God's divine design, and thus, should express appropriate thanksgiving to Him by loving and honoring yourself. For more on this subject, I encourage you to revisit the first book in this series, *The 40 Day Soul Fast.* You have every reason to value the unique individual that God created you to be. This is the very foundation of empowered living and the beginning of setting clearly defined boundaries. Conversely, if you do not love or respect yourself, you live without restrictions and boundaries become meaningless.

> *"True discovery of your value exposes soul attachments for what they are."*

This is one of the reasons why soul attachments are so destructive—especially in relationships. Generally, soul ties distract you from grasping your value. The moment you step into a true discovery of your value, soul attachments are exposed for what they genuinely are.

Again, the key to building personal boundaries, and in turn, honoring the boundaries of others, is an appreciation of your own value and worth. It is impossible to give away what you do not first possess.

It Ends With Honoring Others' Boundaries

If you love yourself enough to establish personal boundaries, you are perfectly poised to honor the boundary lines of other people. You understand that each person has rights, limitations, needs, wants, desires, feelings, dreams, expectations, values, and goals.

Sometimes it is difficult to understand why people do the things they do, so learn how to talk openly, ask questions, and engage in meaningful dialogue. Take a proverbial walk in another person's shoes. View their lives from their perspective rather than yours. As you talk about your needs and limitations, rights, dreams, goals, expectations, etc., encourage others to do the same. Be transparent and receptive. Try to understand them and encourage them to understand and support you. And always, always season your conversations with love, respect, and empathic understanding.

The End-Goal

Respecting the boundaries of other people has a strategic end-goal. When we sincerely listen to one another and take to heart one another's needs and desires, as well as limitations, the understanding that is exchanged *builds up* and *edifies*. It is a sign of both personal maturity and exponential progress toward developing the kind of community that Christ envisioned for His Church.

Apostle Paul sets forth this vision while addressing the church in Ephesus:

We should no longer be children, tossed to and fro and carried about with every wind of doctrine, by the trickery of men, in the cunning craftiness of deceitful plotting, but, speaking the truth in love, may [we] grow up in all things into Him who is the head—Christ—from whom the whole body, joined and knit together by what every joint supplies, according to the effective

275

working by which every part does its share, causes growth of the body for the edifying of itself in love (Ephesians 4:14-16).

By *speaking the truth in love,* we are communicating openly and transparently with one another. No more show. No more pretense. No more hypocrisy. Clear and honest person-to-person communication is absolutely essential if we are going to bring this vision to pass in both our individual lives and in our communities. To work together effectively, we must express mutual honor for one another. The primary place for this transaction of honor to occur is in building healthy boundaries.

POWER POINT

Boundaries were never designed to divide and separate people from one other. On the contrary, they are purposed to enrich our relationships.

As mentioned previously, all of us have limits. This is the normal, human condition. Unfortunately, the *accepted* normal in society has been to push the envelope of these limits, and as a result, destroy countless relationships. If anything, boundaries are relationship preservers. They ensure the maintenance of healthy interactions with the people in our lives. By both establishing these boundaries personally and respecting them in others, we mature into the *body* that Paul describes in Ephesians 4, with every joint working together harmoniously to unveil a clearer picture of Christ in the earth.

POWER THOUGHT

Love others as well as you love yourself (Matthew 22:39 MSG).

ENCOUNTERING
CHRIST

I knew that I had come face to face with some one
whose mere personality was so fascinating that, if I
allowed it to do so, it would absorb my whole nature,
my whole soul, my very art itself. —Oscar Wilde

None I encounter will be able to resist Me
(Isaiah 47:3 AMP).

Last week, we explored the importance of building new
boundaries in our lives. We concluded with Ephesians 4,
where Paul gave us a vision of what we are moving toward—
evolving into a corporate body that releases a fuller, clearer,
more vivid expression of Jesus Christ in the world. Although we
are pressing toward the same goal this week, we are approaching it from a different angle. This week we'll dig deeper as we
establish a more firm and solid foundation upon which we must
build a resilient life.

There are realities that transcend the practical, that dictate
the everyday things we must consistently do. As we work toward
reclaiming the soul by building a more resilient life, I want to discuss the ultimate *soul attachment* that is of utmost importance—
our union and intimacy with Christ.

By building new boundaries, we are protecting ourselves
from the prospect of future harmful soul ties. This is essential,

but remember—we need to ensure that our "house" is not only clean and clear, but also properly filled. The only One worthy of filling our house and possessing our soul is Christ Himself. He heals our past, defines our present, and creates our future. This week, I want to look at how a transformative encounter with Jesus Christ redefines our approach to life.

Remember, Jesus impacted those He encountered by creating a relational, emotional defining moment. He dealt with the issues in the tissues of the soul—the scar tissue of the mind. With laser-like accuracy He spoke to the origin of the problem; no matter how deeply rooted the problem was—whether the symptoms were blindness, deafness, or paralysis—He cut through the bonds of apathy, pride, insecurity, shame, regret, or lack of vision, faith, or hope. He freed those who met Him from the bonds of unforgiveness, bitterness, and offense—and by doing so broke cycles of blindness, lameness, and oppression.

> *Christ's love eclipses your problems by healing the past and giving you a vision for a brighter future.*

By binding the strongman who holds souls captive— *"the accuser of our brethren"* (Revelation 12:10)—Jesus never failed to unlock potential, vision, understanding, and insight. Wherever He shows up in your life today, Christ's love eclipses your problems by healing the past and giving you a vision for a brighter future.

Remember, God's will is to completely break the soul tie cycle in your life. It is not enough for us to be returning to the altar, week after week, petitioning for freedom or deliverance—always *yet again*. Obviously, I am not opposed to any method of healing—for freedom and deliverance are necessary—but they are necessary catalysts intentioned to completely reposition our lives for resiliency. An encounter with the living Christ is a life-transforming moment where these cycles are broken and an entirely new manner of existence is birthed. This week, we will look at five keys to maintaining a lifestyle of encountering Christ.

KEEP A POSITIVE EXPECTATION

We have always held to the hope, the belief, the conviction, that there is a better life, a better world beyond the horizon. —Franklin D. Roosevelt

DISCIPLINE #31 — LET HOPE INTRODUCE YOU TO A NEW WAY OF LIVING

How many times have you heard the phrase, "Don't get your hopes up"? This is often stated in the context of trying to bring someone's unrealistic expectations back "down to earth" in an effort to ground and balance them.

The problem with this approach is that our propensity to treat hope like something ethereal and impossible prevents us from dreaming with a positive expectation. If you want to experience a resilient lifestyle—free from the entanglements of the past that drained your life and energy—you need to *believe* it is possible. You must be able to dream of a reality beyond the one you have been imprisoned in. Dreams flourish in communities and atmospheres of hope. However,

> *Dreams flourish in communities and atmospheres of hope.*

where there is no hope, there is no possibility, and where there is no possibility, there is no substance for dreaming.

Hope is absolutely essential for birthing a reality that is beyond the one we have previously known and experienced. However, you are not going to experience or receive this type of hope from the world; it is only birthed through an encounter with Christ. He is the Author of hope—and as Scripture reveals, the hope He brings into our lives *"does not disappoint"* (Rom. 5:5). Hope, according to Scripture, is the confident expectation of a positive outcome. This is exactly what Jesus released to every person He encountered.

Today we will look at a powerful account from the Gospel of John where an encounter with Christ unleashed hope into an otherwise hopeless situation. We will examine two dimensions of the story, evaluating the impact hopelessness had upon a woman's life, and more specifically, what hope did to elevate her beyond a dysfunctional and dissatisfying existence, characterized by unhealthy soul attachments.

The Encounter at the Well

An ordinary woman going about her business one ordinary day happened upon Jesus at an ordinary well. That brief conversation changed her life forever. Jesus opened her eyes to the Good News: He had come so that anyone could worship God wherever they were *"in spirit and truth"* (John 4:24), drink from the water of eternal life and never thirst again.

Many of us are familiar with the spiritual exchange that took place in this rich narrative. I want to start by specifically examining the present condition of the woman's life and the adverse impact of hopelessness. It is obvious that she struggled with this on several levels. For the sake of time, let's explore three obvious ones: relational, gender, and moral hopelessness.

Relational hopelessness. The woman was astonished that Jesus, a Jew, would interact with not only a Samaritan, but also a divorced woman. The Message version of John 4:9 clarifies that *"Jews in those days wouldn't be caught dead talking to Samaritans."*

Normal rules and custom forbade Jesus from having any type of communication with this woman whatsoever. However, such social conventions never stopped Jesus from bringing hope to the hopeless by helping them embrace their future from a completely transformed perspective.

Gender hopelessness. The paradigm this woman had embraced followed a certain order, where Jews did not interact with Samaritans, and women were regarded in a very low manner in society. Yet, all it took was an encounter with Christ to completely demolish this perspective and redefine her reality—so much so that this woman, after meeting Jesus, proceeded to go *"her way into the city, and said to the men, 'Come, see a Man who told me all things that I ever did. Could this be the Christ?' Then they went out of the city and came to Him"* (John 4:28-30). After one conversation with Christ, the Samaritan woman went from being unsure of who she was to becoming a bold witness of this Man, Jesus.

Moral hopelessness. The woman in this story is most notorious for her checkered past. Jesus boldly calls her out on this, identifying that she was not currently married, but rather, she was presently living with a man out of wedlock after having been married *five times*—yet Jesus does not condemn her. He did not focus on her current circumstances, but gave her a vision of a better future. Jesus said to her, *"Whoever drinks of the water that I shall give him will never thirst. But the water that I shall give him will become in him a fountain of water springing up into everlasting life"* (John 4:14). He gave her a startling new vision of an entirely different kind of life. Overcome and overjoyed, she ran to tell everyone, and as a result of her witness, she became a respected voice in her city. *"Many of the Samaritans of that city believed in Him because of the word of the woman who testified"* (John 4:39).

Jesus did not remain fixated on this woman's shortcomings and failures—He was more intent on exposing her to new realities than dragging her through past memories. By merely speaking with this woman, Jesus opened a significant door of hope into her life, breaking down barriers created by race, gender, and social status, and creating a positive expectation of good things ahead. In one day, she went from being a disreputable tramp to a revered testifier of the Truth.

POWER POINT

This is the power of hope in action. The key is not defining hope by the standard of the world, where there is no substance, so the thing we "hope" for may or may not come to pass. It is impossible for us to be confident and positive if what we are believing for is an unsure reality. This is not what Jesus gave the Samaritan woman.

What Jesus offers is the vision of a completely new version of reality. This vision creates a positive expectation within us that what He revealed as possible can and will come to fruition in our lives.

POWER THOUGHT

Now faith is the substance of things hoped for...
(Hebrews 11:1).

Day 32

SEE PAST BARRIERS

Assuredly, I say to you, if you have faith as a mustard seed, you will say to this mountain, "Move from here to there," and it will move; and nothing will be impossible for you (Matthew 17:20).

DISCIPLINE #32 — BREAK THROUGH BOUNDARIES BY FOLLOWING THE SPIRIT

An encounter with Jesus elevates your understanding of what is both possible and available to you. Suddenly, the vision for your future and destiny become larger because you are no longer viewing through a mere mortal lens. You recognize the current availability of what was previously impossible. Your encounter with the Divine actually creates a deposit—*the Spirit of God dwelling within you.* Though Jesus left the earth bodily, He did not leave the planet without His Spirit, and His Spirit specializes in releasing impossibilities into the natural realm. He was the force behind creation in Genesis 1:2, as well as the *same* Spirit who raised Christ from the dead (see Rom. 8:11).

> *An encounter with Jesus elevates your understanding of what is both possible and available to you.*

Before the Holy Spirit, there was a significant barrier preventing us from accessing the mind, thoughts, and will of God.

This barrier was a human condition that remained incompatible with an indwelling habitation of the Holy Spirit. Under the Old Covenant, encounters with God did not have the ability to release a deposit into the core of humanity, for humankind was still under the vicious tyranny of sin.

The barrier of our sin condition thus created a barrier with God. This barrier was broken because of Jesus' blood, but sadly, many of us still live with a barrier mentality.

A New Lens to See New Life

To enjoy the resilient life God has purposed for us, it is foundational that we first believe such a reality is *accessible* and *available* to us. Many never step into their destiny, not because of God's unwillingness, but because they refuse to see beyond the barrier of covenantal transition. There was a significant transition that took place between the Old and New Covenants, making provision for you and I to experience a new way of seeing and living from God's perspective. Unfortunately, many believe that this lifestyle is inaccessible to them—even though Jesus purchased it on their behalf and made it available through the Holy Spirit.

Isaiah 64:4 similarly states, *"For since the beginning of the world men have not heard nor perceived by the ear, nor has the eye seen any God besides You, who acts for the one who waits for Him."* Here we confront the barrier of mystery and inaccessibility. While there are entire realms of knowledge that are veiled from our eyes, there is also a new possibility of access to what was previously inaccessible and unknowable. Apostle Paul made this very clear in First Corinthians 2, where he cites Isaiah 64:4 and follows it up with a new reality: *"But as it is written: 'Eye has not seen, nor ear heard, nor have entered into the heart of man the things which God has prepared for those who love Him"* (1 Cor. 2:9). He continues by adding, *"But God has revealed them to us through His Spirit"* (1 Cor. 2:10).

Every barrier has been removed for you and me because we have become inhabited by the Spirit of God. The very Spirit that wrought the impossible through the miracles and wonders of Christ dwells inside you. Just as nothing was impossible for the disciples who trusted in Jesus of Nazareth, such is the case for those today who follow the leading of the Holy Spirit.

Here are the three barriers that Jesus broke through so you could live a resilient life.

Opened Heavens

From the beginning of His ministry on earth, Jesus broke through the barriers of time and space. He brought the supernatural, eternal dimension to bear on the natural and time-bound world we live in. He defied the forces of nature by walking on water, turning water into wine, raising the dead, and then returning from the dead. In His famous encounter with John the Baptist, upon rising up from being baptized, *"The heavens were opened to Him, and He saw the Spirit of God descending like a dove and alighting upon Him"* (Matt. 3:16). Everyone present heard God's voice break through to the earth from heaven declaring, *"This is My beloved Son, in whom I am well pleased"* (Matt. 3:17). That was a defining moment for Jesus. From that point forward, wherever Jesus went, the heavens opened—and God's voice could be heard and His Spirit felt on all He touched. Because of Jesus, the supernatural realm of hearing God's voice and experiencing the miraculous has become possible to all who are filled with the Holy Spirit.

The supernatural realm of hearing God's voice and experiencing the miraculous is possible to all who are filled with the Holy Spirit.

Opened Minds

When a religious scholar by the name of Nicodemus secretly came to confer with Jesus, he was given the keys to salvation.

Jesus told him that only by being born again—born not of the flesh, but of the Spirit—could anyone enter into the Kingdom of God. This was a revolutionary concept that would shatter all former religious beliefs—that *whomsoever* is born of the Spirit will see God's Kingdom. Not only that, but Jesus also made clear that there are two systems in operation—the fleshly, temporal, visible, world system, and the heavenly, eternal, invisible, spiritual system. For *"That which is born of the flesh is flesh, and that which is born of the Spirit is spirit"* (John 3:6). Jesus went on to inquire, *"If I have told you earthly things and you do not believe, how will you believe if I tell you heavenly things?"* (John 3:12).

Let's make sure we don't doubt Him when He speaks to us—even if what the Holy Spirit speaks seems beyond our ability to process and comprehend. Remember, the Spirit has made access to the supernatural thoughts and ways of God possible. Yield to Him; He will lead you into *all* truth (see John 16:13).

Opened Potential

In John chapter 5, a man lay paralyzed beside a pool along with many other people who were blind, lame, and paralyzed, *"waiting for the moving of the water"* (John 5:3). The key word here is *"waiting."* This man was surrounded by people who had no vision—who were unable to make any progress, blind, no goals or aspiration for the future; halted, stagnated, withered, and atrophying—all "waiting" for something to happen. These were wounded souls who had been emotionally handicapped by shame, pain, rejection and bitterness.

For thirty-eight years this man watched other people move out ahead and take what they needed. For thirty-eight years, he gave his personal power away and resigned himself to be a product of his environment. For thirty-eight years he lived with self-imposed limitations capping his potential. Jesus came along and asked him what it was he wanted, then told him, *"Rise, take up your bed and walk"* (John 5:8). Jesus' question challenged him.

With no crutch, he gained strength and resilience to defy the odds, surmount his condition, and live the life of his dreams. As a result, the man got up and went on his way. The Holy Spirit is still asking the same question today, "What do you want?"

Power Point

The Spirit of God lives inside you; He offers access to an endless source of supernatural potential. Press through the barriers and embrace the resilient life that God has waiting for you on the other side!

Power Thought

Only those who attempt the absurd can achieve the impossible. —Albert Einstein

Day 33

FOLLOW GOD'S LEAD

Prayer is putting oneself in the hands of God, at
His disposition, and listening to His voice in the
depth of our hearts. —Mother Teresa

DISCIPLINE #33 — TRANSFER COMPLETE
CONTROL TO THE HOLY SPIRIT

Yesterday, we discovered that we are indwelt by the very Spirit
that empowered the Lord Jesus Christ. The same Spirit that
breaks through natural barriers, opening our eyes to new possibilities, is the very One Jesus sent to divinely direct our lives.
That is how He works. First He graces our minds to embrace
new realities, and then shows us how to actually walk in these
new realities.

Today you are in a position to break the cycles of "former
realities" and in exchange, embrace an entirely upgraded lifestyle characterized by empowerment, victory, and resiliency.
Under the "old way" of living, things tended to be haphazard,
visionless, and accidental. *Life happened.* There was no intentionality or specific focus. Whatever soul ties you had, be it a
relationship, state of being, allegiance, or way of life—those ties
dictated the course of your life. I pray by this point you see that
this is not the reality God wills for you.

As you have been studying these different exchanges and
dysfunctions, my prayer is that the Holy Spirit has been working

with you to break old habits and old lifestyles, thus preparing your mind to receive fresh vision of a new way of living—*resilient living*. For this to become a lifestyle and not merely a temporary high, there are some best practices we should apply.

Follow Divine Direction

When Jesus encountered a man who was paralyzed—unable to move—stuck in the same place year in and year out, He gave that man direction. He said to the paralytic, *"Arise, take up your bed, and go to his house"* (Matt. 9:6), and immediately the man *"arose and departed for home"* (Matt. 9:7).

When you feel paralyzed by life's circumstances, ask Jesus to raise you up and point you in the right direction. Jesus said, *"Ask, and it will be given to you; seek, and you will find; knock, and it will be opened to you"* (Luke 11:9). For *"the steps of a good man are ordered by the Lord, and He delights in his way. Though he fall, he shall not be utterly cast down; For the Lord upholds him with His hand"* (Ps. 37:23-24). Reach up from wherever you are and receive direction for your life.

Remember, God's direction for your life does not include you remaining trapped in a vicious soul cycle of bondage, deliverance, and a temporary season of freedom, only to return to a previously paralyzed state of being. His good plan is to *completely break the cycle*, and show you how to experience an entirely new way of life.

Listen to the Holy Spirit and obey His voice. He speaks through Scripture. He speaks to the deep places of your heart. He speaks through a renewed mind. Value the voice of the Holy Spirit, for this is *God speaking to you!*

Receive Fresh Vision

Jesus came across a blind man begging in the street. His disciples asked whether his blindness was a result of the man's sins or the sins of his parents. Jesus answered, *"You're asking the wrong question. You're looking for someone to blame. There is no such cause-effect here. Look instead for what God can do"* (John 9:3 MSG). What God can do includes giving vision. Jesus went on to say, *"I came into the world to bring everything into the clear light of day, making all the distinctions clear, so that those who have never seen will see"* (John 9:39 MSG).

Luke gave an account of Jesus proclaiming, *"The Lord has sent me...to give sight to the blind"* (Luke 4:18 CEV). Jesus came so that you would never lack vision or insight into your situation. In the same way, the Holy Spirit carries on the vision-releasing ministry of Jesus, revealing God's perfect plan and purpose for your life. He is setting

> *The Holy Spirit carries on the vision-releasing ministry of Jesus, revealing God's perfect plan and purpose for your life.*

you up for a vision transition. Previously, under the tyranny of soul ties, your vision was clouded. Clarity was scarce, as you were yoked to destructive people, cycles, and circumstances. As you are now free from this old way, I encourage you to begin seeing yourself as a free person. You have not merely tasted or experienced freedom—you *are* free. Let this be your new vision of life.

I encourage you to seek the Holy Spirit to restore perfect sight and clarity where you are having trouble adjusting your focus. Ask Him to open your eyes as He did for the man in Bethsaida—*"Jesus placed his hands on the man's eyes again, and his eyes were opened. His sight was completely restored, and he could see everything clearly"* (Mark 8:25 NLT).

Mix God's Word with Faith

An officer whose ailing servant was *"paralyzed, dreadfully tormented"* (Matt. 8:6). sought out Jesus on his servant's behalf. Jesus offered to go to the man's house to heal his servant, but the officer knew Jesus only needed give the command and the servant would be healed. Encountering Christ gave the officer the kind of faith that impressed Jesus. He declared to the on-looking crowd, *"I have not found such great faith, not even in*

Israel" (Matt. 8:10). Then Jesus said to the officer, *"Go your way; and as you have believed, so let it be done for you"* (Matt. 8:13).

Encountering the Christ will empower you to grab hold of the Word of God in faith. Many routinely and religiously study the Scriptures, but simply continue to read a book rather than encountering a Person. This was especially true for the religious leaders of Jesus' time, as He called out their condition: *"You search the Scriptures, for in them you think you have eternal life; and these are they which testify of Me"* (John 5:39). They could probably recite entire portions of Scripture from memory, but the page remained powerless. The author of Hebrews lets us in on the secret of living an empowered life by properly applying the Word of God—*"but the word which they heard did not profit them, not being mixed with faith in those who heard it"* (Heb. 4:2).

Jesus taught that your faith mixed with God's Word makes things happen. You, too, can hear Jesus say, *"Go your way; and as you have believed, so let it be done for you"* (Matt. 8:13).

POWER POINT

The Holy Spirit not only empowers you to see past restrictive barriers, but He will show you how to walk into the new life God has prepared for you. The key is transferring complete control of your life into His most capable hands!

POWER THOUGHT

God's Spirit beckons. There are things to do and places to go!
(Romans 8:14 MSG)

Day 34

LEAN IN

Embrace this God-life. Really embrace it, and nothing will be too much for you (Mark 11:22 MSG).

DISCIPLINE #34 —
BEGIN TO LIVE LIFE GOD'S WAY

To enjoy the benefits of the "God-life," we need to adhere to His standards of living. Rather than loads of effort, it's more of a *leaning in*; more than work-laden, it is driven by intimacy. Jesus said, "*He does only what he sees the Father doing. Whatever the Father does, the Son also does*" (John 5:19 NLT). Where did Jesus "see" what the Father was doing? I believe it was during those refreshing times of solitude and intimacy where, in a place of love and communicating, Jesus caught vision of the lifestyle the Father desired to express through Him. Likewise, we are not trying to live a certain way or follow certain standards because we are endeavoring to earn divine favor. Favor was extended to you and me because of the atoning work of Christ. The cross is the loudest demonstration of God's favor imaginable, and those who receive its work become inheritors of this favor.

Today, we are not looking at tools to help us gain God's approval. Rather, we are reviewing three specific characteristics of a God-modeled life that not only attract supernatural blessing, but also position you to live the resilient life you were always designed to live.

Lean In to a Lifestyle of Forgiveness

As we discovered earlier, one of the most crippling forces on the planet is shame. Jesus came to lift up your head, clear the slate, and put you in right standing with God. He humbled Himself so that you wouldn't be humiliated. He endured the shame of the cross so you wouldn't have to ever be ashamed again. He covered your disgrace with His grace. The psalmist asked, *"How far has the Lord taken our sins from us? Farther than the distance from east to west!"* (Ps. 103:12 CEV).

Christ's most beloved apostle, John, wrote with this purpose in mind, *"Because your sins are forgiven you for His name's sake"* (1 John 2:12). Forgiveness is a powerful force, and it is what God set all of the events of the Bible in motion to do. Only second to the power of His forgiveness toward you is the power He has given you to forgive others. Never forget, *"he who hates his brother is in darkness and walks in darkness, and does not know where he is going, because the darkness has blinded his eyes"* (1 John 2:11).

And in the eloquent words of 19th century American preacher, Edwin Hubbel Chapin, "Never does the human soul appear so strong as when it forgoes revenge and dares to forgive an injury."

Lean In to a Lifestyle of Provision

If you are poor in spirit, or poor in substance, Jesus said the Spirit of God is upon Him for such as you. He demonstrated that not only is He the lifter of your soul, providing His joy and comfort whenever you're in need of spiritual comfort, but He is well able to provide for you materially as well. *"Those who seek the Lord shall not lack any good thing"* (Ps. 34:10)—and Paul reminded us that *"God shall supply all your need according to His riches in glory by Christ Jesus"* (Phil. 4:19). Look at all He was able to do with a fish or two and a couple small loaves of bread—He fed the five thousand in Matthew 14 and the four thousand in

Matthew 15. He provided money for taxes in the mouth of a fish in Matthew 17; and in Luke 5, He sent Simon Peter out to fish until his nets tore from the size of the catch. Whatever He touched prospered, and whatever He touches through you will prosper, too.

You are a conduit for Him to flow through. In the same way we receive and thereby extend forgiveness, the model is for us to receive and ultimately release provision. We stagnate when we simply store up the blessing of God for ourselves. Once again, we return to the model of Jesus, which is reinforced by His mandate. He freely received from the Father and then freely gave out of this divine resource. Likewise, His charge to you and me is, *"Freely you have received, freely give"* (Matt. 10:8). The Message translation speaks directly to the specific issue of provision—*"You have been treated generously, so live generously"* (Matt. 10:8 MSG).

Lean In to a Lifestyle of Deliverance

One Sabbath day as Jesus was teaching in a synagogue, he saw a woman who had been crippled by an evil spirit. She was completely bent over and had been unable to stand up straight for eighteen years—eighteen years!

> *When Jesus saw her, he called her over and said, "Dear woman, you are healed of your sickness!" Then he touched her, and instantly she could stand straight. How she praised God!* (Luke 13:12-13 NLT)

This work of healing outraged the leader of the synagogue. He loudly stated to the whole crowd, *"There are six days of the week for working...Come on those days to be healed, not on the Sabbath"* (Luke 13:14 NLT). Rebuking him, Jesus replied:

> *You hypocrites! Each of you works on the Sabbath day! Don't you untie your ox or your donkey from its stall on the Sabbath*

and lead it out for water? This dear woman, a daughter of Abraham, has been held in bondage by Satan for eighteen years. Isn't it right that she be released, even on the Sabbath? (Luke 13:15-16 NLT)

An encounter with Jesus will always set you free from whatever holds you captive. This is what we have been moving toward throughout our journey together—a lifestyle of deliverance. You are actually able to sustain deliverance as your position rather than an experience when you live *leaned in* to Christ.

> *Yesterday's experience is not sufficient to supply today's deliverance.*

Yesterday's experience is not sufficient to supply today's deliverance. Many try to survive on "old manna" when in fact, the Spirit of God desires our relationship with Him to be vibrant, dynamic, and exciting. God intends deliverance to be a lifestyle, not an isolated experience. The way to discover what a delivered life actually looks like is by leaning into the Father, beholding the example of Jesus, and asking the Holy Spirit to guide you further into this Truth.

POWER POINT

The God-life is not a dreary black and white—it is vivid and colorful. He is undeniably a God who upholds certain standards and models of living, but all with good reason. His structures are life-enriching and life-enhancing. He is not a mafia boss or power-seeking dictator; His agenda is not to withhold, diminish, or overpower. He is not the proverbial "Cosmic Killjoy"—He came to bring *abundant* life. The only thing He wants to restrict you from is small living. Sin is the gateway to small living. Soul attachments are gateways to small living. Unforgiveness and greed are gateways to small living.

As you continue to lean in to Jesus, and catch a fresh vision of His example, you will discover the extravagant freedom and liberty that accompany a lifestyle yielded to the Holy Spirit and committed to modeling the Lord. Remember, we are not working for God's favor. We are *already* favored, pressing in to enjoy greater intimacy with our beloved Savior. These encounters cannot help but produce transformation in our lives!

POWER THOUGHT

Lovers will always outwork workers in the long-run in the Kingdom of God. —Mike Bickle

Day 35

STEP OUT

All the forces in the world are not so powerful as
an idea whose time has come. —Victor Hugo

DISCIPLINE #35 — ACTIVATE THE POWER
OF GOD WITHIN YOU

On our last day together this week, I want to empower you
to take the next step on your journey to reclaiming your soul.
I am not content with this merely being a study or overview of
exchanges, dysfunctions, and disciplines. My vision is to arm
you with tools that will take you from a place of bondage to a
new life of liberation. The key to making this essential transition is drawing from the life source and power of God inside
you. This is the point in our study where I want the power of
God to go from being a concept or idea, to "an idea whose
times has come" that manifests in your life!

There are three principles that will help you activate the
power of God within you and thereby successfully transition
into the resilient life:

The Potential of Hope

Hope exposes you to the potential of a resilient life. Without hope,
you have no vision of a desired end to work toward. You remain

caught in soul attachments and destructive cycles until you encounter living hope. Remember—*Hope is a Person.*

A woman who had suffered for twelve years with an issue of blood had spent her life's savings seeking a cure. There wasn't a doctor who could help her. She had given up hope until she heard that Jesus was on His way through town. Considered unclean, she risked everything going out into public. She slipped through the crowd and struggled to get near enough to see Him.

> *Just then a woman who had suffered for twelve years with constant bleeding came up behind him. She touched the fringe of his robe, for she thought, "If I can just touch his robe, I will be healed." Jesus turned around, and when he saw her he said, "Daughter, be encouraged! Your faith has made you well." And the woman was healed at that moment* (Matthew 9:20-22 NLT).

All hope was lost until she met the Master of Hope Himself. He met her there on the street where she was unannounced unclean and undesirable—and that one brief encounter transformed her future.

Hope is a game-changer. Until you have hope, there is no possibility for transformation. Hope introduces previously unrealized possibility and potential.

As we move toward the conclusion of this study, I want you to remain mindful of the dire need for hope, as well as its Source and divine origin. Any assurances of hope outside of Jesus Christ are unsubstantial, for He is our only *sure* hope. Remember, hope as defined by Scripture, is a confident, positive expectation. It is not wishing. It is not idle. It is not maybe. Hope latches on to the potential of a resilient life and refuses to let go until this reality becomes a lifestyle.

> *Hope introduces previously unrealized possibility and potential.*

The Promise of Abundant Life

Hope exposes you to the potential of a resilient life, but the assurance or *promise of abundant life* compels you to pursue this lifestyle until it starts to define your world. People around the planet are exposed to hope as they encounter Christ. How we steward this precious gift of hope is determined by our understanding of God's will for our lives.

Of life and more life—abundant life—Jesus said, *"I came so they can have real and eternal life, more and better life than they ever dreamed of"* (John 10:10 MSG). Not only did Jesus raise the physically dead, but more importantly, He came to raise the spiritually dead.

In John we read how Jesus spoke to the people saying, *"I am the light of the world. If you follow me, you won't have to walk in darkness, because you will have the light that leads to life"* (John 8:12 NLT). Allow Jesus to shed light on whatever is dead or dying or lying dormant in you—give Him access to those places and they will begin to flourish once more.

We must believe God's plan is good, His purpose is for our best interest, and His overall agenda for our lives is one of victory, freedom, and resiliency—*life and more life*. I am convinced that we are entering an age when Christians are becoming increasingly discontent with substance-less spirituality. As believers experience the life-giving power of Jesus, they are exposed to greater demonstrations of God's goodness. They are not only reading and hearing that God is good—they are tasting of this reality for themselves. These "tastes" of the abundant life will drive them to pursue it until it becomes less of a "once in a while" mountain-top experience, and more of a consistent way of being.

The Power of Authority

The third truth that positions you for resilient living is the *power of authority*. When you have hope and are assured that God's will for you is an abundant life, you will evaluate everything else by those standards. Anything that threatens to release death, torment, or bondage into your life is branded as enemy-originated and confronted with the authority of Christ within you. You will step into a greater understanding of this authority as you increase in intimacy with Jesus, as the authority you received is not your own—it is His. To walk in this authority, you must intimately acquaint yourself with how Jesus did.

One of the keys Jesus wanted to leave with His disciples was the knowledge of the authority they had as a result of being in relationship with Him. *"I give you the authority to trample on serpents and scorpions, and over all the power of the enemy, and nothing shall by any means hurt you"* (Luke 10:19). He promised them they would do even greater works than He did—*"I tell you the truth, anyone who believes in me will do the same works I have done, and even greater works, because I am going to be with the Father"* (John 14:12 NLT).

When we are in relationship with Jesus, *"we are more than conquerors through Him who loved us"* (Rom. 8:37). With Christ at your side, *"No weapon turned against you will succeed. You will silence every voice raised up to accuse you"* (Isa. 54:17 NLT). Remember this as we prepare to move into the final week of our time together and you take authority over your own soul—as you *"work out your own salvation with fear and trembling"* (Phil. 2:12).

POWER POINT

Understand that relationship is a fundamental principle of success. When it comes to stepping out and reclaiming your soul, you must begin with a deep and abiding relationship with Jesus. Wherever there was weakness, bondage, lack, or sorrow, Jesus entered in and brought strength, freedom, abundance, and joy. In each instance, a shift occurred.

Why is an encounter with Christ so powerful and transformative? Due to His union with God the Father, who *is* love (see 1 John 4:16) and because Jesus is the embodiment of that love. God's love is only made evident in relationship. It is the kind of

> *God's love is only made evident in relationship.*

love that never insists on its own rights, seeks its own, or gets offended. It is an unconditional love that always believes the best *of*—and hopes the best *for*—a person. God loves you too much to let you remain in a place of bondage and hopelessness. It is in this next and final week that we will review some practical steps to living free from destructive soul attachments, and establish once and for all the abundant life of resiliency God intends for you.

Step out with confidence, knowing that throughout the journey—in all of its highs and lows—God's love is constant toward you and *will never fail!*

POWER THOUGHT

Love is kind and patient, never jealous, boastful, proud, or rude. Love isn't selfish or quick tempered. It doesn't keep a record of wrongs that others do. Love rejoices in the truth, but not in evil. Love is always supportive, loyal, hopeful, and trusting. Love never fails! (1 Corinthians 13:4-8 CEV)

Week Eight

RECLAIMING
YOUR SOUL

Why do you hasten to remove anything which
hurts your eye, while if something affects your soul
you postpone the cure until next year? —Horace

*So I will restore to you the years that the swarming locust
has eaten* (Joel 2:25).

Don't postpone the care of your soul one more day. Seize the
moment, right here, right now to reclaim everything that has been
stolen! Take time to pause and reflect—take note of where you've
been, what has influenced you, where you are now, and how you
would like to be tomorrow. It does not matter if what happened
to you was your fault or the doing of someone else. By this point
in our journey, I hope that you're convinced that it's God's will to
set you free and on a course to a more empowered life.

This week will be very different from the previous seven
weeks. Each day's entry will be short and very practical. You have
already been armed with all of the information you need to
break whatever cycle of bondage your soul has been caught in
and reclaim what rightfully belongs to you—a life of empowerment and resiliency. This is what we have been working toward.

Asa Don Brown so aptly describes my vision for the intended
end of this book:

"Resiliency is the essence of a global positive framework." Healed people *heal* people. We are working toward building a *global positive framework*—a new way of life for souls across the world. Your ability to demonstrate an unhindered, victorious, and stable lifestyle is the refreshing glimpse that an often beaten-down world needs. I want you whole so you can *be* this glimpse to the world; that your transformation would stir others to pursue and experience the same resilient way of living.

The high vision of the resilient life that we are pursuing is this:

> All of us get knocked down, but it's resiliency that really matters. All of us do well when things are going well, but the thing that distinguishes athletes is the ability to do well in times of great stress, urgency and pressure.
> —Roger Staubach

This section is about equipping and positioning you to create a new normal.

What sets resilient people apart is their ability to flourish in times of opposition and difficulty. Let's elevate our vision, if we have not already. Forbid quick fixes or superficial solutions from being an option for you. Dare to live authentically. Dare to be exceptional. Stand out in your generation

> " *Stand firm in pressing toward a total soul renovation.* "

as one who refused to settle for "good enough"—and stand firm in pressing toward a total soul renovation.

People often experience breakthrough, victory, and freedom, but seldom allow these characteristics to define their lifestyle. This is what separates the resilient from the complacent; my prayer and desire for you is to be one who is set apart that offers hope for change to *everyone else* who is watching your life.

> People who soar are those who refuse to sit back, sigh and wish things would change. They neither complain of

their lot nor passively dream of some distant ship coming in. Rather, they visualize in their minds that they are not quitters; they will not allow life's circumstances to push them down and hold them under. —Charles Swindoll

Day 36

LISTEN

Put your ear down close to your soul and listen hard. —Anne Sexton

Discipline #36—Honestly Evaluate Your Soul's Condition

I want to give you some simple steps to evaluating the present condition of your soul. Take a few moments to pause and reflect upon everything you have learned on this journey:

One: *Become still and quiet in God's presence.* What are you hearing? Does anything immediately come to mind that the Holy Spirit has been trying to highlight and direct your attention to?

Two: *Pray and ask for the Holy Spirit to show you the danger zones regarding the health of your soul.* Ask the Lord to direct you to those encumbrances and attachments that are holding your soul captive. Listen for that "still small voice." Take this opportunity to act on whatever comes up in your spirit.

Three: *Repent* if you need to, *pray* for deliverance, and *praise Him* for complete restoration and liberty *"by which Christ has made us free, and do not be entangled again with a yoke of bondage"* (Gal. 5:1). If the soul tie or attachment was the result of your personal choices, simply repent and receive God's abundant forgiveness. If not, pray for deliverance from the consequences of others' actions.

Most importantly, as you pray, hear Him coaching you to relax—to trust Him with the care of your soul—and above all, as God instructs, to *"be still, and know that I am God"* (Ps. 46:10). We will focus more on the prayer of *breaking free* in the days to come, but for now, simply approach the Lord in a posture of repentance and receiving.

Four: Be intentional as you deliberately seek Him on behalf of your own soul. Purposefully seek His cleansing presence and peacefully allow yourself to enter into His rest—*"For we who have believed do enter that rest.... Let us therefore be diligent to enter that rest, lest anyone fall according to the same example of disobedience"* (Heb. 4:3,11).

As you enter into this time of reflective prayer, do so with confidence and expectation that the Holy Spirit will bring to your attention the specific attachments that need to be addressed.

POWER POINT

While the process of confronting years, decades, and even lifetimes of bondage should not be oversimplified, it is equally problematic to overcomplicate it. This week, you are going to honestly evaluate the condition of your soul and receive freedom from the One who sets you free *"through and through"* (John 8:36 MSG).

POWER THOUGHT

And behold, the Lord passed by, and a great and strong wind tore into the mountains and broke the rocks in pieces before the Lord, but the Lord was not in the wind; and after the wind an earthquake, but the Lord was not in the earthquake; and after the earthquake a fire, but the Lord was not in the fire; and after the fire a still small voice (1 Kings 19:11-12).

Day 37

FORGIVE

Remember, the Lord forgave you, so you must forgive others (Colossians 3:13 NLT).

DISCIPLINE #37—EXERCISE YOUR AUTHORITY TO FORGIVE

Unforgiveness keeps you bound on several dimensions. By refusing someone forgiveness, you are continuing to maintain agreement with the offense, with the offender, and ultimately, with satan's tyrannical influence over your life. The very things that continue to poison your soul are often the very things you are unwilling to let go of through forgiveness. One of the fundamental keys to breaking dangerous soul attachments is letting that person and offense go by exercising your power to forgive.

Too many of us are deceived into believing that by extending forgiveness, we are letting our enemies off the hook. Such is not the case. Rather, forgiveness is your way of removing them, along with their hurtful activities, *out of your life*—completely. I am convinced that if we clearly understood the dangerous strongholds that unforgiveness produces in our lives, we would be *"quick to forgive an offense"* (Col. 3:13 MSG) as Scripture tells us to do.

Forgiveness, however, is nothing short of a supernatural exercise. To extend it, you must draw from the well of the Holy

Spirit within you. He enables you to accomplish the impossible, and in most people's minds, the offer of forgiveness to an undeserving party is an impossible act. That said, all of us are ultimately undeserving when it comes to receiving forgiveness, but Scripture reminds us that *"while we were still sinners, Christ died for us"* (Rom. 5:8). Truly, there is no greater picture of extending forgiveness to the undeserving than what Jesus provided at Calvary's cross.

It is absolutely essential that you exercise the supernatural authority you have received in Christ and verbally forgive those who have wronged you.

Call out their names before the courts of heaven, and release them into the Father's hands. As I said earlier, my aim is not to oversimplify the process. I understand that there are many factors that go into the process of extending forgiveness. My aim is not to minimize what you have gone through, but to maximize the life-giving, bondage-breaking power contained in your *choice to exercise forgiveness.* You may need to undergo a season of counseling to deal with the fruit of what you have experienced. My objective here is to simply help escort you to a place where you recognize the need to break the cycle of unforgiveness in your life because of how it keeps you bound to the past, to traumatic experiences, and ultimately, tied to the very soul attachments you long to break.

> *The electromagnetic field of a soul creates a powerful force that exerts itself into every realm to bring about continuing change.*

If you have experienced a rift in a friendship, a marriage, or even a business partnership, *exercise your power to forgive today.* Your experience is interwoven with the life dynamic of everyone with whom you have ever had an emotional connection. As we discussed earlier, the electromagnetic field of a soul creates a powerful force that exerts itself into every realm to bring about continuing change.

Take some time and ask the Lord to bring to mind people you need to forgive. As you get names and memories, write them down, then go through the list one by one and forgive each person. Tear up the list when you are finished.

Another important person you might need to forgive is yourself. Ask the Lord to show you if there is anything you need to forgive yourself for.

Be on the alert—*"Be sober, be vigilant; because your adversary the devil walks about like a roaring lion, seeking whom he may devour"* (1 Peter 5:8). *"Be serious and watchful in your prayers"* (1 Pet. 4:7). Even though the enemy wants to keep you bound, the ability and authority to break free from his snare of unforgiveness is right there in your heart, and often, released upon your lips.

Power Point

In the words of John Bunyan, "Pray often; for prayer is a shield to the soul, a sacrifice to God, and a scourge for satan." And as Mark 11:25 tells us, *"Whenever you stand praying, if you have anything against anyone, forgive him, that your Father in heaven may also forgive you your trespasses."*

Power Thought

To forgive is to set a prisoner free and discover that the prisoner was you. —Lewis B. Smedes

Day 38

ABIDE

However strong the branch becomes, however far away it reaches round the home, out of sight of the vine, all its beauty and all its fruitfulness ever depend upon that one point of contact where it grows out of the vine. So be it with us too.
—Andrew Murray

DISCIPLINE #38—KNOW GOD'S WILL BY REMAINING IN GOD'S WORD

Today, I want to give you a key to praying with precision and power. I'm sure at this point you are ready to pray for freedom—and hope to experience what you are praying for. The problem is, many people pray with uncertainty because they are not abiding in God's Word and therefore remain ignorant of His will. On the other hand, there are many who earnestly believe they are praying effectively and confidently, but are not receiving answers. They pray, cry out, confess, and declare, but continue to experience a gap between their prayers and the answer coming to pass.

In order for you to experience complete breakthrough and to pray with assured effectiveness, I want to share with you the secret to praying for *and* seeing results. This is what Jesus had in mind when He connected the necessity of "abiding in" Him to our prayers being answered. He said:

> *Abide in Me, and I in you. As the branch cannot bear fruit of itself, unless it abides in the vine, neither can you, unless you abide in Me. "I am the vine, you are the branches. He who abides in Me, and I in him, bears much fruit; for without Me you can do nothing. If anyone does not abide in Me, he is cast out as a branch and is withered; and they gather them and throw them into the fire, and they are burned. If you abide in Me, and My words abide in you, you will ask what you desire, and it shall be done for you* (John 15:4-7).

Therein lies the secret. When you pray, plug into the true source of an empowered life—God and His Word. Get powered up, and then shine that light with laser-like accuracy into every situation and circumstance.

> *When you spend time in the Word of God, you come face to face with the will of God.*

Confidence in prayer is unlocked and unleashed when you are assured that your prayers are in agreement with God's will. Abiding in Christ, remaining in that place of intimacy with Him, demands that you know His Word. You don't have to be a Bible scholar or memorize the entirety of Scripture—but the truth is, the Scripture unveils God's will. When you spend time in the Word of God, you come face to face with the will of God. As you "abide in Christ," meditate on His words, and study His example in the Gospels, you are further exposed to God's will.

POWER POINT

Ask yourself—*what is God's will for my soul?* I pray the answer comes quickly. Our time together has been an exploration of the diabolical plot of the enemy to enslave your soul—but only insofar as he can keep you blind to the life-giving, redemptive agenda of the Lord Jesus to set it free.

This redemptive plan is clearly expressed in today's meditation passage.

POWER THOUGHT

May God himself, the God who makes everything holy and whole, make you holy and whole, put you together—spirit, soul, and body—and keep you fit for the coming of our Master, Jesus Christ (1 Thessalonians 5:23 MSG).

BIND

And I will give you the keys of the kingdom of heaven, and whatever you bind on earth will be bound in heaven, and whatever you loose on earth will be loosed in heaven (Matthew 16:19).

DISCIPLINE #39—IDENTIFY ENEMIES OF YOUR SOUL THAT NEED TO BE BOUND

Over these final two days, I will walk you through steps you can take to sever the tentacles entangling your soul from every mal-associative experience, word, or deed you may have been ensnared by. I will show you how to take authority over the domain of your interior life—how to reign as king and priest in the realm of your own soul—and infuse it with the Light and Truth of the Kingdom of God. The Kingdom *is* within you! The first step is binding the enemies of your soul—the intruders who trespassed upon property that does not belong to them.

As we abide in Christ, His words become more and more clear to us. With this clarity comes understanding of what God is *for* and what He is *against*. We become acquainted with what is allowed in His Kingdom, and what is forbidden. There are things we are called to release—which are present realities in heaven—and then there are those we are instructed to bind. Cancel. Forbid.

I am excited to walk you across the "finish line" in this process, but there is one step you must take before we pray together and officially disengage any weapons locked and loaded against your soul.

The Bible says you cannot take dominion over an area until you have first bound the strongman of that area. Before you bind him you must blind him! Blind him with the light of Truth—then you can overpower him. He must be recognized in order to be confronted and dethroned. Jesus taught, *"For when a strong man like Satan is fully armed and guards his palace, his possessions are safe—until someone even stronger attacks and overpowers him, strips him of his weapons, and carries off his belongings"* (Luke 11:21-22 NLT).

This "strong man" is not a specific person or malevolent spirit. The concept that Jesus teaches describes more of a sustained place of bondage than any particular individual. That is the enemy's goal for your life. He wants to do everything in his limited power to deceive you to remain in bondage. His great deception is preventing you from shining light on the dark areas, thus exposing their identity and arming you to overcome them.

POWER POINT

The strong man maintains a place of dominion over your soul *only* as long as your condition remains shrouded in darkness. Anything under enemy jurisdiction prefers the darkness. Why? As long as you do not shine light upon these areas, you cannot bind them. You remain blind and therefore incapable of binding. That said, as soon as light is cast upon the darkness, you acknowledge the area, relationship, or exchange for what it is, and it becomes another *name* that is subject to the authority of *the Name* of Jesus (see Phil. 2:9-10).

That is what you must learn to do in regard to your own house—and your own soul. You have the authority to blind and bind the strong man and strip him of his weapons.

POWER THOUGHT

Darkness cannot drive out darkness: only light can do that. —Martin Luther King Jr.

Day 40

PRAY

Men and women are needed whose prayers will give to the world the utmost power of God; who will make His promises to blossom with rich and full results. God is waiting to hear us and challenges us to bring Him to do this thing by our praying. —E.M. Bounds[1]

DISCIPLINE #40 — RECLAIM YOUR SOUL USING THE WEAPON OF PRAYER

We have come to the final day of our journey together. It has been an honor walking alongside you and taking you to a place where, I believe, you are on the brink of shifting seasons and stepping into a new way of life. Lifestyle transformation is what *The Soul Series* is all about.

The key to successfully breaking past cycles and establishing a lifelong soul transformation is *prayer*. This is not just any prayer. Resiliency is fueled and sustained by what I call *Authoritative Prayer*.

Authoritative prayer must be practiced daily. Regarding this life, not one day goes by that the enemy is sleeping or that your flesh is on vacation. Exercise your authority daily in order to strengthen it, just as Paul told Timothy to do regarding godliness, *"exercise yourself toward godliness"* (1 Tim.4:7).

I want to give you a few practical keys about prayer before we actually go through the process together.

You Are Worthy to Pray

There is nothing the enemy would like you to believe more than the lie that you are inadequate to pray. His plot is to maintain the reins on your soul as long as possible. He well knows that the longer it takes for you to approach God's throne in prayer, the longer he maintains the right to keep you in bondage.

Revivalist Charles G. Finney provides the following insight considering your "worthiness" for prayer: "Persons never need hesitate, because of their past sins, to approach God with the fullest confidence. If they now repent, and are conscious of fully and honestly returning to God with all their heart, they have no reason to fear being repulsed from the footstool of mercy."[2]

Earlier this week, you repented for any sins or practices you engaged in that might have brought you to a place of bondage. Repentance not only gives you legal standing before the throne of grace, but the very fact that Jesus shed His blood on the cross and authored your redemption gives you the ability to confidently stand before God—even in the midst of your sin or iniquity.

You are needy after you sin, because you *need* to repent. This is not a bad, shameful, or disgraceful place to be. Rather, acknowledging this need positions you to act on Hebrews 4:16, which extends this powerful invitation: "*Let us therefore come boldly to the throne of grace, that we may obtain mercy and find grace to help in time of **need**.*" Never flee His presence after sin, for His presence is the very place you need to run toward. Remember, "*If we confess our sins, He is faithful and just to forgive us our sins and to cleanse us from all unrighteousness*" (1 John 1:9). You are worthy to approach His throne in prayer, backed by the guarantee that He is listening and ready to act on your behalf.

Effective Prayer is a Habit

The whole point of our study has been to reframe your entire way of living—your lifestyle. Lifestyle is a product of daily habits. Those who do not view prayer as a habit—or way of living—but rather, as a go-to remedy when they are experiencing trouble, tend to experience seasonal blessing, breakthrough, and victory—if any at all. Apostle Paul invites you to an alternative lifestyle of faith where you *"pray without ceasing"* (1 Thess. 5:17). I want to help you build prayer into your life as a habit, for the habits we cultivate position us for either success or failure, breakdown or breakthrough.

As the 19th century theologian Horace Bushnell stated, "Habits are to the soul what the veins and arteries are to the blood, the courses in which it moves." Revelation warns, *"Let the one who is righteous, still practice righteousness; and the one who is holy, still keep himself holy"* (Rev. 22:11 NASB).

It is a daily challenge, but with the Spirit of God working in you, it is what you were "recreated" to do. *"Let the Spirit change your way of thinking and make you into a new person. You were created to be like God, and so you must please him and be truly holy"* (Eph. 4:23-24 CEV).

Effective Prayer is Natural for the Supernatural

As you develop this prayer habit in your life, I assure you that what once was unnatural and abnormal will become very normal. Why? You are a spiritual being, first and foremost. Prayer is a means of supernatural communication. As I noted, you were recreated to commune and fellowship with the Divine. Though there are habits we need to develop to recalibrate our lives to come into alignment with God's purpose for our life in Christ, the reality is that for a believer, prayer becomes a natural way of living. We cannot limit it to a formula or particular style. After all, to *pray without ceasing* implies a lifestyle of continuous communion with God.

Author Richard Foster comments, "Countless people pray far more than they know. Often they have such a 'stained-glass' image of prayer that they fail to recognize what they are experiencing as prayer and so condemn themselves for not praying." We need to move past the religious, "stained glass" perspective, as it places a ceiling on how we define prayer.

As we conclude our study, I want you to apply these principles of prayer to the following prayers, confessions, declarations, and renunciations. These are not meant to be read through or recited only once. I want you to live, ever mindful, of the soul-stealing agenda of your enemy—and be equipped in the heat of battle over your soul to always remain in command. You must remain in firm possession of your soul (see Luke 21:19), for your enemy is relentless in his agenda to entangle your soul through soul attachments, and progressively deplete your very life force until you are rendered a powerless tool in his diabolical grasp. I pray you have a stern resolve in your spirit that says, "This has gone on long enough!"

POWER POINT

Through the power of authoritative prayer and by purposefully developing the habit of prayer, I believe you will not only break every soul tie, but will experience the renewed, resilient life Jesus died for you to enjoy.

MEDITATION

…The earnest prayer of a righteous person has great power and produces wonderful results (James 5:16 NLT).

PRAYERS
OF RECLAMATION

Transformational living begins by living in the moment and letting go of the past. Paul said in Philippians 3:13-14, *"one thing I do, forgetting those things which are behind and reaching forward to those things which are ahead, I press toward the goal for the prize of the upward call of God in Christ Jesus."* Fully embrace every present moment by continually pressing toward the goal *"of the upward call of God"* by repenting, changing how you relate, and by receiving the grace of God's love. Right now, where you are, this very moment:

- Acknowledge your current condition,
- Ask the Spirit of God within you whether you have any soul ties that need to be broken, and
- Discern what types of ties and in what areas you need deliverance.

You must *want* to be free, and then you must willingly yield yourself to God through:

- Acknowledgment
- Disengagement from the source of attachment
- Demonstrating voluntary rejection by verbally renouncing the tie
- Letting go of any past associations remotely related with the attachment
- Repenting now and purpose to change how you relate in the future

- Receiving the grace of God—His love, restoration, and divine enablement to live free
- Re-establishing healthy boundaries through forgiveness and the principles of love (see 1 Cor. 13:4-7)
- Totally submitting to the Lordship of Christ
- Asking the Holy Spirit to lead and guide you into all truth
- Establishing prayer shields, firewalls, and divine hedges of protection around your life

Prayer Points (pray out loud):

Today I take full responsibility for where I am. I refuse to blame or project my emotions, feelings, or attitude onto others. I refuse to allow repressed emotions to go unaddressed. I renounce all destiny-altering emotional, physical, psychological, spiritual, and social dependence upon anything and anyone who sabotages or undermines my relationship with God, healthy relationships with family and friends, and the fulfillment of my God-given purpose and assignments. I break soul ties with _____ (recall names of past lovers, perpetrators, violators of covenants, molesters, dysfunctional and diabolical relationships). I break ungodly rule and control over my soul by evil agents.

Read the following Psalm aloud:

Have mercy on me, O God, because of your unfailing love. Because of your great compassion, blot out the stain of my sins. Wash me clean from my guilt. Purify me from my sin. For I recognize my rebellion; it haunts me day and night. Against you, and you alone, have I sinned; I have done what is evil in your sight. You will be proved right in what you say, and your judgment against me is just. For I was born a sinner—yes, from the moment my mother conceived me. But you desire honesty from the womb, teaching me wisdom even there.

Purify me from my sins, and I will be clean; wash me, and I will be whiter than snow. Oh, give me back my joy again; you have broken me—now let me rejoice. Don't keep looking at my sins. Remove the stain of my guilt. Create in me a clean heart, O God. Renew a loyal spirit within me. Do not banish me from your presence, and don't take your Holy Spirit from me. Restore to me the joy of your salvation, and make me willing to obey you. Then I will teach your ways to rebels, and they will return to you.

Forgive me for shedding blood, O God who saves; then I will joyfully sing of your forgiveness. Unseal my lips, O Lord, that my mouth may praise you. You do not desire a sacrifice, or I would offer one. You do not want a burnt offering. The sacrifice you desire is a broken spirit. You will not reject a broken and repentant heart, O God (Psalm 51:1-17 NLT).

Continue to pray:

Father,
According to Psalm 51, I break and sever all attachments, associations, and dependence upon:

- Drugs, alcohol, addictive substances, and activities
- Acquaintances, friendships, and intimate relationships with those who do not embrace my core values
- Perverted/deviant relationships, past and present deviant behaviors
- Lewd, promiscuous, immoral, unethical activities
- Adulterous relationships
- Incest
- Cultic and anti-God, anti-Christ religious organizational activities and practices
- Witchcraft
- Blood covenants
- Verbal and written agreements entered into through ignorance, coercion, manipulation, or deception

- Bribes
- Pornographic materials (including books, Internet, movies, etc.)
- Controlling family members
- Controlling relationships
- Destiny-altering activities
- Inordinate affections toward people, things, possessions, and money
- Sexual relations with ex-spouses
- Money illegally and inappropriately gained

Father, wash away the residual effects of repression and every soul tie by the blood of the Lamb and by the washing of the water of the Word:

- Deliver me from evil affection and lustful desires and fantasies
- Shatter strongholds and blow them to smithereens by the winds of the Spirit
- Remove persistent grudges, hidden resentments, unutterable hurts, disappointments, deep-seated offenses, and vendettas
- I renounce soul ties associated with inheritances, generational curses, and parental contracts (contracts entered into by parents or my parents' parents)

I break soul ties with:

- Old habits
- Seasonal relationships
- Abusive leadership
- Addictive cultural environments
- Smothering relationships
- Dysfunctional and self-destructive mindsets

- Old, limiting paradigms
- Non-productive business dealings and partnerships
- Grant me new life strategies, life skills
- Grant me new ways of thinking, new ways of working, and new ways of living
- Give me a hunger and thirst for righteous living
- Sanctify me wholly, as I give to You my affections, and desires, my mind, will, and emotions

As you lay hands on the top of your own head:

- Command the reticular formation, limbic system, and frontal lobe to come into divine alignment.
- Declare that you have the mind of Christ and that your thoughts will no longer be polluted by demonic inferences, fantasies, and lewd imagery.
- Declare that the glory and power of God will fall upon you in a new way.

Declare:

- I have a right to say "no" to others if it is an invasion of my space or a violation of my rights.
- I have a right to take the risk to grow in my relationships with others.
- If I find that my space or rights are being violated or ignored, I have the right and will assertively protect myself to ensure I am not hurt.
- I have the right to do things that emanate from my free will so that I do not become so overly enmeshed with others that I lose my identity.
- I have a right to explore my own interests, hobbies, and outlets so that I can bring back to my family or group my unique personality to enrich our lives rather than be lost in a closed and over-enmeshed system.

- I will never again allow my space and rights to be violated.
- I will stand up for myself and demand my rights be respected and not violated. If I am ignored, I have the right to leave or ask those infringing on my rights to get out of my life.
- I have the right to be visible—to be seen and heard.
- I will stand up for myself so that others can learn to respect my rights and my needs—and so that others can learn they are not allowed to violate my space.
- I choose to no longer disassociate from my feelings when I am being treated in a negative way. I choose to be aware of what is happening to me and assertively protect myself from further violation or hurt.
- I do not need to be cold and distant or aloof and shy to protect myself from being hurt.
- I choose to open myself up to others trusting that I will be assertive when necessary to protect my rights and my privacy from being violated.
- There is a line I have drawn over which I do not allow others to cross. This line protects my uniqueness, autonomy, and privacy. It allows me to be the way I really am rather than the way other people want me to be.
- This line lets others know that this is who I am and where the dividing line exists between where my personhood begins and another person's influence on me ends.
- This line defines who I am, who they are, and where we meet as two distinct individuals.
- As complete and whole individuals before God, I purpose to never cross over this holy line so that we can forever maintain a healthy and edifying relationship with one another.

Today, I stand in the liberty, where Christ has set me free. I accept Jesus Christ as both my Lord and Savior.

Today I refuse to be held captive by yokes of bondages ever again. Whom the Son sets free is free indeed!

I seal this prayer in Jesus' name.

Amen.

The Lord is my shepherd; I shall not want.
He makes me to lie down in green pastures;
He leads me beside the still waters.
He restores my soul;
He leads me in the paths of righteousness
For His name's sake (Psalm 23:1-3).

But what happens when we live God's way? He brings gifts into our lives, much the same way that fruit appears in an orchard—things like affection for others, exuberance about life, serenity. We develop a willingness to stick with things, a sense of compassion in the heart, and a conviction that a basic holiness permeates things and people. We find ourselves involved in loyal commitments, not needing to force our way in life, able to marshal and direct our energies wisely (Galatians 5:22-23 MSG).

The most powerful weapon on earth is
the human soul on fire. —Ferdinand Foch

Appendix A

A PERSONAL CONTRACT FOR LIVING A RESILIENT LIFE

LIVING DECLARATIONS

The following is a daily declaration. Speak it out loud over your life every day.

I have the courage and personal integrity to:

- Set clear boundaries for myself and to help others to respect them accordingly
- Be myself
- Dream of a better life
- Wake up and live the life of my dreams
- Enjoy today
- Believe that tomorrow will be better than today
- Voice my opinion
- Pursue my goals
- Change my mind
- Break self-destructive activities, thoughts, and cycles of failure
- Change for the better
- Continuously improve on a daily basis
- Always be my very best, give my very best, do my very best
- Put my best foot forward
- Fully enjoy giving and receiving love

- Boldly face my fears and weaknesses with courage
- Seek and ask for help and support when I need it
- Spring free of the superwoman/man trap
- Stop being all things to everyone
- Set clear boundaries
- Trust myself to know what is right for me
- Make my own decisions based on my perception of options
- Befriend myself
- Be kind to myself
- Be totally honest with myself
- Respect my vulnerabilities
- Heal old and current wounds
- Acquire new, good, and useful habits and eliminate the bad
- Complete unfinished business
- View my failures as life lessons
- Turn my losses into gain
- Realize that I have emotional and practical rights
- Honor my commitments
- Keep my promises
- Give myself credit for my accomplishments
- Love the little girl/boy in me
- Overcome my addiction to and need for approval
- Grant myself permission to laugh out loud, love out loud, and live out loud
- Play as hard as I can
- Dance like no one is watching
- Sing at the top of my voice
- Catch butterflies
- Color outside the lines
- Watch mother nature as she tucks the sun in for a good night sleep and then turns the nightlights on for my enjoyment, security, and pleasure

- Witness the dawning of a new day as the sun rubs the lingering sleepiness from its eyes
- Choose life over death
- Choose success over failure
- Live with an attitude of gratitude
- Quit being a trash receptacle and dumping bin
- Rid myself of toxic relationships
- Pursue and develop healthy and supportive relationships
- Renegotiate the terms of all relationships
- Nurture myself like I nurture others
- Take "me moments"
- Be alone without feeling lonely
- Demand people give to me as much as I give to them
- Manage my time
- Value the time God gives me by using it wisely
- Demand that others value my time
- Be more objective about my feelings and subjective about my thoughts
- Detoxify all areas of my life
- Take an emotional enema when necessary
- Nurture others because I want to, not because I have to
- Choose what is right for me
- Insist on being paid fairly for what I do
- Know when enough is enough
- Say "no" and mean it
- Put an end to toxic cycles
- Set limits and boundaries
- Say "yes" only when I really mean it
- Have realistic expectations
- Take risks and accept change
- Live morally
- Conduct my affairs ethically
- Grow through change

- Grow through challenges
- Give others permission to grow and to be themselves
- Break glass ceilings
- Live beyond the limits
- Set new goals
- Savor the mystery of the Holy Spirit
- Pray and expect an exceptional, favorable outcome
- Meditate in order to unclutter my mind
- Wave goodbye to guilt, self-doubt, rejection, and insecurity
- De-weed the flower bed of my thought life
- Treat myself with respect and teach others to do the same
- Fill my own cup first, then refresh others from the overflow
- Demand excellence from myself and others
- Plan for the future, but live in the present
- Value my insight, intelligence, and wisdom
- Know that I am loveable
- Celebrate the differences in others
- Make forgiveness a priority

I have the courage to:

- Accept myself just as I am now and forever
- Live within my means
- Love God
- Manifest His divinity
- Move beyond innate fears by living in the realm of faith
- Embrace His Spirit that is stronger and wiser than mine
- Prosper beyond my imagination
- Give more than I receive
- Give to those who can never return the favor
- Love unconditionally
- Live consciously

Therefore:
- I will give God the time He needs
- I will give my mind the order it needs
- I will give my life the discipline it needs
- I will give my spirit the freedom it needs
- I will give my soul the love it needs
- I will give my body the nourishment and exercise it needs
- I will give my voice the platform it needs
- I will take a stand for what I believe
- I will give myself the love and attention I need
- I will pursue my dreams and accomplish my goals
- I will give to others
- I will pursue my purpose and maximize my potential
- I will stand on truth and take a stand for truth
- I will positively impact my generation
- I will positively influence a system and/or an institution
- I will live, learn, love, serve, and then leave a legacy
- I am on a collision course with destiny
- I am at the intersection of truth
- I am on the avenue of opportunity
- I am traveling the boulevard of passion
- I am residing on a street named courage
- All lights are green
- I choose to proceed
- I choose to walk with purpose, success, and nobility
- Today and always, I alone accept and own full and total responsibility for being my genuine and true self and therefore vow to live authentically, to grow and care for my best and nobler self, to reflect the power of God's glory and divinity working in and through me
- Today, I shall be blessed with all good things
- I will have good success

- My joy, peace, prosperity, and success shall be as abundant as the stars in the sky
- Friendship, favor, affluence, influence, health, happiness, support, beauty, and abundant living shall be my constant companions
- I am unconditionally loved, celebrated, revered, appreciated, and honored beyond measure and human comprehension
- I make a difference in this world
- I am moving, breathing, blessing, alive, and at work on this earth
- This is my contract with the eternal soul and spirit within me
- Today, I give myself permission to be all God has created me to be—and to push until I succeed!

Signed

_____

SIGNATURE

_____ Day of _____ 20 _____

Send me an email and let me know you did it. Here's to a life of freedom in Christ Jesus. God bless!

ENDNOTES

Introduction

1. Proverbs 23:7 KJV.
2. Proverbs 4:23 NLT.
3. Proverbs 4:27 NLT.
4. See John 7:38.
5. Luke 21:19.

Preface

1. W.E. Vine, Merrill F. Unger and William White Jr., Vol. 1, *Vine's Complete Expository Dictionary of Old and New Testament Words*, 96 (Nashville, TN: T. Nelson, 1996), s.v. "To go out, go forth."

Chapter One

1. Theories by the Institute for Creation Research suggest it is possible that when God created the earth, the entire planet was enclosed in a water vapor canopy that would cause a greenhouse effect on the earth evenly distributing temperatures the world over—even at what are now the polar icecaps. This canopy is what fell during the flood, also suggesting that there is much more water on the surface of our planet today then there was during the time of Adam and Eve in the Garden. For more information on this, see the ICR web-site. I would suggest starting with the article at http://www.icr.org/article/long -summertime/.

2. See Ezekiel 1:16; 10:10, though the context I am using this allusion in is not the same, so these Scriptures do not really apply to what I am saying here. I am using their illustration to help create a picture.

Chapter Two

1. Walter Chen, "How to Rewire Your Brain for Positivity and Happiness." Lifehacker.com. Retrain Your Brain, 6 February 2013. http://lifehacker.com/5982005/rewire-your-brain-for-positivity-and -happiness-using-the-tetris-effect.

2. Janet Reed, "Creative Emotion." Enchantedmind.com. 1998; http://enchantedmind.com/html/science/creative_emotion.html.

Chapter Three

1. The Commission on Children at Risk, *Hardwired to Connect: The New Scientific Case for Authoritative Communities* (New York: The Institute for American Values, 2003), 14.

2. *Merriam Webster's Collegiate Dictionary*, Eleventh ed. (Springfield, MA: Merriam-Webster, Inc., 2003), s.v. "electromagnetism."

3. Lisa Wimberger, *New Beliefs New Brain* (California: Divine Arts Media, 2012), x.

Chapter Four

1. Brene Brown, *Daring Greatly: How the Courage to be Vulnerable Transforms the Way We Live, Love, Parent, and Lead* (New York: Gotham Books, 2012), 23.

2. Ibid.

3. see 2 Corinthians 5:17 and Galatians 6:15.

4. see 2 Corinthians 3:18.

5. see Romans 12:12.

6. Proverbs 24:5 AMP.

7. Hosea 4:6.

8. http://thinkexist.com/quotation/not_everything_that_is_faced_can_be_changed-but/7880.html.

9. 2 Corinthians 3:17.

10. Hebrews 12:2.

11. Song of Solomon 2:15.

12. Psalm 140:4.

13. Colossians 1:23 MSG.

14. 2 Corinthians 9:8.

15. Philippians 2:13.

16. 1 John 2:16.

17. *Merriam-Webster's Collegiate Dictionary*, s.v. "exchange." .

18. Microsoft Corporation, *Encarta® World English Dictionary* (New York: Bloomsbury Publishing Plc., 1999), s.v. "exchange."

19. Proverbs 18:21.

20. Proverbs 18:20.

21. See Matthew 6:21.

22. Hebrews 11:1.

23. Isaiah 33:15-16.

24. Numbers 11:4-5.

25. Ezekiel 18:27.

Day 1

1. For further study, secure a copy of my book *Commanding Your Morning*.

2. http://www.goodreads.com/quotes/217207-watch-your-thoughts-they-become-words-watch-your-words-they.

Day 4

1. Read *The Rules of Engagement for Spiritual Battle* for an in-depth study on this subject.

Day 6

1. Colin Powell.

Day 7

1. See my book, *Binding the Strongman*, for a comprehensive list of subordinate spirits that can infiltrate your mind, finances, family history, health, future, and nation.

Day 18

1. Michael Bayer, "Understanding Codependent Behavior," Treatment4Addictions.com, http://www.treatment4addiction.com/conditions-disorders/mood/codependency.

2. "Fact-Sheet: Co-dependency," Mental Health America, http://www.mentalhealthamerica.net/go/codependency.

Day 40

1. E.M. Bounds, *The Weapon of Prayer*.

2. "An Approving Heart—Confidence in Prayer" from *The Way Of Salvation*, Chapter XXII; Charles G. Finney 1792-1875.

ABOUT DR. CINDY TRIMM

Cindy Trimm has dedicated her life to serving God and humanity. A best-selling author, high-impact speaker, and former senator of Bermuda, Dr. Trimm is a sought-after empowerment specialist, thought leader, and catalyst of cultural change. Listed among *Ebony* magazine's *Power 100* as the "top 100 doers and influencers in the world today," Dr. Trimm is a consultant to civic, nonprofit, and industry leaders around the world. With a background in government, education, psychotherapy, and human development, Dr. Trimm translates powerful spiritual truths into everyday language that empower individuals to transform their lives and their communities. Her message brings new meaning, purpose, dignity, and hope to a global audience.

THE SOUL SERIES

The 40 Day Soul Fast is a comprehensive teaching on the nature of the soul, properties of thought, power of identity, words, and actions. This is an introductory "foundation-laying" book on how your inner life affects your outer world.

Reclaim Your Soul is a more in-depth study on the nature of emotional attachments/entanglements and how to break free from or avoid them. It categorizes the various types of relational soul ties that might be holding you back and weighing you down.

The Prosperous Soul offers insight into how the health of your soul affects the health and healing of your body. The health of your body and soul are inter-related. (Scheduled release Spring 2015)

Heal Your Soul, Heal the World brings it all together into the context of your role in the larger world as a leader and catalyst for change. (Scheduled release Spring 2016)

OTHER BOOKS BY DR. CINDY TRIMM

Commanding Your Morning Daily Devotional

Til Heaven Invades Earth

When Kingdoms Clash

The Prayer Warrior's Way

The Art of War for Spiritual Battle

Commanding Your Morning

The Rules of Engagement

CindyTrimm.com
Let's stay connected!

CINDY TRIMM

Be sure to visit us online at *CindyTrimm.com* for lots of online resources to empower, equip and encourage you daily!

Videos • Blogs • Articles
Speaking Event Schedule • TV Broadcast Information
Online Resources • Email Subscribe
...and more!

@cindytrimm

facebook.com/drtimm

CINDY TRIMM

Explore **Core4**
The Life Empowerment System

Dr. Cindy Trimm has compiled a lifetime of empowerment strategies and success principles in her revolutionary Core 4 Empowerment System.

The Core 4 Empowerment System will help you unleash the potential locked inside of you and breakthrough the limitations and barriers holding you back. No matter where you are in life, no matter how far you need to go, no matter how limited you might feel, the Core 4 Empowerment System will propel you to higher levels of meaning, purpose, and fulfillment.

Each month you'll receive two DVDs and a daily study guide that will walk you through Dr. Trimm's 4 Pillars of Empowerment, including Self-Knowledge, Success, Significance, and Service. Your annual subscription will deliver 24 DVDs and 12 workbooks, more teaching in a single program than Cindy Trimm has ever offered before!

Join the thousands of people who have experienced the power of the principles taught in this all new Empowerment System! Improve the quality of your life and position yourself for breakthrough, growth, and abundance.

Become the best version of YOU starting today!
I'll be right there with you every step of the way!

Dr. Cindy